NATO'S TRANSFORMATION

The Changing Shape of the Atlantic Alliance

NATO'S TRANSFORMATION

The Changing Shape of the Atlantic Alliance

Edited by Philip H. Gordon

Rowman & Littlefield Publishers, Inc.
Lanham • Boulder • New York • London

UA
646.3
ROWMAN & LITTLEFIELD PUBLISHERS, INC.   N2459
1997

Published in the United States of America
by Rowman & Littlefield Publishers, Inc.
4720 Boston Way, Lanham, Maryland 20706

3 Henrietta Street
London WC2E 8LU, England

British Cataloging in Publication Information Available

Library of Congress Cataloging-in-Publication Data

NATO's Transformation : the changing shape of the Atlantic Alliance / edited by Philip
    H. Gordon.
        p. cm.
    Includes bibliographical references and index.
    ISBN 0–8476–8386–9 (alk. paper). — ISBN 0–8476–8385–0 (pbk. : alk. paper)
    1. North Atlantic Treaty Organization. 2. Europe—Foreign relations. 3. Europe—
Politics and government—1989– I. Gordon, Philip H., 1962– .
    UA646.3.N2459   1997
    355'.031091821—dc21   96–46278
                                                                            CIP

ISBN 0–8476–8386–9 (cloth : alk. paper)
ISBN 0–8476–8385–0 (pbk. : al. paper)

Printed in the United States of America

⊖™ The paper used in this publication meets the minimum requirements of American
National Standard for Information Sciences—Permanence of Paper for Printed Library
Materials, ANSI Z39.48–1984.

17992

Contents

Credits

The following chapters first appeared in these issues of *Survival*:

Autumn 1996: 'The Costs of NATO Enlargement', Ronald D. Asmus, Richard L. Kugler and F. Stephen Larrabee [under the title 'What Will NATO Enlargement Cost?'].

Summer 1996: 'NATO Enlargement and the Baltic States', Ronald D. Asmus and Robert C. Nurick.

Spring 1996: 'Recasting the Atlantic Alliance', Philip H. Gordon.
'Common European Defence and Transatlantic Relations', Nicole Gnesotto.
'France's New Relationship with NATO', Robert P. Grant.
'The Masque of Institutions', Philip Zelikow.
'Combined Joint Task Forces in Theory and Practice', Charles Barry.
'Partnership for Peace: Permanent Fixture or Declining Asset?', Nick Williams.
'NATO's Role in Counter-Proliferation', Robert Joseph [under the title 'Proliferation, Counter-Proliferation and NATO'].

Spring 1995: 'NATO Enlargement: A Framework for Analysis', Ronald D. Asmus, Richard L. Kugler and F. Stephen Larrabee [under the title 'NATO Expansion: The Next Steps'].
'The Flawed Logic of NATO Enlargement', Michael E. Brown.
'Can Containment Work Again?', Dana H. Allin.

Chapter 13 first appeared in the Winter 1996–97 issue of *Washington Quarterly* [under the title 'Does the WEU Have a Role?'].

Preface

At their landmark summit in Brussels in January 1994, leaders of the North Atlantic Treaty Organisation agreed on a package of measures designed to adapt the Alliance to a new strategic situation. After more than four years of debate about how – or if – NATO should evolve, Alliance leaders agreed on four critical elements of reform: Partnership for Peace (PFP), a programme of military and political cooperation with former members of the Warsaw Pact; Combined Joint Task Forces (CJTF), a military command arrangement by which some members could act militarily with NATO assets but without necessarily involving all the Alliance's members; a non-proliferation and counter-proliferation programme, the first time the Alliance had become involved in either field; and the formal recognition of a European Security and Defence Identity (ESDI), a true 'European pillar' of the Alliance. In short, what NATO leaders proposed at the beginning of 1994 was no less than a transformation of the Alliance – from a US-dominated, integrated, Cold War machine to a more flexible, more inclusive and more European alliance with new roles and missions.

This book is about that transformation. It is a collective study of what NATO has accomplished, what still remains to be done, and what might go wrong. The authors – from the US, the UK and France – are all leading analysts of European security, many of whom have also held senior positions in government or international organisations, including NATO itself. All but one of the chapters in this book originally appeared in *Survival*, the quarterly journal of the International Institute for Strategic Studies. I commissioned most of them for a special issue on NATO, European Security and Transatlantic Relations in spring 1996 and for this book have added others to cover three important themes: transatlantic relations after the Cold War; the debate about NATO enlargement; and the new functional tasks adopted in January 1994. Because nearly all of the chapters were written in 1996, and the few from 1995 (chapters 5–7) were conceptual analyses, significant revisions were unnecessary, and the essays are printed here in their original form (with the date of publication noted on p. vii). The only significant step in NATO's transformation that has taken place since most of the chapters were written was the June 1996 Berlin summit, the implications of which are analysed in the concluding chapter.

I have made great efforts to ensure the coherence of the volume, but no attempt at all to present any sort of consensus about the Alliance's future. Some authors believe that NATO enlargement is a critical step for European security; others think that it is at best superfluous and at worst dangerous and expensive. Some authors call for a new treaty between the US and Europe, while others think such a step would be largely irrelevant. Some believe that institutional adaptation is critically important, while at least one sees institutions as a 'masque' that diverts analysts from the real security issues in Europe. Readers, I hope, will both learn from the wealth of factual material and sound analysis presented and make up their own minds as to which side possesses the best logic.

I am responsible both for the choice of subjects analysed here and the main substantive editing of the chapters, but others have played important roles in creating this book. Most helpful was Petra Green, the Assistant Editor of *Survival*, who not only played her usual essential role in the initial editing and preparation of articles for the journal, but did an exceptional job of ensuring the consistency, coherence and quality of the book. I would also like to thank the organisers of and participants in several of the conferences where most of these articles were presented and debated. These include Anne Deighton of St Antony's College, Oxford, who ran a conference on the Western European Union's role in European security in June 1996; Joseph Fromm, Chairman of the US Committee of the IISS, and Hans Binnendijk, Director of the Institute for National Security Studies of the National Defense University (NDU), who organised a conference on the future of NATO at NDU in June 1996; and Henri Cavanna of the Forum International des Sciences Humaines, who organised a conference on 'The Future of the Atlantic Alliance' held at the Paul H. Nitze School of International Studies in Washington DC in December 1995. Mike Spirtas was also extremely helpful in working on the book at the IISS, as was Helga Haack, who provided valuable assistance throughout, and IISS Production Supervisor, Mark Taylor. The original impetus for doing this book came from Susan McEachern of Rowman & Littlefield, who, as always, was a highly professional and pleasant editor to work with.

Philip H. Gordon

Introduction:
NATO's Transformation

A few years ago, *NATO's Transformation* would have seemed an unlikely title for a book to be published in 1997. For many, the end of the Cold War had ended NATO's main *raison d'être*, and, although the Alliance was widely expected to endure in some form, it was hardly expected to flourish. Book and article titles from the early 1990s – 'The End of NATO?', 'Europe After an American Withdrawal', 'NATO's Last Mission', 'The Graying of NATO' – reflected the mood of the times.[1] Liberal scholars expected NATO to wither because the dawn of peace in Europe undermined the need for big military organisations, and collective security would be given new life. Thus Richard Ullman could write in 1991 that NATO was faced with 'growing irrelevance', and that 'it would be surprising if Europe's alliances outlive the century'.[2] Realist scholars, on the other hand, did not abandon their belief in the utility of military force, but they were convinced that no alliance could hold together in the absence of a clear threat. Kenneth Waltz was confident in 1990 that 'NATO is a disappearing thing. It is a question of how long it is going to remain as a significant institution even though its name may linger on'.[3]

Predictions of NATO's inevitable demise, however, have so far proven mistaken. The Cold War threat has indeed disappeared, and with it NATO's primary mission, but the organisation's usefulness has endured. Only 14 months after the fall of the Berlin Wall in November 1989, a major war in the Persian Gulf reminded the West that military conflicts were perhaps not obsolete after all, and that a transatlantic military organisation might be worth preserving. NATO was not officially involved in the 1991 Gulf War, but few doubted that the legacy of 40 years of close military cooperation, standardisation, and training among the Western allies was crucial in assembling the international coalition that defeated Iraq.

In 1992, the Alliance again found itself called upon to act, this time by creating and policing a 'no-fly zone' over Bosnia-Herzegovina and enforcing a maritime arms embargo on former Yugoslavia, both in support of the UN peacekeeping mission there. These were limited missions, and NATO's critics argued that the Alliance should have been doing much more to stop the fighting in the Balkans. The debate about whether an early NATO intervention in 1991 would have stopped the warring parties from carrying out their aims will continue for years, but here the relevant point is simply that the very existence of NATO and its fire-power probably deterred what could have been an even more aggressive assault by Bosnian Serbs and their allies in Serbia, who tended to back off each time NATO made military threats. NATO leaders may well have failed to act as decisively as they should have in the early stages of the war; had NATO not existed, however, decisive action would not even have been an option. That NATO was useful became clear in 1995 when the Alliance finally undertook a decisive military operation, heavily bombing Bosnian Serb positions in August and September 1995 and forcing the warring parties to the negotiating table. By the end of the year, NATO found itself with almost 60,000 troops deployed in former Yugoslavia, alongside new partners from Eastern Europe and even Russia – a far cry from the obsolescent 'Cold War dinosaur' that some had claimed it would become.

Political scientists and international-relations scholars have long debated whether institutions primarily adapt to the changing needs and interests of their members or whether the institutions themselves shape those needs and interests. The case of NATO from 1990–97 seems to suggest that the institution adapts to needs more than the other way around – as NATO's members' requirements changed, so did the Alliance. In 1990–91, NATO jettisoned its Cold War military doctrine and opened itself up to the East by creating the North Atlantic Cooperation Council with the former members of the Warsaw Pact. During 1992, after the resistance of some of its members to new missions eroded in the wake of the crisis in former Yugoslavia, NATO formally adopted peacekeeping and peace-enforcement missions on behalf of the United Nations or the Conference on Security and Cooperation in Europe (CSCE, now OSCE). By 1993, NATO leaders realised their own adaptation was not advancing as quickly as the international system itself, and they called the January 1994 summit in Brussels to speed up internal reform. At the summit they announced the Partnership for Peace programme that would integrate the Central and East Europeans more completely and lay the basis for enlargement; adopted the concept of Combined Joint Task Forces (CJTFs), in order to undertake the sort of mission they were already executing in an ad-hoc fashion in the Balkans more efficiently; accepted the creation of a European Security and Defence Identity (ESDI) within NATO as a goal; and announced a comprehensive approach to the new challenges posed by the growing proliferation of weapons of mass destruction. By 1996, NATO's work in all four areas had advanced considerably, and, at the Berlin meeting of the North Atlantic Council in June that year, ministers accepted the basic principles of the CJTF concept, agreed on ways to give ESDI more visibility within NATO, and pledged to finish their work on new command structures for the Alliance by the end of the year.

As 1997 begins, the Alliance that seemed to be without a mission six years ago has thus come a very long way. It has informally contributed to victory in one major war (in the Gulf), and formally contributed to the ending, at least temporarily, of another (in Bosnia). The Alliance has pledged to name its first new members in the course of 1997, and already has formal partnerships with 27 of its former enemies or neutral countries, many of whose troops participated together with NATO's in the Bosnian Peace Implementation Force (IFOR) in former Yugoslavia. NATO has become more flexible through CJTF, and has given its European members a potentially greater voice by allowing them, theoretically at least, to undertake missions with NATO assets without US participation. NATO may well eventually fail, wither and die, but for now, the Alliance seems in remarkably good health. It is perhaps not surprising that recent articles about NATO – 'Why NATO is Still Best', 'NATO's Functions After the Cold War', 'Why NATO Should Grow' and 'NATO's Persistence After the Cold War' – are very different in tone from the earlier, pessimistic ones.[4]

The progression from 'NATO will fall apart' to 'NATO has enduring value' has not been linear, and there are still analysts today who think the Alliance is fated to dissolve, just as there were those in 1990 who expected it to endure. But a clear trend exists, and NATO has surely come further in its adaptation, and has been more effective in performing the roles given to it, than seemed likely even a few years ago.

Why has NATO proven more useful than expected? The first reason, alas, is that the hopes expressed as the Cold War was coming to an end in 1989 – most notably in Francis Fukuyama's essay 'The End of History' – that cooperation was replacing conflict as a norm of international relations has, at best, proven premature.[5] As the Cold War ended, security studies seemed to be a dying field, and military alliances anachronistic. But the view that the Cold War alone was responsible for international conflict and the need for military balance was an inversion of cause and effect. The disappearance of the Soviet Union and the effective end of communism had huge implications for NATO and its military posture, but they did not mean – as some prematurely hoped – that international conflict in and around Europe had become impossible. The first decade of the post-Cold War period was not the peaceful, cooperative era many assumed it would be – instead it saw the largest air–land battles since the Second World War take place in Iraq; four years of brutal war in South-eastern Europe that left an estimated 200,000 dead and several million refugees; a civil conflict in Algeria that resulted in over 10,000 deaths; and numerous civil and ethnic conflicts in Africa, some of which reached genocidal proportions. NATO no longer seemed necessary to do what it was primarily made for – containing the Soviet threat – but it continued to perform many deterrence, humanitarian and even war-fighting missions.

A second reason NATO has proven more useful than anticipated is that the hope that it could be replaced by some exclusively European organisation has proven as fanciful – or at least premature – as the hope that no security organisation would be needed at all. In the heady days of 1989–90, with the Soviet menace gone and the European Community (EC) forging ahead with its planned unity, some in Europe believed the EC could itself take the lead in securing Europe, especially since the sort of massive military force and nuclear deterrence provided primarily by the United States no longer seemed necessary. In a famous and no doubt since-regretted phrase, Luxembourg Foreign Minister Jacques Poos announced that the EC's intervention in Yugoslavia was 'the hour of Europe, not the hour of the United States'.[6] In December 1991, at their summit in Maastricht, EC leaders proclaimed a Common Foreign and Security Policy (CFSP) that was to endow them with more effective means to act together beyond their borders, and the EC for the first time adopted the goal of a common defence policy.[7] These ambitions proved excessive, and the CFSP's first few years were disappointing. The failure to put an end to the war in Bosnia – a nearly impossible task – could not fairly be blamed on Europe, but the denouement of the Bosnian war – with an American negotiator (Assistant Secretary of State Richard Holbrooke) bringing the warring parties to a negotiating table in Dayton, Ohio – underlined just how important the roles of NATO and the United States were. The US brought to bear military power, relative unity, credibility and a willingness to use force that the European Community simply did not have. Unless or until Europe has the means to act alone, decisively and with military force, NATO – shorthand in this case for US involvement in European security – will remain indispensable.

Finally, NATO has proven useful because its members – a group of liberal democracies with similar interests and values in the world – were willing to maintain it and tailor it to the requirements of the new era. It is perhaps ironic that some of those most convinced in the early 1990s that NATO should be scrapped were the same ones who were furious a few years later that it was not being used, or was not effective enough, in former Yugoslavia.

Reform and preservation of the Alliance – perhaps incomplete, perhaps imperfect – has not been inevitable. Less-thoughtful leaders in 1990 might have decided to dismantle NATO in the face of the criticism that it no longer had a role. Alternatively, they might have chosen to enlarge it quickly to new members including Russia, turning it into an OSCE-style collective-security organisation with no capacity to act. They might have opposed reform and new roles like peacekeeping and peace-enforcement, and concentrated on the old (and obsolete) mission of central defence. Or they might have kept the Alliance intact but cut its budgets so severely as to render it incapable of acting. All these options were at one moment or another supported, often by serious and influential people. But they were not adopted. If NATO has proven useful over the past five years, it was largely because Alliance leaders had a sense that an integrated, organised political-military organisation with a successful track record should not be given up lightly. Even when it was hard to say exactly what NATO was for – 'instability' never seemed to be as compelling a justification as Soviet tanks – NATO leaders were right to believe that the Alliance was worth preserving. That no one expected crises in the Persian Gulf, Yugoslavia or Rwanda to arise how and when they did – and to draw in, in one way or another, Western military forces – might serve as a useful lesson in thinking about what to do with NATO in the future.

Complacency about NATO's future, of course, would be as misplaced as the presumptions of NATO's imminent demise. While the Alliance has come a long way since 1990, no one can guarantee that it will not, ultimately, decline, and there are still some good reasons to believe that it might. In Bosnia, for example, NATO has been effective at limiting the use of military force, at forcing the Bosnian Serbs to the negotiating table, and, since its ground deployment in December 1995, at separating and keeping the peace among warring factions. It has not, however, been very successful in bringing about the national reconciliation that is a prerequisite of an enduring peace. NATO may ultimately be faced with a potential no-win decision about how long and in what form it will stay in Bosnia: to leave could lead to renewed war among the parties to the conflict and again raise questions about what NATO is good for, but to stay could lead to a costly, frustrating and potentially indefinite mission that would erode support for the Alliance, especially in the United States.

Another potential danger for the Alliance is enlargement itself, seen by some as a sign of NATO's vitality and future relevance.[8] NATO is an organisation that operates by consensus, which has been difficult enough with 16 members. If and when the Alliance expands to take on up to 25 new members, potentially from the Baltic states to Bulgaria, it may become tricky to preserve its necessary cohesion; any single member, for internal political or any other reasons, could potentially prevent the Alliance from acting or evolving. Managing an Alliance that includes one set of adversaries such as Greece and Turkey is one thing, but if Central Europeans do not overcome their own historic rivalries, the management of internal conflict might become even more problematic. If NATO cannot preserve its internal cohesion and does become more like a collective-security pact like the OSCE, key partners like the United States, the UK, France and Germany might begin to ignore it, and take decisions in bilateral or 'contact-group'-like forums.

Finally, NATO may eventually fall prey to a new version of the old 'burden-sharing' dispute, but without the 'glue' of the Cold War to keep itself together. During the Cold War, Americans and Europeans argued constantly about who should pay how much for what, but both sides ultimately knew that the stakes involved were too important to let such disputes cause the Alliance to fall apart. Now, while European security is still critically important, crises in and around Europe are not of the same 'existential' nature as when there was a Soviet threat, especially to the United States. In the context of a debate over who should do what in the coming years in former Yugoslavia, for example, Americans (especially in the US Congress) might hold their support for NATO hostage to a European willingness to bear more risks and costs than Americans, and Europeans might well refuse, trying to deny the US a political role if they are unwilling to share the risks on the ground. If Europeans resent Washington's attempts to impose its leadership on its allies without flexibility, and Americans resent Europe's failure to spend more on its own defence or support the US in regions such as East Asia or the Persian Gulf, NATO will suffer.

The year 1996, then, may not have been the turning point in NATO's renewal that it seemed – the step forward that would thrust the Alliance ahead to another half-decade of useful service – but the calm before the storm, the last gasp of an Alliance striving for relevance, albeit destined in the end to decline. This book does not pretend to predict or provide any consensus about which of these fates is more likely. Each of the authors has his or her own ideas about what is the most likely and most desirable future for NATO. What the book does attempt to do is to provide informed analysis and discussion of an alliance that has changed profoundly over the past five years. NATO's transformation is clearly under way. If readers of these chapters gain a better sense of why that transformation has come about, where it might be headed, and what shape it should ultimately take, the authors will have achieved their main goal.

Notes

1. See Henry Kissinger, 'The End of NATO?', *The Washington Post*, 24 July 1990; Jane M. O. Sharpe, *Europe After an American Withdrawal* (Oxford: Oxford University Press, 1991); Ronald Steel, 'NATO's Last Mission', *Foreign Policy*, vol. 69, no. 4, Autumn 1989, pp. 83–95; and Hugh de Santis, 'The Graying of NATO', *Washington Quarterly*, vol. 14, no. 4, Autumn 1991, pp. 51–65.

2. By 'Europe's alliances' Ullman was referring to NATO and the Warsaw Pact. See Richard K. Ullman, *Securing Europe* (Princeton, NJ: Princeton University Press, 1991), pp. 54 and 63.

3. See Waltz cited in congressional testimony, US Congress, Senate, *Relations in a Multipolar World*, Hearings before the Committee on Foreign Relations, 102nd Congress, 1st Session, 26, 28 and 30 November 1990 (Washington, DC: US Government Printing Office, 1991), p. 210. Waltz summed up his view of NATO's future clearly in a subsequent article: 'NATO's days are not numbered, but its years are'. See Kenneth N. Waltz, 'The Emerging Structure of International Politics', *International Security*, vol. 18, no. 2, Autumn 1993, p. 16.

4. See, in chronological order, Charles Glaser, 'Why NATO is Still Best: Future Security Arrangements for Europe', *International Security*, vol. 18, no. 1, Summer 1993, pp. 5–50; John Duffield, 'NATO's Functions after the Cold War', *Political Science Quarterly*, vol. 109, no. 5, Winter 1994–95; Strobe Talbott, 'Why NATO Should Grow', *New York Review of Books*, 10 August 1995; Robert B. McCalla, 'NATO's Persistence After the Cold War', *International Organization*, vol. 50, no. 3, Summer 1996, pp. 445–75.

5. See Francis Fukuyama, 'The End of History?', *The National Interest*, no. 16, Summer 1989, pp. 3–18.

6. Luxembourg held the EC's rotating presidency at the time. Poos cited in Joel Haveman, 'EC Urges End to Yugoslav Violence, Threatens Aid Cut', *Los Angeles Times*, 29 June 1991, p. A11.

7. The compromise wording on defence in the Maastricht Treaty was that the CFSP dealt with 'all questions related to the security of the Union, including the eventual framing of a common defence policy, which might in time lead to a common defence' (Title V, article J. 4). See 'Treaty on European Union' (Luxembourg: Office for Official Publications of the European Communities, 1992).

8. See, for example, Zbigniew Brzezinski, 'NATO – Expand or Die?', *New York Times*, 28 December 1994; Ronald D. Asmus, Robert D. Blackwill and F. Stephen Larrabee, 'Can NATO Survive?', *Washington Quarterly*, vol. 19, no. 2, Spring 1996, pp. 79–101; and Michael Clarke, 'NATO Must Upset Russia or Do Nothing and Die', *Sunday Telegraph*, 7 November 1993. Brzezinski argued that 'failure to address [the issue of NATO enlargement] would compound the danger that the Atlantic alliance may disintegrate'.

Part I
**Transatlantic Relations
After the Cold War**

Chapter 1
Recasting the Atlantic Alliance

Philip H. Gordon

US President Bill Clinton's decision to take a lead in NATO's Peace Implementation Force (IFOR) for Bosnia was like a tonic for the Atlantic Alliance. After more than four years of open disputes about how to deal with former Yugoslavia, transatlantic quarrels over trade policy and the weak dollar, and US–European differences about NATO's organisation, expansion and even *raison d'être*, the US commitment to put American lives on the line was a reassuring sign that it was not 'turning away' from Europe as so many had feared. While transatlantic tensions over Bosnia are still possible – indeed they are likely over issues such as arming the Bosnian government, paying for civil reconstruction and replacing IFOR after one year – even a partial success of the mission will do much to patch up an alliance in alleged disarray.

'Disarray' within the Alliance, of course, is hardly new, and apart from Bosnia the strains of the past few years actually seem less dramatic than some of those experienced in the past.[1] The members of the Atlantic Alliance always had strong differences over 'out-of-area' issues, and even within the North Atlantic area they often found themselves with sharply diverging interests and views. Have the problems of the past five years, then, been nothing more than the latest cycle in an enduring series of passing transatlantic 'crises'? Or were they, on the contrary, a sign of something much more profound taking place in the relationship between Europe and the United States? Has agreement on IFOR put the Alliance back on the same footing it was on in the 1970s and 1980s, or have the bases for the relationship been more fundamentally transformed?

This chapter examines the roots of the recent strains in transatlantic relations and argues that the change now taking place is indeed structural and enduring – not the temporary consequence of a US administration allegedly uninterested in foreign policy, or of a conflict, in former Yugoslavia, over which the Americans and Europeans perceived their interests differently. While acknowledging that unity between Europe and the United States has always been elusive and imperfect, I argue that the transatlantic link is becoming more permanently loosened by such factors as the end of the Cold War, the relative shift in priority from security to economic and other domestic affairs, changing demographic and trade patterns in the United States, and the growing relative importance of other regions to both Europe and the United States. Given such profound changes in world politics, it is only natural that the Alliance, too, is being substantially reordered. In a reordered Alliance, US leadership cannot be taken for granted; when that leadership comes, the US will dictate its terms more than ever before.

To say that the cohesion and even importance of the transatlantic relationship is declining is not to say that the Atlantic Alliance no longer serves an important purpose. Alliances – especially those based on common values and endowed with strong institutions like NATO – provide forums in which shared analyses are fostered and diverging interests can be traded off, and they make joint action possible when alliance members choose to undertake them. Even as their geopolitical and economic interests diverge in the twenty-first century, North Americans and Europeans will continue to be served by an institution in which they discuss common problems, formulate unified strategies and plan, train for and sometimes execute military missions. There is little that Alliance leaders can do to restore a sense of common purpose that is gradually becoming less compelling; what they can and should do is ensure that the lines of communication remain open and that the means for joint action are preserved.

The Sources of Change in Transatlantic Relations
The End of the Cold War

The most fundamental reason why the cohesion of the Atlantic Alliance is weakening is that it is no longer held together by a common threat. Many supporters of a close transatlantic relationship – US Secretary of State Warren Christopher, UK Foreign Minister Malcolm Rifkind and EU Commissioner Sir Leon Brittan among them – have begun to argue that the Alliance was not only about the Cold War, and of course they are right – shared values and economic links were and still are also critically important.[2] But it was the Cold War – more than the Second World War or anything else – that inspired the United States to become a European power, to invest so much commitment and money in Europe's economic rise and to remain engaged in Europe through good times and bad. One might argue that the world has changed since the late 1940s and that even without the communist threat the United States has other, equally compelling reasons to remain committed to Europe; but this proposition remains historically untested.

The logic of the 'Cold War as glue' argument is that, with the United States and Western Europe involved in a global struggle against a clear enemy, both Americans and Europeans needed allies. Whether one interprets the Cold War as a genuinely ideological conflict, or as simply a battle for power with ideology as an excuse (it no doubt had elements of both), the conclusion for Europe and the US was the same: maintaining a close political, military and economic alliance between the US and Europe was vital. Thus, none of the many serious crises that sprung up in Alliance relations during five decades of Cold War – the failure of the European Defence Community (EDC) in 1954; the Suez crisis of 1956; the Middle East war of 1973; or the energy pipeline dispute in the early 1980s, to name just a few – really risked leading to the dissolution of the Alliance itself. A common purpose held the allies together even when their economic, political or even military interests temporarily diverged.

It is not yet clear whether the current problems – and the disputes that arose over former Yugoslavia are clearly the most serious – will lead to a greater erosion of transatlantic solidarity and cooperation than did past disputes. But logic would suggest that, at the very least, the end of the Soviet threat removes much of the insurance against new tensions getting out of hand. There was a Berlin crisis to remind us of the need for the Alliance after Suez, but there may not be an equivalent after Bosnia. It may be politically useful or psychologically comforting to assert that the demise of communism 'will not result in a loss of common interest and commitment', but such a proposition is analytically difficult to defend.[3]

Domestic Priorities in the United States

One of the most important consequences of the end of the Cold War, particularly for the United States, is the resulting relative focus on domestic political, economic and social affairs, as opposed to international security. While domestic-policy frustration and some foreign-policy success have recently reminded President Clinton that leadership abroad can be politically useful, the country's long-term priorities have changed. Decisions that might in the past have been influenced by the need to preserve or strengthen the transatlantic partnership, even at economic cost, will now be based more on economic or purely domestic interests.

US foreign policy under President Bill Clinton has been consistent with the expectation that he would, as he said himself, 'focus like a laser beam' on the economy and make 'strengthening the US economy' a pillar of his *foreign* policy.[4] Under Clinton, whenever the United States has been faced with a choice between apparent domestic or international priorities, it has invariably chosen the former. It has thus been willing to confront Japan forcefully on trade questions, even with the threat of unilateral action, despite the risks posed by such an approach to the Washington–Tokyo security partnership and the need for Japanese support in dealing with Chinese assertiveness or the North Korean nuclear problem. Domestic politics also seems to be relatively more important: by allowing Sinn Fein leader Gerry Adams to visit the United States, thereby lending credibility to the Irish Republican Army (IRA)'s cause, the Clinton administration disregarded the concerns and interests of its close British ally in a way that would have been less likely during the Cold War.

There is an ongoing debate about the extent to which US economic policies were subordinated to security priorities during the Cold War.[5] But it seems undeniable that, if there was ever a tendency in the United States to subordinate perceived economic interests to security priorities, such a tendency no longer exists. Recent US foreign policy seems to be guided by the assertion of Jeffrey Garten, until October 1995 US Under-Secretary of Commerce, that 'the days when we will subordinate our economic interests to political and security alliances – unless we are directly threatened militarily – are over'.[6] For Garten, a leading administration spokesman on foreign commercial relations, 'we are entering an era when foreign policy and national security will increasingly revolve around our commercial interests, and when economic diplomacy will be essential to resolving the great issues of our age'.[7] The message – both in words and actions – to US allies is thus clear, and consistent with that – now known as the Tarnoff Doctrine – put forth in May 1993 by US Under-Secretary of State Peter Tarnoff:

> It is necessary to make the point that our economic interests are paramount … With limited resources, the United States must define the extent of its commitment and make a commitment commensurate with those realities. This may on occasion fall short of what some Americans would like and others would hope for.

Tarnoff's comments were quickly retracted by the State Department, but they have held up pretty well as a guideline for US policy.[8]

Clinton's domestic priorities, it must be noted, are not the isolated views of a particular administration but strongly reflect the opinion of a majority of Americans who feel that their domestic interests were subordinated to foreign-policy goals for too long. Nearly all polling data available suggest that the American public believes that economic interests should be the top priority for the US as a nation.[9] Foreign policy was not listed among the ten greatest problems facing the country in a recent poll of the general public by the Chicago Council on Foreign Relations (among élites, foreign policy came tenth), and that same poll found 'foreign-policy problems' as a percentage of the country's total problems to be lower than at any point since 1978 (which was a year of serious economic problems in the US).[10] Eight of the nine 'élite' groups polled by the Times Mirror Center for the People and the Press said that 'strengthening the domestic economy' should be the top priority for the US government, well ahead of all foreign-policy issues.[11]

Would the domestic focus change under a different President, and might the United States not see a strong revival of internationalism under a new, Republican administration? Such a development appears highly unlikely. As suggested by the polling data above, President Clinton reflects the shift in priorities as much as he is responsible for it. Indeed, the election of the Republican majority in the Congressional elections of November 1994 seemed only to reinforce the domestic emphasis of the American people and the tendency towards unilateralism rather than allied cooperation. If Clinton was elected on the dual planks of domestic focus and activist government, the message of voters in 1994 seemed to be 'keep the domestic focus, but lose the activism'. The Republican-led Congress calls for an even more radical focus on domestic affairs, sharp cutbacks in international aid and involvement, and a break with multilateral engagement.[12] The Republicans' unilateralist inclinations make it improbable that they would be any more willing than the Clinton administration to compromise domestic political or economic interests for the sake of Alliance solidarity.

Trade and Demographic Changes in the United States
Whether the Cold War had ended in the late 1980s or not, the United States would be growing away from Europe. Generational, demographic and economic change are all working to push the US away from its traditional European orientation. Even if one accepts the 'realist' view that national interests are more important in foreign policy than culture or personal relationships, it seems clear that profound and consequential changes are taking place.

One reason for this inevitable development is the effect of generational change, both at a public and leadership level. Even if the Soviet Union had not collapsed in 1991, a new generation of leaders would now be coming to power on both sides of the Atlantic. Just a few years ago, all of the major European and US leaders had played a role in, or were heavily influenced by, the formative experience of the Second World War and its immediate aftermath. Former leaders US President George Bush, UK Prime Minister Margaret Thatcher and French President François Mitterrand all remembered the historic Allied fight against the Nazis and they, along with Germany's Chancellor Helmut Kohl, were products of a period during which the West held firm against Soviet pressure. Within a few years, however, all the Western leaders will be of a new generation. Bill Clinton and current UK Prime Minister John Major were both born after 1945 (UK Labour Party leader Tony Blair is even younger), and Helmut Kohl's eventual successor will doubtless also be from the post-post-war generation. France is a partial exception in this regard, with the 63-year-old Jacques Chirac scheduled to remain in office until the year 2002, but it would be ironic to have to look to a French Gaullist to provide the foundation for a special transatlantic relationship.[13]

All of this, of course, is as true for the public and parliamentarians in Europe and the United States as for their leaders. The past two US Congressional elections, for example, have brought to power more than 200 new members, suggesting a turnover in personnel and direction at least as significant as that which occurred in the post-Vietnam withdrawal elections of 1974.[14] Sooner or later – but probably sooner – leaders and publics in Europe and the United States will be more of the Vietnam generation than of that of the Berlin and Cuba crises.

Demographic factors in the United States are working in the same direction. From 1820–1974, immigrants from Europe made up 76.8% of all immigrants into the United States, compared with just 4.6% for Asians and 9% for Latin Americans.[15] After the 1960s, however, with Western Europe's political and economic stabilisation and Eastern Europe's absorption into the communist bloc, the geographic sources of US immigration changed dramatically. In the 1970s and 1980s, the United States took in more than 5 million legal immigrants from Latin America, nearly 4.5m Asians and only about 1.5m Europeans.[16] Illegal immigration from Latin America and Asia has also been higher than from Europe, as have the birthrates of Asian Americans and Latin Americans within the country. The US population is thus moving away from its European roots: the number of Americans of primarily European origin fell below 80% in 1990 and is projected to be less than 65% by 2020 (see Table 1). There may not be a direct link between the ethnic origins of voters and the policies pursued by their governments, but it is hard to believe that a more Asian/Hispanic US will feel the same ties to Europe as one whose roots were firmly planted there. Times Mirror polls did not break down responses by ethnic background, but it is worth noting that whereas Americans from the Eastern part of the country said Europe was more important than the Pacific Rim by a ratio of 53 to 31%, Americans from the West said the Pacific Rim was more important by 41 to 38%. These regional differences further undermine the idea of a consistent 'national interest' that determines foreign policy.[17]

Even more important than generational or demographic change is economic change, which reflects the growing importance of new markets outside Europe, particularly in Asia. In 1960, Japan and East Asia together represented just 4% of world gross national product (GNP), while the European Economic Community represented nearly 25%. Today, the East Asian and EC shares of world GNP are nearly equal (just under 25%, about the same share as that of the North American Free Trade Association (NAFTA)), but with much higher economic growth rates in East Asia, the figures will continue to shift in Asia's favour.[18] According to the World Bank and other sources, four of the largest five (and seven of the largest ten) economies in the world in the year 2020 will be in Asia.[19] Even if Asian economic growth slows considerably, Asia will enter the twenty-first century as the world's richest region.

Table 1:   Origins of American Citizens, 1980–2050[a]

Year	Europe	Africa	Asia	Hispanic
1980	80%	11%	2%	6%
2000	72%	12%	4%	11%
2020	64%	12%	7%	16%
2050	56%	14%	9%	22%

Source: US Bureau of the Census, *Statistical Abstract of the United States: 1994* (Washington DC, 1994), p. 18. Totals do not reach 100% because figures have been rounded off and small indigenous populations are not included. Mid-range figures are used for projections.

Note: [a] Figures for 2000 onwards are projected.

Table 2:   Projected Asian, European and North American GNP at Constant 1987 Prices ($USbn)

Year	Asia[a]	Europe	North America
1972	1,871	3,591	3,350
1992	4,511	5,583	5,323
2002[b]	8,079	7,503	7,154

Source: World Bank Tables, constant prices (adjusted for inflation) derived by the International Economic Data Bank, Australian National University, Canberra, July 1994, cited in Paul Dibb, *Towards a New Balance of Power in Asia*, Adelphi Paper 295 (Oxford: Oxford University Press for the IISS, 1995), p. 19.

Notes: [a] Includes East, South and South-east Asia, but not Australia or Oceana.
[b] Projection for 2002 based on an estimated 6% growth rate for Asia (less than the past ten years' average) and 3% for Europe and North America (greater than the past ten years' average). The World Bank's regional growth prospects for 1994–2003 are 7.6% for East Asia, 5.3% for South Asia and 2.7% for all developed countries together.

US trade is quite naturally following this pattern of economic growth. US trade with Asia has exceeded trade with the European Community ever since the late 1970s, and the gap is expected to widen. US trade with Asia is worth about $350bn today, compared to $220bn with the European Union (and $232bn with Latin America, surpassing that with Europe). Despite the huge US trade deficits with Asia, that region still takes in more US exports ($130bn) than the European Union ($110bn).[20] In 1992, the share of US exports to Asia exceeded that to Europe by 33% to 26%, and the share of imports from Asia was greater by a ratio of 45% to 21%.[21] The formation of NAFTA, too, with its 385 million consumers and potential for expansion elsewhere into Latin America, will also divert some US trade from Europe.

Table 3:   US Imports from Europe and Asia-Pacific ($USm)

	1950	1960	1970	1980	1992
Europe	1,449	4,268	11,395	46,602	115,282
% of total imports	16.4	29.1	28.5	20.0	20.0
Asia-Pacific	1,846	2,987	10,492	83,691	248,768
% of total imports	20.0	20.4	26.3	36.0	45.1

Sources: US Bureau of the Census, *Historical Statistics of the United States: Colonial Times to 1970,* part 2 (Washington DC, 1975), pp. 905–7; US Bureau of the Census, *Statistical Abstract of the United States: 1982* (Washington DC, 1982), pp. 821–24; and *1993,* pp. 813–16.

Table 4:   US Exports to Europe and Asia-Pacific ($USm)

	1950	1960	1970	1980	1992
Europe	3,306	7,398	14,817	67,512	109,831
% of total exports	32.2	36.0	34.3	30.6	26.1
Asia-Pacific	1,690	4,700	11,216	70,285	140,130
% of total exports	20.1	22.9	26.0	31.8	33.3

Sources: US Bureau of the Census, *Historical Statistics of the United States: Colonial Times to 1970,* part 2, pp. 903–5; US Bureau of the Census, *Statistical Abstract of the United States: 1982,* pp. 821–24; and *1993,* pp. 813–16.

Critics of the US emphasis on Asia point out that transatlantic investment still greatly exceeds transpacific investment, that Asian markets are much less open than European ones and that Asian economic growth, even if regional stability is maintained, will inevitably slow.[22] This is all true, as the fact is that the European Union's single market and eventual expansion will also influence global trade patterns. But it is also true that even slower growth for Asia would still be much faster than expected growth in Europe, and that the potential for liberalising the more closed Asian markets, increasingly likely as economic development takes place, is almost by definition greater than it is in Europe. It is thus not surprising that the great dynamism and potential size of the Asian economies have attracted the attention and excitement of the US business and political communities. If political and military power follow economic growth, as they have throughout history, it is reasonable to expect that Asia's power and importance are on the rise.

Generational and demographic trends, trade patterns and economic interests do not necessarily determine the political or military orientation of a country, and the United States' cultural, historical and institutional relationship with Europe remains far stronger than it does with other regions. But evidence does suggest that an important change is taking place. The US public, it seems, still considers Europe to be the most important world region for the United States, but American élites, including the current government, believe the Pacific Rim to be more important.[23] US Secretary of State Christopher speaks openly of the 'primacy of Asia', and he has criticised his country's overly 'Euro-centric' attitude, an attitude apparently shared by the US business community.[24] Of the ten 'Big Emerging Markets' defined by the US Commerce Department as priorities, only two (Poland and Turkey) are in Europe, and none is in Western Europe.[25]

It is important to dispel the notion that the United States must make a choice among regions or allies. Good foreign relationships and trading partnerships are not zero-sum games, and there is no reason why a country cannot have good relationships with several regions at the same time. Still, a country and its leaders only have so much time, political capital, money and military force. Choices must sometimes be made, and the most important states and regions will have the most influence over those choices. The attention of investors, the capital of businesses, the numbers of languages that students learn and the number of countries to which North Americans can pay attention are also finite. Europe will remain closer culturally to the United States than Asia or even Latin America will, but in relative terms its importance to the United States is declining.

Europe's Own Reorientation

A number of concurrent political and economic changes within Europe are also affecting the cohesion of the Alliance, albeit perhaps less so than changes in the United States or in the international system. First, for many of the reasons already discussed, it seems obvious that, with the disappearance of the Soviet threat, Europe will be less inclined than ever to follow the US lead in response to global challenges. As is clear from their many public pronouncements, most European leaders favour a continuation of the US military role in Europe and most accept that there is not yet a viable European alternative. But the American protectorate, if still useful, is no longer indispensable. Today there is a credible possibility, which did not exist in the past, that if US and European security (or even economic) interests were to diverge – over the Balkans, Eastern Europe or North Africa, for example – the Europeans could respond by seeking military independence from the United States. With persistent double-digit unemployment and their own domestic priorities, Europeans are now less likely to follow Washington's lead on global political problems if it means denying themselves commercial relationships with countries like Iran, Iraq or China.

Second, the opening of Central and Eastern Europe will inevitably shift Europe's attention towards the east. Europe's interest in stabilising Central and Eastern Europe is far greater than that of the United States, just as US interests in Central and Latin America are greater. European resentment over Washington's $40bn bail-out of the Mexican government in January 1995 is a good example of the sort of conflict that may divide the Atlantic allies, and could occur if Europe extends its agricultural policy eastwards when it expands the European Union. If trade barriers are lowered within the NAFTA bloc and within an expanded European Union, but not between the two, the level of trade and commonality of interest between Europe and North America will fall, and the potential for further trade friction and the formation of economic blocs will rise. Those European states not tempted to look east, including Portugal, Spain and France, are increasingly looking south.

Third, European–US differences over the war in former Yugoslavia demonstrated all too clearly the possibility for transatlantic divisions over a major security issue. There are many reasons for these differences, including the US tendency to see conflicts in black-and-white terms, with victims and aggressors, and the Europeans tendency to view conflict in a more subtle – some would say more cynical – manner. But whatever the reasons, the fact is that a war in South-eastern Europe is a much greater danger to Europeans who, subject to refugee flows, feel they cannot permit themselves the luxury of arming one side and not getting more deeply involved. Whether right or wrong, the US determination not to deploy ground troops in Bosnia while the war was still going on, and its later decision not to share intelligence data on the enforcement of the arms embargo against the Bosnian government, sent the message that there may be security crises in Europe that the Europeans have to face without US support. The automatic solidarity of the Atlantic Alliance applied to the contingency of a military threat against one of its members, but it clearly does not apply to cases on which some Alliance members might – indeed will – have different views.[26]

Finally, Europe is being affected by changes even further East – the same Asian economic dynamism that is influencing the US. If the booming markets of the Pacific Rim are overshadowing Europe in the eyes of many Americans, the same is true for Asia and the United States in the eyes of Europeans. Europe's own trade with Asia has grown considerably since the 1960s, and, just as Asian purchasing power will far exceed that of Europe in the year 2020, it will also tower over that of the United States. None of this has been lost on EU leaders, who have recently made a priority of expanding their role in Asia.

Why the Atlantic Alliance is Still Important

Does it matter whether Europeans and Americans have a close political and military alliance? If the Atlantic Alliance was primarily a tool for winning the Cold War, why not just declare victory and let the Alliance fade? If the Europeans and Americans will be less naturally inclined to make concessions to each other for the sake of their alliance, why should their leaders seek to resist the trend? A widely accepted view of international relations suggests that states act in their national interest, largely unaffected by such 'soft' things as perceptions, institutions and personal contacts. American adherents to this school of thought would argue that even if *Europe* matters – since it is obviously an important market and potential military ally – *having a friendly or institutional relationship with Europe* is dispensable, because countries work together when it is in their interest to do so, regardless of their general feelings. Such thinking has much to recommend it as a starting point for international relations theory, and as a description of NATO, but it is incomplete.

Most often, allies act together when they have common interests, not because of an alliance tie or institutional obligations: it is difficult to find many cases of allies acting in conflict with their own interests for the sake of an alliance. The United States did not hesitate, for example, to oppose and force an end to the Suez invasion by Britain and France (1956), unilaterally cancel the *Skybolt* missile and neutron bomb (1961 and 1978), devalue the dollar (1971) or initiate the Strategic Defense Initiative (1983), with little regard for European interests. European states were not much more deferential to the Alliance, and put national interests first when it came to denying the US use of military bases for the Middle East war (1973) or pursuing the natural-gas pipeline contract with the Soviet Union (early 1980s). In a freely maintained alliance – as opposed to an imposed alliance, such as the Warsaw Pact – no one should expect states to deny themselves vital interests for the sake of their partners.

But there are other cases when an alliance does count for something. There are times when leaders need to be able to say to one another 'I really need this', and other times when it goes without saying. Rarely are explicit deals made, such as 'I'll give you this arms contract if you continue to ensure my defence', or 'I'll snub your political enemies if you vote with me at the United Nations', but the existence of an alliance, especially when based on common values, does have a political effect. The United Kingdom, for example, consistently supported US policies – on nuclear strategy, in Central America and Asia, and towards the Soviet Union – even when it was not clear what it had to gain other than the goodwill of the United States. West Germany was even more accommodating, holding back its criticism of US policy in Vietnam despite strong domestic opposition, keeping unwanted dollars in the late 1960s (instead of selling them for gold like the French), and making a heavy financial contribution to the US effort in the 1991 Gulf War, all to keep on Washington's good side. Italy and the Benelux countries, too, were often good allies for the Alliance's sake, and usually supported US positions in international affairs. As Henry Kissinger has pointed out, for all their doubts about US foreign policy, Europeans were the United States' most dependable global allies during the Cold War.[29] And even if less dependent on Europe than vice-versa, the United States sometimes returned such favours, as when it supported the UK in the Falklands War of 1982, despite the potential economic and political costs in Latin America.[28] So long as vital interests are not at stake – and sometimes even when they are – states are sometimes willing to make concessions for their closest allies.[29]

This 'pro-Alliance bias' will no doubt be weaker today than it was during the Cold War, but it is worth noting that, even in the past few years, members of the Alliance have gone out of their way to control their differences. The Clinton administration's policy towards former Yugoslavia, in fact, has been determined as much by a desire to preserve the Alliance as anything else, and on many occasions US actions have been influenced by the notion that NATO was a more important US interest than Bosnia. Although it was itself in favour of lifting the arms embargo against the Bosnian government, for example, the administration forcefully opposed this measure when Congress tried to impose it unilaterally, arguing that doing so would cause unacceptable damage to NATO.[30] Similarly, despite its strong reluctance to introduce ground troops to the Balkans, the US was prepared throughout 1994–95 to deploy up to 25,000 soldiers to assist in a withdrawal of the United Nations Protection Force (UNPROFOR) (a policy not contested even by Europe's harshest critics in Congress) and later to deploy a similar number of US troops for a peace-implementation force. Clearly this willingness had something to do with the importance Washington placed on preserving the Atlantic Alliance, a point made explicitly by the administration as it tried to sell the policy to a reluctant legislature.[31]

The simple view that countries cooperate militarily when their interests converge and do not do so if and when their interests diverge also overlooks the importance of a permanent institutional structure, which is useful in several ways. First, common institutions and frequent meetings of officials within those institutions can help to foster a common analysis of a given situation. National interests, the supposed guidelines for national policy, are not always 'given' but are derived from the perceptions and interpretations of those interests, which can be influenced by the perceptions and interpretations of others. There are obvious limits to how far leaders or representatives of the Alliance can harmonise their policies against the tide of diverging geopolitical trends; but making no attempt whatever to do so, and dispensing with the mechanisms to try, would be a perverse response to these trends. Second, and even more important, institutions are necessary to implement common action if and when analyses and perceived interests do converge. Indeed, after 45 years of NATO,

Americans take interoperability with Europeans, forward bases and transatlantic military trust so much for granted that they sometimes forget what the world would be like if the Organisation did not exist. But as NATO Supreme Allied Commander Europe (SACEUR) General George Joulwan recently reminded Congress, the existence of NATO provides the US European Command (USEUCOM) with basing, infrastructure and prepositioned equipment that has proven essential in several post-Cold War contingencies, and was indispensable during the 1991 Gulf War.[32] Cooperation within NATO has also proved indispensable in the execution of military operations in former Yugoslavia, including the no-fly zone, the September 1995 air-strikes and now *Operation Joint Endeavour* (IFOR). If US and European forces are ever going to be called upon to act together in the post-Cold War world – and US forces in Europe have planned 32 operations and actually executed 13 of them since 1993 – their cooperation in NATO will be essential.[33]

Arguments that the United States should give up forward basing in Europe and elsewhere and instead rely on US-based assets miss this important point.[34] They also fail to recognise that there may come a time (if that time has not already arrived) when the United States is simply incapable of mounting major operations alone, and that European assets – intelligence, force projection capabilities and troops – might be necessary to the United States. It is possible that, even in the absence of an Atlantic military organisation, the United States and Europe might be able to count on each other's support if both sides' interests were threatened; but the cooperation seems far more likely to take place – and might only be possible – if alliance structures were already in place.

The continued existence of a formal alliance for security reasons may be even more important to the Europeans than to the US. Today, Europe seems safe from attack, and it is hard to imagine the re-emergence of a Cold War-type threat. But five years after the collapse of communism is too soon to assume that no new ideology, nationalism or threatening instability will emerge in Europe or North Africa. It is probably exaggerating to say (as did former NATO Secretary-General Willy Claes) that Islamic fundamentalism is 'at least as dangerous as communism was', but it would be equally unwise to dismiss serious instability in North Africa as something by which Europe – and thereby the United States – would remain unaffected.[35] Europeans continue to try to develop their own means for dealing with security and will undoubtedly be spurred on in their efforts by the lessons of Yugoslavia. But the fact that NATO was unable to produce transatlantic solidarity on one security crisis means neither that it did not help at all, nor that it might not prove essential in the future. Europeans may regret that they were not able to invoke Alliance solidarity and count on full US support for their policies in Yugoslavia, but it would be a mistake to conclude that such support will never be there or that Europe will soon be able to do without it. Recent assessments have conservatively placed the cost of Europe building its own communications, logistics, force-projection and satellite capabilities at around $107bn per year, requiring a rather unlikely increase in the share of GDP spent on defence by most European countries from 2.5% to 4%.[36]

There is probably little that can be done to counter the trends that are inevitably undermining the relative alliance cohesion that existed during the Cold War. But it would be dangerous to conclude that a looser alliance is a dispensable one. Interests common to Europeans and North Americans include preventing a new hegemonic challenge in Europe; assisting the anchoring of stability and security to Eastern Europe; ensuring continued access to energy supplies; preventing or coping with instability in North Africa and the Middle East; and containing the spread of weapons of mass destruction. The Atlantic Alliance is not as obviously necessary as it once was, but it continues to provide residual defence insurance, the means for proactive security policy on behalf of its members, and the foundation of a 'pluralistic security community' in which war among its members has all but been abolished.[37] Cold War or no Cold War, these are not unimportant functions.

Preserving and Adapting the Alliance

This chapter's basic assertion is that structural changes are diminishing both the cohesion and the perceived value of the Atlantic Alliance. Trends within the Alliance place the burden of demonstrating its utility on those who want to maintain it. It is not surprising that leaders on both sides of the Atlantic are actively searching for ways to revitalise an apparently fading partnership – if the Alliance were not perceived to be 'broke', no one would be trying to fix it.[38] What should – and should not – be done?

• *Do Not Expect Free Trade to Save the Alliance.* One of the most frequently heard recommendations for how to promote post-Cold War transatlantic relations is the creation of a free-trade zone between Europe and North America (TAFTA). The issue has been on the agenda for a long time, but a number of both US and European senior officials – including US Secretary of State Warren Christopher, German Foreign Minister Klaus Kinkel, President of the EU Commission Jacques Santer and Canadian Prime Minister Jean Chrétien – have begun to throw new weight behind it.[39]

While a successfully negotiated TAFTA would have some economic advantages, including that of economic specialisation, it has a number of problems and limits.[40] First, the impact on existing transatlantic free trade, especially if limited to manufactured goods and tariff reduction, would be relatively small. Trade and investment between North America and Europe is highly integrated, and there is not much scope for further liberalisation. (Average tariff rates on industrial goods in most sectors are no more than 2–3%, and average customs duties are 4.1% in the EU and 3.4% in the US.)[41]

Second, there is by no means any guarantee that in the areas where liberalisation might have real meaning – notably agriculture, textiles, aviation and audio-visuals – the negotiations would be successful, given the political constraints on both sides. Far from enhancing transatlantic cooperation and understanding, negotiations on a TAFTA could thus simply stimulate quarrels that would not be resolved and might be better left untouched. A far-reaching agreement between governments that was later rejected by a parliament on either side of the Atlantic would probably be worse than no agreement at all. Finally, beyond the risks of failure there are the risks of success. A free-trade pact between North America and the EU, as with any regional trading arrangement, would be a step away from the goal of creating a global free-trade order embodied by the nascent World Trade Organisation. It could alienate developing countries and push Asians to retaliate with their own preferential arrangements. A TAFTA might lessen the chance of a NAFTA–EU bloc arrangement, but it could increase the possible formation of Asian and Atlantic blocs.

Even more important, a TAFTA is not a panacea for transatlantic relations under strain, and those who seek to replace the old security community with a new economic partnership will be disappointed. In security cooperation, the ultimate goal was always the same or at least similar, but economic relations are inherently more competitive. The fact that both sides gain from trade does not help to resolve the question of relative perceived gains, which is always at the centre of trade negotiations. Adding an economic emphasis to the Atlantic Alliance always failed in the past, and it is unlikely to be much more successful today. TAFTA may well be in the economic interests of the transatlantic partners, but it is not going to be NATO's salvation.

• *Forget New Charters, Just Act Like Allies.* NATO does not need a new legal or institutional basis, such as those proposed by a number of leading officials and analysts.[42] In the absence of a common will or perceived common interests, such a grandiose effort would only serve to highlight the gap between leaders' rhetoric and their actions, a problem that has plagued the Alliance since the end of the Cold War. In 1990 and 1991, Americans and Europeans proceeded with a Transatlantic Declaration between the US and the EC and a new Strategic Concept for NATO, neither of which has produced the sort of cooperation proponents of some new formal charter desired.[43] If Europeans and Americans do prove that they are willing to maintain a genuine alliance, there might be a case at some point to consecrate the new relationship in treaty form. But after the countless failures of international institutions (such as NATO, the EU and the UN) to uphold their pledges recently, the establishment of a new relationship on the ground should precede any attempt to formalise such a relationship in treaty terms. Actions speak louder than words.

Instead of grand principles or new documents, the allies might simply make more of an effort to act like allies. What does acting like allies mean? It means, first of all, resisting the temptation, so evident from 1991 to 1995, to pander to domestic public opinion and place blame for foreign-policy problems on foreign allies or international institutions. It might also be useful to consider the code of alliance behaviour once articulated (if not always followed) by Henry Kissinger: the allies best strategically placed to influence the outcome of a crisis situation should be given the chance to lead.[44] Kissinger's line was not always adopted and he, making foreign policy for a superpower, found it hard to resist acting otherwise, but the principle is a sound one. In Bosnia, it would have meant the United States letting Europe take the lead instead of publicly opposing European policy without being willing or able to change it. The US might have announced that it had a different approach but, unwilling to impose that approach on reluctant allies, it was prepared to stand by those allies and help avoid the worst of all worlds, in which Americans and Europeans pursue contradictory policies. When vital interests are not at stake, the importance of the alliance itself becomes greater than that of the regional crisis. This principle seems at least partly to have been applied in the US decision to participate in IFOR.

Admittedly, resisting the temptation to blame others publicly and sometimes deferring to allies will not always be possible, and it is certainly unlikely so long as political leaders are weak at home. But one should not overlook the fact that failing to cooperate itself contributes to weakness, and shifting the blame will inevitably take its toll. A modest effort to stand by allies where their interests are far greater than one's own and to resist the temptation to blame them for failure would be a helpful contribution to the functioning and preservation of the Alliance. We should at least understand that the failure to do so will only contribute to its erosion.

• *Forego Congressional Forums, and Encourage Public Understanding.* Concerned that the transatlantic allies are growing apart, a number of senior Alliance officials have proposed various forums for bringing policy-makers closer together. Malcolm Rifkind, for example, has suggested a new Atlantic Assembly of 150 US Congress members and 150 European parliamentarians that would deal not only with security affairs (as does the current North Atlantic Assembly (NAA)), but also with trade, broader economic issues and other 'potential areas of discord'.[45] Others – such as Leon Brittan, German Defence Minister Volker Rühe and the Transatlantic Policy Network (a coalition of European parliamentarians and multinational companies) – have made similar proposals.[46] The logic behind these ideas is no doubt sound, but one wonders whether a new body would have any more impact than the existing NAA, which has been largely ignored by leading parliamentarians in both Europe and the United States. With their overwhelmingly domestic focus and the lack of any 'transatlantic' constituency, there seems little reason why senior legislators would take a week from their busy schedules, and also grounds for doubt as to whether anything but posturing would result.[47]

If the goal is mutual understanding, it might make more sense to pursue transatlantic exchanges at a more public level, such as through the existing Fulbright programmes, United States Information Agency (USIA) and European Union Visitors Programmes, the UK's new Atlantic Fellowships and Germany's Bundeskanzler Scholarships – an exchange modelled on Rhodes Scholarships set up by Chancellor Kohl. The next generation of US and European business, policy-making, media, academic and cultural élites will be less inclined to preserve a close transatlantic relationship than their predecessors were, and if the perceptions of these groups are being pulled in opposite directions the politicians who represent them will not be able to stem the tide. To the extent that government-to-government exchanges are pursued, an earlier, more limited proposal by Rifkind to exchange senior civil servants would probably be more constructive, particularly if it involved exchanges among government policy-planning staffs who would seek to harmonise national assessments before they diverged. Finally, a broader sense of shared transatlantic interests can be reinforced through the joint pursuit of cooperation in such new domains as transnational crime prevention, counter-terrorism and non-proliferation, as provided for in the EU–US Transatlantic Joint Action Plan of 2–3 December 1995. If European and American interests in other areas are diverging relative to the Cold War, their common interest in these areas seem more pertinent now than ever.

• *Enlarge NATO Deliberately, and Not Too Widely.* When the Cold War ended and NATO's original mission was largely undermined, many saw its expansion as a promising way to save an otherwise imperilled alliance.[48] A new NATO was to have the mission not only of defending its members and going 'out of area', but it would also take on responsibility for consolidating democracy in Central Europe and, in the words of proponents of enlargement, 'extending stability across the continent'. After an initial period of hesitation, and pulling sometimes reluctant Europeans along, President Clinton finally announced in January 1994 that the question was 'no longer whether NATO would take on new members, but when and how'.[49]

There were always good arguments both for and against NATO enlargement. In its favour, it is true that extending military guarantees to Central Europe would help alleviate some of the understandable security concerns of the states of that region, and that taking the new democracies into this exclusive club would contribute to their feeling of belonging in the West (especially given the European Union's reluctance to take them in quickly). Expanding the Alliance would be a statement to Russia that, while NATO members wanted good relations with Moscow, they were not prepared to subordinate their foreign and security policies to Russian wishes, and that the long period of Russia's unwanted domination of its Western neighbours had ended. The arguments of those who claimed NATO enlargement would 'strengthen Russian hardliners' or freeze out states in the 'grey zone', such as Ukraine or the Baltic states, were often exaggerated: the Russian nationalists were doing well anyway for domestic reasons, and just because an alliance might extend a security guarantee to some states hardly means that it would be indifferent to an invasion of others.

On the other hand, NATO could not be expanded without costs and risks. It might well be irrational, short-sighted and counter-productive for Moscow to react to enlargement by taking hostile countermeasures (such as backing out of arms-control agreements or deploying more troops further West), but that is no guarantee that it would not do so. Indeed, especially having raised the level of rhetoric in order to protect themselves from hardliners in the course of the Russian legislative and presidential election campaigns, even pro-Western Russian leaders like President Boris Yeltsin might feel obliged to take countermeasures simply for the sake of 'credibility', an argument that NATO leaders should certainly understand (having made similar arguments so often themselves). And there was also the risk that, if enlargement were undertaken simply as a temporary political expedient or to 'save the Alliance' without a full acceptance of its implications – a willingness to risk nuclear war over Central Europe – the extended guarantee might not be so valuable; Central Europeans already had plenty of experience with guarantees that were not backed by the will or means to uphold them. Contrary to the arguments of those who say it is necessary to enlarge the Alliance while security prevails, perhaps a guarantee to Central Europe might be more credible if extended in a period of genuine military threat – as was the situation with NATO in the first place.

Whatever the case, it has now been widely accepted that NATO will take in new members, and it was probably never realistic to imagine that it could put off enlargement forever. But if the principle of an open Alliance is and should be accepted, there seems no need to rush, nor to go too far. Indeed, a deliberate process of enlargement – beginning no sooner than 1997 – could have some advantages: it would allow Russia to complete at least another electoral cycle and further adjust to its new geopolitical situation; it would avoid accusations that the US was pushing enlargement for political reasons in an election year; it would enable Central Europeans to demonstrate their democratic and Western 'credentials' as responsible potential members of the Alliance (as they are currently doing in IFOR); and it would allow, ideally through membership in the European Union, Central Europe as a region genuinely to integrate itself economically, politically and culturally with the rest of Europe, thereby making any eventual military guarantees or commitments more plausible.

The impatience of those who want to enlarge NATO sooner is understandable. But with the Soviet threat gone, the Alliance can be more discerning about which members it lets in, and when it does so. The NATO of the future will be less about protecting its members from an all-out assault and more about consulting among like-minded nations that sometimes have similar interests and values to protect around the world. NATO still operates by consensus, and the more members it takes in the greater the chance that parochial interests or petty grievances prevent progress towards otherwise common goals; the Alliance should not forget the problems it had with obstreperous members in the past, and that was when there was a common threat. There are good reasons to proceed with NATO enlargement, and by cooperating so well in Bosnia the Central Europeans are already establishing their credentials. Those Central European states that demonstrate they belong to the West through democracy, media freedom, civilian control of the military, market economies and commitment to liberal values should be invited to join NATO when current NATO members are genuinely prepared to defend them; but no more, and no sooner.

• *Preserve Military Structures and Capabilities.* Perhaps the most important role Alliance leaders can play today is to ensure that the institutions, patterns of communication, command structures and shared military capabilities built up over the last 40 years are preserved. More than anything, NATO was a forum where an international bureaucracy and military forces from 16 countries could assemble to plan and train together, and develop an infrastructure to be used if their political masters so decided. No military organisation like it has ever existed in the past, and it would be rash to do away with the trust, common procedures, interoperability and experience that exists within NATO.

Obviously, without the massive Soviet threat, NATO's structure and bureaucracy will have to be scaled down, and some of this has already been accomplished. But so long as it is plausible that European and US forces might be called upon to undertake military tasks together – and they keep having to do so, from the Persian Gulf to the Balkans – it makes sense to preserve an integrated command structure and shared assets. Without a single, common threat, it will be necessary to find ways of allowing 'coalitions of the willing' to use those assets even when all NATO members do not agree to participate – this was the principle accepted at NATO's January 1994 Brussels summit in the US acceptance of a European Security Identity and the adoption of the Combined Joint Task Forces (CJTF) concept.[50] But these goals must be pursued without creating unaffordable redundancies or damaging the principle of NATO primacy.

Agreed to in theory more than two years ago, CJTFs have still not been finalised. The main dispute within the Alliance over CJTFs pits France, which sees CJTF primarily as a way to enable the Europeans to undertake eventual military operations without the US but with NATO assets, against the United States and most of the other allies, which see it primarily as a way of ensuring the continued centrality of NATO's integrated military command and avoiding the duplication of resources and structures. With such incompatible goals, it is not surprising that the allies have been unable to agree on the details of the means.[51]

Yet CJTF, or something like it, must be made to work if NATO is going to achieve the flexibility it needs in the new environment. The United States should accept, as it already has in principle, France's main goal of making NATO assets available in certain contingencies for uniquely European deployments. Yugoslavia has already demonstrated that there might be military actions Europeans want to take without the United States, and it is not only unreasonable to expect Europe to contribute the bulk of the resources for common assets without having access to them, but it might be in the United States' own interest to facilitate the success of those actions while reducing duplication of means. On those occasions when the US does want to get involved or take the lead, the creation of European-only options does not seem a great risk; European states would be unlikely to refuse US leadership if it was genuinely offered.

France, on the other hand, should give up its desire to ensure that CJTFs at the European level be distinct from NATO's integrated structures, which the other allies clearly want to preserve. So long as European-only CJTFs are indeed 'separable', as declared in the original concept, France should not oppose NATO involvement in them. The United States would be unlikely (and unwise) to 'sabotage' operations that the entire WEU wanted to undertake with NATO assets, for doing so would be the surest way to undermine support in Europe for the continuation of NATO. Continued French intransigence over the role of the integrated command will confirm the suspicions of some that France's true goal is to demonstrate that Europe cannot count on the support of the United States, and, thereby, that it must develop its own autonomous means.

Even if the CJTF debate is resolved and successfully decides the fate of common NATO assets (which include an air-defence system; command, control and communications (C^3) assets; oil pipelines; and 18 airborne warning and control systems (AWACS)), the fact is that Europe will remain dependent on national US assets (such as long-range heavy transport aircraft, air-refuelling capabilities and satellite intelligence systems) for everything but very small-scale interventions. Since automatic access to US national means is out of the question – no country will make its national assets automatically available to an alliance without a veto over their use – Europe must accept the dilemma that the French have (intentionally or not) underlined: it must either put the resources behind developing independent capabilities or accept dependence on the United States. This is a reality that CJTFs cannot be expected to resolve.

The Alliance might, however, consider some sort of leasing arrangement, by which purely US assets lacked by the Europeans might be rented out or lent for a specific mission, with financial and other arrangements settled in advance. The precedent of US air-lifting of troops for French deployments in Africa, or the leasing or sale of KC-135 airborne refuelling aircraft, would be a basis from which to work, and could be supplemented by co-training European pilots and troops on the sorts of US aircraft, helicopters or air-defence systems they might need to borrow.

Conclusions

It is legitimate to be concerned about the future of the Atlantic Alliance. Not only has the military threat that made this alliance necessary in the first place disappeared, but other geopolitical, economic and demographic factors are also leading Americans and Europeans apart. Every other military alliance in history was disbanded after its main *raison d'être* disappeared, and there is no guarantee that this Alliance will have a different fate.

The Atlantic Alliance, however, will probably not disappear. Many challenges to shared US and European interests remain, and common culture and values, while not a sufficient condition for partnership, will continue to create a bias towards transatlantic cooperation. US and European leaders should, however, accept the consequences of a recast Alliance and avoid the complacent view that nothing has changed. If Americans want to preserve the credibility of a proven Alliance and count on European support in times of need, they should demonstrate their continued commitment to the Alliance, even when that commitment has a cost. Europeans, in turn, should do all they can to ensure that the Americans remain involved – while preparing for the inevitable occasions when US commitment will not be as strong as Europe would like.

Notes

1. As one unnamed former US Secretary of Defense once asked: 'When has NATO ever been in array?'. See David G. Haglund, 'Must NATO Fail? Theories, Myths, and Policy Dilemmas', *International Journal*, vol. 50, no. 4, Autumn 1995, p. 651. The original quote is cited in François Heisbourg, 'Europe/Etats-Unis: le Couplage Stratégique Menacé', *Politique Etrangère*, no. 52, Spring 1987, pp. 111–12, the title of which itself is indicative of past concerns about Alliance cohesion.

2. See Warren Christopher, speech at the Casa de America in Madrid, 'Charting a Transatlantic Agenda for the 21st Century', 2 June 1995 (Washington DC: Department of State, Office of the Spokesman); Malcolm Rifkind, 'The Atlantic Community', speech to the Pilgrims Society, 15 November 1994; and Sir Leon Brittan, 'The EU–US Relationship: Will it Last?', speech to the American Club of Brussels, 27 April 1995.

3. The citation is from Malcolm Rifkind, who claims that common interest and

commitment 'predated the Cold War and will live on after it' and that 'those who say that the end of the Cold War will lead to a parting of the ways between the United States and Europe do not understand history'. One might make the same criticism of those who believe the Cold War was not the most important cause of the common transatlantic interest. See Rifkind's arguments in 'The Atlantic Community', pp. 3–4.

4. See Bob Woodward, *The Agenda* (New York: Simon and Schuster, 1994). Indeed, the very shift from George Bush – a former Second World War fighter pilot, US representative to the People's Republic of China, US Ambassador to the United Nations, and Vice-President – to Clinton – the governor of a small southern state with little experience or responsibility in international affairs – was a powerful symbol of America's new post-Cold War focus.

5. See, for example, the debate between Alfred E. Eckes, who argues that US presidents for 45 years 'consciously subordinated domestic economic interests to foreign policy objectives', and his critics, who assert that this was not the case. See Alfred E. Eckes, 'Trading American Interests', *Foreign Affairs*, vol. 71, no. 4, Autumn 1992, p. 135; and the letters to the editor by Francis M. Bator and Richard N. Cooper, 'Free Trade', *Foreign Affairs*, vol. 71, no. 5, Winter 1992–93; and Philip H. Trezise, 'Trade Policy: Myths of Altruism', in *Foreign Affairs*, vol. 72, no. 4, September–October 1993, pp. 187–89.

6. See Jeffrey F. Garten, 'Trade and Foreign Policy: Reflections on Economic Diplomacy', presentation at the IISS, London, 11 July 1995, p. 16. US Trade Representative Mickey Kantor has used almost the exact same language in testimony to Congress. See Kantor cited in Trezise, 'Trade Policy', p. 188.

7. See Garten cited in John Stremlau, 'Clinton's Dollar Diplomacy', *Foreign Policy*, no. 97, Winter 1994–95, p. 18, which is a good assessment of the United States' new economic priority.

8. See Tarnoff quoted in John M. Goshko, 'Reduced US Role Outlined but Soon Altered', *Washington Post*, 26 May 1993.

9. See John E. Rielly (ed.), *American Public Opinion and US Foreign Policy 1995* (Chicago, IL: The Chicago Council on Foreign Relations, 1995). Much has been written about the shift from foreign to domestic priorities in the US. For a few good examples, see Peter Peterson with James K. Sebenius, 'The Primacy of the Domestic Agenda', in Graham Allison and Gregory F. Treverton, (eds), *Rethinking America's Security: Beyond Cold War to New World Order* (New York: W. W. Norton and Co., 1992), pp. 57–93; Stanley Sloan, *The US Role in the Post-Cold War World: Issues for a New Great Debate*, Congressional Research Service Report for Congress, 24 March 1992; and Stremlau, 'Clinton's Dollar Diplomacy'.

10. See Rielly, *American Public Opinion*, pp. 7, 10.

11. The Times Mirror selected groups of 'influentials' in various categories such as 'business', 'media', 'foreign affairs', 'science' and 'security'. The only group that did not choose 'strengthening the domestic economy' was the 'cultural' élite, which placed protecting the global environment first, and strengthening the domestic economy second. See Times Mirror Center for the People and the Press, 'America's Place in the World: An Investigation of the Attitudes of American Opinion Leaders and the American Public About International Affairs', November 1993, pp. 18–19.

12. See 'The US: The Unilateralist Temptation', in *Strategic Survey 1994–95* (Oxford: Oxford University Press for the IISS, 1995), pp. 53–63; and 'US National Security:

Revitalisation or Isolation?', *Strategic Comments* (London: IISS), no. 3, 22 March 1995.

13. And yet this is already happening. See columnist Thomas L. Freedman's recent speculations along these lines in 'A Leadership Partner for America?', *International Herald Tribune*, 24 July 1995.

14. The 117 freshmen elected to the 103rd Congress (1992) was the highest number ever, followed by the 85 new members elected in 1994. See Kevin Merida, 'Many Democratic House Freshmen Won't Be Returning', *Washington Post*, 10 November 1994.

15. US Bureau of the Census, *Statistical Abstract of the United States: 1975* (96th edition) (Washington DC, 1975), p. 101.

16. US Bureau of the Census, *Statistical Abstract of the United States: 1994* (114th edition) (Washington DC, 1994), p. 11.

17. For the poll results, see Times Mirror Center, 'America's Place in the World', p. 34.

18. According to the International Monetary Fund and other organisations, Asia will produce more than 30% of world GNP by the year 2000. See Kenneth S. Courtis, 'The Centre of the World Economy Shifts to the Asia-Pacific: Challenges and Opportunities for Canada', address to the Pacific Basin Economic Council of Canada, Toronto, 18 April 1994; Kishore Mahbubani, 'The Pacific Impulse', *Survival*, vol. 37, no. 1, Spring 1995, pp. 105–6; and Paul Dibb, *Towards a New Balance of Power in Asia,* Adelphi Paper 295 (Oxford: Oxford University Press for the IISS, 1995), pp. 18–19.

19. See the figures cited in 'War of the Worlds: A Survey of the Global Economy', *The Economist*, 1 October 1994, p. 4. The top ten in 2020 by GDP at purchasing-power-parity estimates and using the growth forecasts of the World Bank's *Global Economic Prospects* are China, United States, Japan, India, Indonesia, Germany, South Korea, Thailand, France and Taiwan.

20. See International Monetary Fund, *Direction of Trade Statistics*, (Washington DC: International Monetary Fund, 1993), p. 111.

21. See 'US Trade Policy Review', *General Agreement on Tariffs and Trade (GATT)* (Geneva: GATT, June 1994) vol. 1, pp. 21, 23. Here 'Europe' includes Eastern Europe and the former Soviet Union. 'Asia' includes Australia and Oceana.

22. For an argument that 'Europe remains by far the most important economic partner for the United States', see Robin Gaster and Clyde B. Prestowitz Jr, *Shrinking the Atlantic: Europe and the American Economy* (Washington DC: Economic Strategy Institute and North Atlantic Research Inc., July 1994).

23. When asked which part of the world, Europe or the Pacific Rim, was most important to the United States, 50% said Europe, compared to 31% for the Pacific Rim. Among the élites, however, this view was only shared by the defence and security and the scientific communities, albeit by a lower ratio. All of the other élite groups believed the Pacific Rim to be more important. See Times Mirror Center, 'America's Place in the World', p. 6.

24. The US 'business and finance élite' found the Pacific Rim to be more important to Europe by a ratio of 51% to 26%. See Times Mirror Center, 'America's Place in the World', p. 6. For Christopher, see the *New York Times*, 25 July 1993.

25. The countries are China (including Taiwan and Hong Kong), India, Indonesia, Brazil, Mexico, Turkey, South Korea, South Africa, Poland and Argentina. See Stremlau, 'Clinton's Dollar Diplomacy', p. 18.

26. None of this should be surprising, given the Alliance's poor record in dealing with 'out-of-area' crises. See Douglas T. Stuart and William T. Tow, *The Limits of Alliance: NATO Out-of-Area Problems Since 1949* (Baltimore, MD: The Johns Hopkins University Press, 1990).

27. See Henry Kissinger, 'Die Atlantische Gemeinschaft Neu Begründen', *Internationale Politik*, no. 1, January 1995, p. 22.

28. The existence of the Atlantic Alliance was not the only reason the United States opposed this aggression by a dictatorship – principle was also involved. But one of the reasons US government supporters of Britain in the Falklands dispute prevailed over their colleagues who called for a neutral stance was surely the UK's status as a close US ally. As the then Under-Secretary for European Affairs Lawrence Eagleburger put it: 'I was driven essentially by one very simple argument – an ally is an ally'. US Defense Secretary Caspar Weinberger's strong feelings about the UK were also said to have played an important role. The Eagleburger quote is originally from Chaim Kaufman, *US Mediation in the Falklands/Malvinas Crisis: Shuttle Diplomacy in the 1980s* (Pittsburgh, PA: Pew Program in Case Teaching and Writing in International Affairs, 1988), p. 13. On Weinberger ('a passionate Anglophile'), and for an excellent general analysis, see Lawrence Freedman and Virginia Gamba-Stonehouse, *Signals of War: The Falklands Conflict of 1982* (London: Faber and Faber, 1990), especially pp. 161 and 189–90.

29. For an account of how the Atlantic allies tried – albeit with mixed success – to stand by each other in crises, see Elizabeth D. Sherwood, *Allies in Crisis: Meeting Global Challenges to Western Security* (New Haven, CT: Yale University Press, 1990).

30. Even the US Congress tempered its embargo legislation to avoid negative consequences for the security of European troops. The so-called 'Dole amendment' gave the President the authority to waive the embargo legislation if he deemed that its implementation would compromise the 'safety, security and successful completion of the withdrawal of UNPROFOR personnel from Bosnia'. See 'Bosnia and Herzegovina Self Defense Act, Amendment no. 1801', 18 July 1995.

31. See President Clinton's assertion in a letter to Congress in November 1995 that 'if we do not do our part in a NATO mission, we would weaken the alliance and jeopardize American leadership in Europe'; and US Secretary of Defense William Perry's argument (made in testimony to Congress and in a later speech in Philadelphia) that whereas US 'vital interests' themselves were not threatened in Bosnia, US involvement there 'affects the vital national security interests of the US by maintaining the strength and credibility of NATO'. A Pentagon spokesman clarified the point that using US forces to implement a peace settlement was essential because 'we're protecting NATO – that's vital'. *Time*, 27 November 1995, p. 42.

32. Joulwan noted that the existence of NATO 'gives [the United States] access to basing and infrastructure necessary for force projection both [in Europe] and in [the Persian Gulf]. This proved critical during *Desert Shield* and *Desert Storm*, where 95% of the strategic airlift, 90% of the combat aircraft and 85% of the naval vessels were staged from or through USEUCOM's [area of responsibility]. This would have been practically impossible without USEUCOM basing and infrastructure, to include equipment prepositioned in theatre to supply reinforcing forces'. See 'European Theater Remains One of Conflict and Transition', prepared statement of Gen. George A. Joulwan, USA, Commander-in-Chief, US European Command, to the House National Security

Committee, 2 March 1995, in *Defense Issues* (Washington DC: American Forces Information Service, Office of the Assistant to the Secretary of Defense, March 1995), vol. 10, no. 40, p. 7. Joulwan also points out the advantages of access to common NATO infrastructure, 72% of which is paid for by the Europeans.

33. *Ibid.*, p. 4. These figures are as of March 1995 and therefore do not include the IFOR operation.

34. For an example, see Charles Krauthammer, 'Don't Let "Cheap Hawks" Shoot This Weapon Down', *International Herald Tribune,* 11 July 1995.

35. See Roger Boyes, 'Muslim Militancy is Next Big Threat says NATO Chief', *The Times*, 3 February 1995.

36. See, for example, the Royal United Services Institute's estimate cited in *The Economist*, 25 February 1995. Another estimate gives £70bn per year for Europe as a whole, with £15bn and 25 years necessary for a complete European panoply of radar, infra-red and communications satellites that would still not equal what the United States has. See Ian Bruce, 'Europe Counts Cost of Fighting its Own Battles', *The Herald,* 16 May 1995.

37. The concept of security communities is discussed in Karl Deutsch, *Political Community and the North Atlantic Area: International Organization in the Light of Historical Experience* (Princeton, NJ: Princeton University Press, 1957). Also see the discussion in Gebhard Schweigler, 'Driftet die Atlantische Gemeinschaft Auseinander?', *Internationale Politik*, no. 6, June 1995, p. 55.

38. For some of the more important recent proposals, see Christopher, 'Charting a Transatlantic Agenda for the 21st Century'; Rifkind 'The Atlantic Community'; Brittan 'The EU–US Relationship'; and the speeches by French Prime Minister Alain Juppé and German Defence Minister Volker Rühe at the 1995 Wehrkunde Conference in Munich discussed in Joseph Fitchett, 'Western European Proposes New Transatlantic Pact', *International Herald Tribune*, 7 February 1995. There is an interesting (and ominous) parallel here with 1973 – dubbed the 'Year of Europe' by Henry Kissinger (for many of the same reasons that are motivating leaders today) but which turned out to be a year of crisis in the Alliance instead.

39. For Christopher, see 'Charting a Transatlantic Agenda'; for Kinkel, 'Kinkel Favors Transatlantic Free Trade Area', Foreign Broadcast Information Service WEU-95-116, 16 June 1995, p. 3; and for Chrétien, Nathaniel C. Nash, 'Is a Trans-Atlantic Pact Coming Down the Pike?', *New York Times*, 15 April 1995. Canadian Minister for International Trade Roy MacLaren has also been a prominent proponent. See MacLaren's speech to the Royal Institute of International Affairs, London, 'The Occident Express: Towards Transatlantic Free Trade', 22 May 1995 (text provided by the Canadian Department of Foreign Affairs and International Trade).

40. Economically, a free-trade zone would expose industries on both sides of the Atlantic to greater competition, resulting in increased efficiency and thereby greater competitiveness with other regions. And the further lowering of agricultural barriers and subsidies could result in significant consumer and government budgetary savings that could usefully be used in other ways. See Thomas J. Duesterberg, 'Prospects for an EU–NAFTA Free Trade Agreement', *Washington Quarterly* , vol. 18, no. 2, Spring 1995, pp. 71–82.

41. See Brittan, 'The EU–US Relationship', p. 7.

42. See Jacques Santer's proposal in his inaugural speech to the European Parliament

for a 'genuine transatlantic treaty' (January 1995). Cited in Lionel Barber, 'Niggling Trade Disputes Threaten US–EU Relationship', *Financial Times*, 13 March 1995. Also see Gunther Hellmann, *Die Europäische Union und Nord-amerika nach Maastricht und GATT: Braucht die Atlantische Gemeinschaft einen neuen Transatlantischen Vertrag?*, Internal Studies no. 70 (Bonn: Konrad Adenauer Foundation, December 1994); and Hellmann, 'EU and USA Need Broader Foundation: The Case for a "Transatlantic Treaty"', *Aussenpolitik,* English Edition, vol. 45, no. 3, 1994, pp. 236–45.

43. In the Transatlantic Declaration of November 1990, the US and Europe 'solemnly reaffirmed' their 'determination further to strengthen their partnership' and pledged to 'inform and consult each other on important matters of common interest'. NATO's Strategic Concept of a year later similarly reaffirmed Alliance solidarity and reiterated the continued validity of the essential purpose of the Alliance. The objective elegantly expressed in both documents is honourable, but the impact on government policies has been difficult to discern. Both documents are reprinted in Nanette Gantz and John Roper (eds), *Towards a New Partnership: US–European Relations in the Post-Cold War Era* (Paris: Institute for Security Studies of the Western European Union, 1993), pp. 201–17.

44. In discussing the 'proper conduct of allies in an emergency when they sincerely disagree with one another either about causes or about remedies', Kissinger asks: 'Should they use the occasion of their partners' embarrassment to vindicate their own views? Or do they have an obligation to subordinate their differences to the realisation that the humiliation of the ally who, for better or worse, is *most* strategically placed to affect the outcome weakens the structure of common defence and the achievement of joint purposes?'. Kissinger always asserted that allies have an interest in deferring to each other when vital interests are not at stake and long argued that the US was wrong to oppose its allies in the Suez crisis for this reason. See the discussion in the second volume of his memoirs, Henry Kissinger, *Years of Upheaval* (Boston, MA: Little, Brown and Company, 1982), pp. 708 and 729–30.

45. See Peter Almond, 'Rifkind calls for Atlantic Forum', *Daily Telegraph*, 31 January 1995.

46. See Brittan, 'The EU–US Relationship'.

47. As an EU trade official reportedly remarked, 'put parliamentarians from France and the US mid-West together, and they'll simply squabble over agriculture'. See Lionel Barber and Guy de Jonquières, 'US and Europe Eye Each Other Up', *Financial Times*, 12 May 1995.

48. See Ronald D. Asmus, Richard L. Kugler and F. Stephen Larrabee, 'Building a New NATO', *Foreign Affairs*, vol. 72, no. 4, September–October 1993, pp. 28–40; Zbigniew Brzezinski, 'NATO – Expand or Die?', *New York Times*, 28 December 1994; Michael Clarke, 'NATO Must Upset Russia or Do Nothing and Die', *Sunday Telegraph*, 7 November 1993; and Asmus *et al.*, chapter 5.

49. See Clinton quoted in 'Clinton Hints NATO Would Defend East from Attack', *International Herald Tribune*, 13 January 1994.

50. CJTF are a means for putting together multinational and multi-service forces and command structures for specific tasks as they arose. CJTFs would be able to deploy either as a NATO force (involving those NATO members which chose to participate); a WEU force (thus creating the possibility for Europeans to undertake operations using NATO assets but without the involvement of the United States); and as either of the

above along with non-NATO members (such as the countries participating in Partnership for Peace or others). See Barry, chapter 10. Also see the excellent report of the North Atlantic Assembly Defence and Security Committee by Rafael Estrella, General Rapporteur, NAA International Secretariat, *After the NATO Summit: New Structures and Modalities for Military Cooperation*, November 1994.

51. On France and CJTF, see Grant, chapter 3.

Chapter 2
Common European Defence and Transatlantic Relations

Nicole Gnesotto

The organisation of a common European defence policy is no longer the controversial issue that it was during the Maastricht Treaty negotiation in 1991. Europe's lack of unity at the time of Maastricht is evident in the highly conditional (and often contradictory) language of the Treaty on European Union. It defines the Common Foreign and Security Policy (CFSP) as including 'the eventual defining of a common defence policy which might in time lead to a common defence' (Article J4). This diplomatic phraseology betrayed the lack of consensus in Europe about a CFSP at the time.[1]

Five years later, the evolution of the strategic context – with regard to Bosnia, US foreign policy or France's new attitude towards NATO – has made new compromises possible. Yet numerous differences remain, and it is still not clear whether these apparent convergences are any more than technical or marginal adjustments. As the European Union's Inter-governmental Conference (IGC) opens in 1996, the debate about European defence remains conflictual, and the questions it raises – in particular about the future of Euro-American relations – are all too often being ignored.

Uncertain Convergence on European Defence

The debate about European defence and the US role in Europe no longer leads to ideological quarrels, because many of the factors that had blocked consensus have disappeared. In 1991, any suggestion of European autonomy in defence (especially when made by France) immediately raised suspicions of competition with NATO, an organisation already uncertain about its mission in the wake of the Soviet collapse. US suspicions, of course, were most prominent, as demonstrated by the many criticisms and warnings put forward by the administration of President George Bush.[2] But in Europe, too, leaders in the UK, Portugal, the Netherlands and (sometimes) Italy were sceptical about any Franco-German initiative in the area of common security or defence.

Since 1994, however, there has been a relative convergence of views in both the US and Europe. In the United States, the Clinton administration claims to support genuine European cohesion: the NATO summit of 10–11 January 1994 gave a real endorsement to the creation of a European defence and security identity (ESDI) under the Western European Union (WEU).[3] In backing ESDI, the Americans – perhaps even more than the Europeans themselves – are taking note of the lessons of the Bosnian conflict, which made clear that there will be crises in Europe in which the US does not want to intervene. If Washington does choose to intervene militarily, as it has in the case of the NATO-led Peace Implementation Force (IFOR) in Bosnia, then the supremacy of American leadership is not in question. But because the new crises of post-communist Europe, whether caused by restive minorities or state disintegration, do not imply the automatic engagement of the US, it is in the US' own interest for Europeans to be sufficiently organised to provide at least minimal management of the crises on their periphery.[4]

This new US pragmatism in task-sharing implied more pragmatic European positions, the best example of which so far is the recent convergence between the UK and France. Here, too, the case of Bosnia was fundamental. The two countries, traditionally among the most opposed to European integration (and especially to a common European defence), found themselves aligned – both stuck in the Yugoslav quagmire, sharing the same risks, subject to the same criticisms and confronted with the dilemmas of reluctant intervention and elusive neutrality. Their soldiers dying together brought them together: the French discovered the utility of operational cooperation with NATO and agreed to build the still-desired ESDI within the Alliance; and the British, having for three years experienced the volatility of US engagement in European conflicts, became more conscious of what a 'European card' might have to offer. By December 1995, the French had made their new pragmatism official, fully joining the NATO Military Committee that they had left in 1966, and announcing further participation by their Defence Minister in NATO bodies.[5]

Other European countries also experienced the US unpredictability that, combined with great uncertainty about the situation in Russia, leads to a general European consensus on at least the following points for 1996:

- the need to 'do something' in the area of defence;
- the use of the WEU as the framework for this common defence;
- the need to reinforce the operational capacities of this organisation;

- the maintenance of inter-governmental decision-making in foreign and defence policy; and
- the need for complementarity with NATO, which will remain the provider of collective defence, while the WEU limits itself, for the time being, to crisis management.

Despite these convergences, much remains to be done. The extraordinary complexity of the problems and a number of latent ambiguities make genuine progress in building a new European security order practically impossible. At a time when the political stakes call for the definition of a truly new global contract between Europe and the United States, the institutional priority currently given to preparing the IGC seems artificial – if not ridiculous.

The Dilemmas of a Common European Defence
The Defence Role of the European Union

The first critical debate is that of the European Union's legitimacy as a political-military actor. Should the EU have a defence role, a common defence policy being the logical result of a common foreign and security policy? Or should the Union remain a 'civil power' without a political-military role, and leave the building of a European defence outside the EU framework? The choice is not a new one. In 1990–91, the British view that the EU should not have a defence role competed with an alternative Franco-German vision of the future – two irreconcilable projects that led to the ambiguity of the Maastricht Treaty. Today, on the eve of the IGC, the UK maintains (even more strongly, in fact) its opposition to any political and military integration in the framework of the EU, whereas Germany – now ahead of France as the motor of Europe – sees political union as an indispensable complement to monetary union.

This ideological division about the objectives of European integration would be unimportant to the IGC if it did not have so direct an impact on the question of the WEU's future. The UK is refusing, even more strongly than five years ago, all political subordination of the WEU to the Union, as well as the placing of European defence in the framework of the 'common policies' of the Union.[6] London would at most permit, under certain conditions and in very limited cases, a European defence policy for which the WEU would be the only political and executive body. Germany, however, along with France, wants to institutionalise a certain degree of political dependence of the WEU on the EU Council, which would be the highest decision-making body and would establish general directives for European military actions. These two approaches are contradictory. To be sure, the UK's veto of the link between the WEU and the Union cannot alone delay the entire IGC (institutional channels between the two institutions can always be reinforced), but London's enduring reservations about military competences for the EU are so serious that any pragmatic compromises reached will likely be no more than cosmetic.

National Sovereignty and Collective Efficiency

The second major dilemma concerns the link between the desire to preserve national sovereignty and the need for collective efficiency. How can national control over armed forces – meaning a veto right for states and their national parliaments – be maintained without paralysing the decision-making capacity of a Union eventually consisting of 20 or more members, all with the right to veto? Where defence is concerned, this classic dilemma between 'deepening' and 'widening' cannot be resolved by resorting to majority votes: no state will ever accept that its soldiers be sent to die as the result of a qualified majority vote. Even Germany, the advocate of European federalism, would admit this, and inter-governmentalism will therefore remain the rule. But if the consensus principle is useful because it preserves the freedom of national abstention (so that no state is forced to participate in a military operation against its will), it nonetheless creates a huge problem: the need for consensus can also limit the freedom of action of those states that might want to intervene, but that run the risk of being blocked by another state's veto, even if just one of the 15 in the Union. The question is therefore a delicate one: how can inter-governmentalism be rendered effective by making it unequal, when the golden rule of European integration is precisely fundamental equality among all its members?

The United Nations, with its five-member Security Council, works on the principle of inegalitarian inter-governmentalism. But the conditions of its creation after the Second World War no longer correspond to current realities, and are particularly inappropriate for the democratic states of the European Union. NATO was also able to create a form of unequal multilateralism, the weight of the United States making that country *de facto* more influential than any other member in joint decision-making. But such a disproportion of power, between a leader and the rest, does not exist in Europe, nor is it desired.

The numerous variations on the theme of a 'hard core' for Europe, limiting integration in certain areas to those countries willing and able to move ahead, were designed to resolve this dilemma between sovereignty and efficiency. But can a military hard core be built in the same way as the monetary one, when Germany remains reluctant to get deeply involved in military crisis management and when, without the UK, a European defence would be like a duck without feet? It is essential and normal that Germany participate in the Union's decision about military intervention, but could it also claim a right of political control of a military mission in which it could not participate? Moreover, how could the primacy of certain (large) states over other (small) states be justified, when it is often the small – indeed, neutral – ones that traditionally provide the most blue helmets for UN peacekeeping?

However useful the debate about 'hard cores', then, it is unlikely to lead to great innovations for 1996. The reform of decision-making for security policy – which must also prepare the way for future enlargement of the EU to the countries of Central and Eastern Europe – should nonetheless respect the following four principles:

- no state should be obliged to participate in a military operation against its will;
- a majority of states should not thereby be prevented from acting by the veto of one or two partners;
- the neutral countries of the Union (and those, like Denmark, that refuse to adhere to the WEU) should not have a right of veto on the decisions of the EU in military matters; and
- the shared risk of casualties is a determining criterion for sharing decision-making power, political control and military command.

These principles could take two institutional forms. One is the rule of 'consensus minus five', meaning that the five EU members that are not members of the WEU could not exercise a veto in the European Council when the decision calls for the WEU to be used; and the other is qualified majority voting, not to decide a military operation, but, on the contrary, to prevent one.

European Defence and the Atlantic Alliance

The third challenge is to reinforce European defence while at the same time preserving and revitalising the Atlantic Alliance. The complementarity of the two processes is unanimously accepted in principle, but significant differences remain when it comes to translating this general formula into concrete terms. To build a European defence without operational capacities would be absurd, but to build such capacities by duplicating those of NATO would be both too expensive and politically unacceptable. No European country, not even France, supports such an option. Whereas a minimal operational reinforcement of the WEU is necessary and inevitable, if only to define how to place soldiers under European command, sharing NATO's means remains the most natural solution, as adopted officially by the Alliance in January 1994.[7] Even so, the Combined Joint Task Force (CJTF) concept, intended to enable Europeans to use NATO assets when the US decided not to intervene in a local crisis, is still, like the project of building a European pillar itself, unfulfilled.

The lessons of the war in Bosnia are essential here. On the one hand, by unilaterally withdrawing from enforcing the arms embargo on former Yugoslavia in November 1994, the US should logically have left the political and military control of the operation in the Adriatic to the Europeans, all the more so as nearly all of the ships involved were European. The Supreme Allied Commander Europe (SACEUR), however, kept the command of this European operation to himself. The situation in Bosnia also created the unfortunate precedent by which one country, the United States, had two policies towards the same conflict – a national one (non-application of the embargo), and an Alliance one (the order given to US officers in NATO to implement NATO policy). Is it possible to imagine a European country supporting one belligerent nationally and another as part of a European defence? Finally, the Bosnian crisis was one in which the United States was not only reluctant to intervene, but in which Washington found itself in a major political disagreement with its main European allies, about both the analysis of the conflict and its consequences. If the sharing of NATO military means is hard enough in the case of US abstention or indifference, what will it be like in cases of fundamental political disagreement between Europe and the United States?

Thus the debate about the devolution of collective NATO means to the Europeans, in case of US abstention, cannot be limited to a technical debate, to be resolved by some structure of the military organisation. The autonomy of a European military operation can only be the product of a major political negotiation between European WEU members and Washington, not with Supreme Headquarters Allied Powers Europe (SHAPE) or NATO headquarters in Brussels.

The Dilemmas of Enlargement

The fourth dilemma is how to enlarge Western institutions to encompass the Central and East European countries without either provoking Russian hostility or destroying, through concessions, the force and the credibility of these institutions. This dilemma applies to both the enlargement of the EU/WEU and to that of NATO. The eastward extension of the two organisations is in effect inevitable, necessary and irreversible. Logically, and in the best of the possible scenarios, the two processes should be simultaneous and convergent; the enlargement of Western institutions should represent the progressive political integration of all the European democracies into the same institutional network, with its different economic, political and military dimensions. In reality, however, the reconciliation of these processes is problematic, for at least three reasons.

The first problem is the timing: NATO enlargement, to two or three of the so-called Visegrad Four countries (Poland, the Czech Republic, Hungary and Slovakia), may well take place more rapidly than that of the EU. This is so because certain Americans seek in Central Europe a way to reinforce the mission of the Atlantic Alliance, and also because other Americans refuse to allow NATO's destiny to depend on the decisions of the EU – a European body in which the US has no rights. The paradox would be that Poland would become a member of NATO without being a member of the EU and therefore without being able to join its common defence dimension, the WEU.

This leads directly to the second problem, because the Maastricht Treaty establishes a strong legal link between membership in the EU and membership in the WEU: any EU country can, at least theoretically, become a WEU member (or observer).[8] But the WEU, in turn, has a formal link with NATO, with Article 5 of the two organisations intimately related – all WEU states now accept that NATO membership is a prerequisite for WEU membership, even though the reverse is not true.[9] Thus, if Austria, for example, asked to join the WEU – and this will also be true for the Central and East European countries and Baltic states when they are members of the Union – it would only do so by also joining NATO, and therefore with the agreement of the United States. The paradox would be that Europe could not enlarge completely, that is, including its common defence dimension, without the agreement of the United States, which is not a member of the Union.

The third problem lies with NATO's own organisation. NATO enlargement requires, on the one hand, the transformation of its structures and operations, if only to make it acceptable to Russia: if enlargement were to take place by a simple geographic extension of the current military organisation, with all the concrete implications of its Article 5, this might provoke Russian aggressiveness. NATO's credibility, on the other hand, particularly in the eyes of its European members, requires the maintenance of its primary collective defence function – including nuclear deterrence. The risk, then, is that in order to enlarge, the Americans might show too much flexibility in their interpretation of Article 5, thereby leaving some states better protected than others within the same Alliance. This would raise questions about the value of Article 5, and about that of NATO itself.

Some may be tempted to suggest purely institutional responses to these questions, by reinforcing the autonomy of the WEU *vis-à-vis* the Union, by separating the common defence policy from the CFSP, and by trying to win time by delaying NATO's own expansion as long as possible. If the WEU were independent from the EU, the latter could certainly expand freely and practically indefinitely, without the problem of new WEU members ever being raised. NATO and the WEU could thus enlarge before the EU or not at all, but in either case as a function of their own rhythm and according to their own criteria, and not as a result of the EU's internal dynamics.

But what is the value of such institutional manipulations when it comes to the major political solidarity that constitutes the heart of European integration? If some future member of the EU – such as Finland, for example – were to be attacked by some great power – Russia, for instance – the European Council could obviously not limit its response to institutional orthodoxy. The European Union could not refuse to defend a member threatened by attack, under the pretext that it was not a formal member of NATO or the WEU. In other words, the entirety of the security relationship between Europe and North America must be rethought.

Major Negotiation or Lost Opportunity?

Given the many – and often contradictory – issues raised by the question of European defence, it seems rather undesirable to limit the 1996 IGC to an exercise in institutional renovation. This, however, is unfortunately the most likely scenario. It would be more useful to make the IGC 1996 the forum for a new debate, at Europe's initiative, about the future of the Atlantic Alliance and notably task-sharing between Europe and the United States.

Euro-US Political Negotiations

In operational terms, it is necessary to begin political negotiations with Washington – and not with NATO – about the conditions under which Europe would exercise autonomy in matters of defence. The debate should focus on two points, the first of which concerns US assets in NATO. It seems obvious that Europeans should be able to use NATO assets, since they already provide 80–90% of NATO's conventional forces. The absolute minimum to expect for 1996 is that Europeans commit all of their means not only to NATO, but also to the WEU. The more delicate issue, however, concerns means earmarked to NATO that are either exclusively or primarily American (such as intelligence, and command, control and communications equipment) or that are fully integrated (such as the NATO air-defence network). Under what conditions, in the case of US abstention, is the United States prepared nonetheless to provide these assets in support of a European operation? Even worse, in case of US opposition to a European intervention, how can European autonomy be ensured, knowing that only the United States possesses certain means that are essential for any serious military operation?

The second sensitive point concerns the NATO chain of command. On the one hand, to disintegrate it in favour of a European operation poses not only the problem of potentially undermining NATO's main mission of collective defence, but it might also raise questions for US public opinion or in Congress, which might not see why they should support the continued deployment of American troops in Europe if the European command becomes too prominent. On the other hand, if the shared risk of death is really the foundation of the Atlantic contract – it justified US leadership during the 40 years of nuclear risk for Washington – it is hard to see how a European operation in which only Europeans took real risks would not be under the exclusive command and control of Europeans, via the WEU or even the EU. A certain degree of disintegration of NATO's military apparatus is thus inevitable in order to bring about the compromise agreed in January 1994. The question remains how to organise the European pillar without either destroying NATO or, at the other extreme, transforming the Europeans (and the WEU) into little more than foot soldiers under SACEUR's control.

These difficult points – which have continued to block the implementation of CJTFs – make future discussions about the creation of a European pillar of NATO delicate and controversial, but also essential. In case of a US–Europe strategic agreement, it is necessary and in the interest of both parties for Europeans to be able to use US means devoted to NATO, just as they must be able, if necessary, to allocate certain NATO integrated military commands already staffed by Europeans to the WEU. The entire operation would be placed under WEU command, with the agreement of and in association with Washington. Alternatively, in case of Euro-US strategic disagreement, or even of US opposition to the European use of NATO means, Europe risks being paralysed by its dependence. There is thus no other solution to compensate for this eventuality that the Bosnia crisis has made all too plausible, but to build – in addition to NATO – the means for European strategic autonomy. In other words – and this is the most sensitive point – the construction of a European pillar *within* NATO does not make the construction of a European pillar *outside* NATO superfluous, especially when it comes to strategic transport, intelligence gathering and the structures necessary for political control and military command.

These stakes are crucial not only for the operational credibility of European defence, but also for the future of NATO itself. Indeed, one cannot exist without the other. The Bosnia experience demonstrates, if it was not clear already, that NATO has an uncertain future as an organisation of crisis management if it remains completely dependent on the military engagement of the Americans. As for Europe, the notion of a 'European pillar of the Alliance' will only have any meaning if the WEU has the means truly to become the Europeans' political *and* military structure within NATO – not to substitute some absurd notion of 'European Europe' for the Atlantic Alliance, but to preserve the pertinence of that Alliance in the face of post-Cold War realities.

This more egalitarian rethinking of NATO's military procedures would also be the prerequisite for a far-reaching revision of transatlantic institutions. NATO's eventual enlargement will not itself suffice to revitalise the Alliance, including in the eyes of US public opinion. Even if enlargement remains consistent with NATO's collective defence function and non-discriminatory against current member-states, the sharing of military means for crisis management will remain problematic. If, on the contrary, enlargement is accomplished to the detriment of Article 5, it is difficult to see how this newly enlarged NATO could remain credible as the political organ of Europe's security, thereby creating the risk that resentment, disappointment and suspicion come to define Alliance relations more than solidarity among member-states. At a time when the common threat has disappeared, and while the United States will not always inclined to intervene in peripheral crises, it will also become more and more difficult to limit the US role in Europe to military affairs, which would make the American presence a burden for both sides. The NATO framework, enlarged or not, is restrictive by nature, and the Transatlantic Declaration that redefined European–American relations in 1990 is far too informal.[10] The only credible option for the long term is a new, bilateral treaty of mutual defence and global economic and political cooperation, between equal partners, the EU and the United States.[11] There is no need today, as in the 1960s, to fear an 'Atlantic Europe', but rather to maintain the tradition of an America that remains 'European'.

The United States and European Union Security

The second question about Euro-US relations is whether and under what conditions the United States is prepared to guarantee the defence of a European Union of 18, 20 or even 25 members. In other words, what is the US interpretation of NATO's Article 5? Whether one likes it or not, it will be increasingly difficult to avoid this potentially painful debate as the process of enlargement goes ahead.

For the answer is less obvious than it might seem, and three cases are theoretically possible, depending on the threats and the countries in question: the US could decide to defend all EU countries against all threats; it could agree to defend all EU countries, but only in the case of a new Russian threat; or it could defend only some EU states against an eventual Russian threat.

The first case is the least problematic. It simply requires that EU and NATO enlargement take place simultaneously. The two other options, however, would require the Union itself to have the means to stand in for the US and defend all its members against all potential threats, whatever their origin. If this were not the case, the very notion of common defence policy would be meaningless. And yet the current consensus among European countries avoids the question altogether, or pretends that the first option is the most likely one.

This consensus rests, in fact, on the limitation of the tasks for European defence to crisis management (non-Article 5 missions), reserving for NATO the first responsibility for collective defence (Article 5). This minimalist definition of European defence was the leitmotiv of the British position at the time of the Maastricht negotiation, and it was supported by nearly all the countries in Europe. It has also become, as expressed in the 1994 *White Paper on Defence*, France's official position.[12]

This consensus certainly has some political merit, in the sense that it calms the diffuse fears of disloyal competition between the European defence project and the Atlantic organisation: even the French can no longer be suspected of wanting Europe *instead of* NATO. And it is true that, at a time when the United States is uncertain of its own European vocation, the modesty of the European approach is reassuring to everyone.

But there are a number of reasons to doubt whether this common wisdom, however tactically reasonable, is rational, or even tenable. In operational terms, this distinction between collective defence and crisis management is far from pertinent: the experience in Bosnia – especially the debate about an eventual withdrawal of the blue helmets by NATO forces in spring 1994 – showed that a peacekeeping mission can demand combat operations similar to those required of a collective defence force. The great ambiguity of new, post-Cold War risks – which are neither like inter-state conflicts nor traditional peacekeeping – requires an external intervention to be undertaken with all the necessary military means, including the means for heavy combat or forced withdrawal.

In institutional terms, the distinction between crisis management and defence is equally impractical. To reduce European defence to a crisis-management role, even if placed in the legal framework of the WEU, contradicts the WEU treaty itself. The WEU treaty is based on its own Article 5, which is even more far-reaching in its obligations than NATO's, and contains nothing whatever obliging its member-states to manage crises collectively. In this area, in fact, the decision of the member-states is completely free and sovereign. If the WEU could limit itself to crisis management, it could actually expand immediately to Finland, Austria and Poland, without that expansion posing any problem at all for NATO. In other words, if the minimalist version of European defence were to become the rule, it would make sense to situate it outside the framework of the WEU. If, however, the WEU is to be considered the normal framework for a common European defence policy, this can only be as part of a global interpretation of defence, including Article 5.[13]

Finally, NATO's own evolution does not seem to suggest an Alliance that will limit itself to Article 5 contingencies. Since the Rome summit in November 1991, the Atlantic Alliance has given itself a new strategy of collective security and crisis management (IFOR is the most obvious example) at the same time that its objective of enlargement raises questions about what will remain of Article 5. In the long run, can Europeans leave the collective defence mission to NATO alone, when NATO seems to want to be able to do everything, without being certain that it will always be able to do collective defence?

In truth, where enlargement is concerned, the EU will no longer be able to avoid the question of its own collective defence capacity, in case of excessively restrictive US interpretations of NATO's Article 5. Far from being premature, this question is crucial (even if controversial) because it requires one of two things: either the eventual inclusion of a defence 'Article 5' in the Treaty of European Union (which, after all, would be normal practice); or the acceptance of a coexistence, in the same Union, of different zones of security. In the first case, it is the potential for competition with NATO that causes problems; in the second, it is the principle of discrimination within the Union that cannot be admitted. But, whatever the tactical considerations and the low profiles that all are adopting during the preparation for the 1996 IGC, this question is and will remain fundamental. In the long run, in fact, Europe's political union, in parallel with its monetary union, requires the reciprocal engagement of all the EU member-states to defend each other collectively, with or without the United States.

Conclusion

The current consensus among Europeans for the preparation of 1996 is fragile, artificial and not very productive. The revision conference of the Treaty on European Union is hardly seen today as the opportunity for a true renovation of US–European security relations. France's new inclination towards British pragmatism may reinforce these modest goals. But that is hardly a reason to rejoice. With Germany at the heart of European integration and the main *raison d'être* of NATO itself, is it not time for France, together with Germany and then with the UK, to elaborate thoroughly a global European defence project that takes post-Cold War considerations into account? Tactical prudence and bilateral Franco-British *rapprochement*, however necessary, is no substitute for a true European security policy.

As for the common values and principles such a policy would be designed to defend, one can only hope that Europe's dismal performance in Bosnia at least leads it to rethink its role. While Europe's political credibility will be a function of its institutions and means to act, its legitimacy is of another nature altogether. This European schizophrenia between abstract institutional battles and a real war in which Europeans failed to uphold the very values that they seek to incarnate and promote must now be cured.

Notes

1. See Nicole Gnesotto, 'European Defence: Why Not the Twelve?', *Chaillot Papers*, no. 1, Western European Union Institute for Security Studies (Paris: Institut d'Etudes de Sécurité de l'UEO, March 1991).

2. The most eloquent illustration of US suspicion was the 'Bartholomew telegram' sent to the 11 NATO members of the EC in February 1991.

3. 'We give our full support to the development of a European Security and Defence Identity which, as called for in the Maastricht Treaty, in the longer term perspective of a common defence policy within the European Union, might in time lead to a common defence compatible with that of the Atlantic Alliance'. North Atlantic Council Declaration, Press Communiqué, M-1(94)3, Brussels, 11 January 1994, para. 4.

4. Until the creation of IFOR in December 1995, the operational American contribution to the management of the Bosnian crisis involved only air operations, not ground deployments.

5. See the 5 December 1995 announcement in Brussels of Foreign Minister Hervé de Charette at the North Atlantic Council – the first such meeting attended by a French Defence Minister (Charles Millon) since 1966.

6. See the British memorandum of March 1995 on relations between the WEU and the EU: 'we should create a new WEU body at Head of State and Government level involving Full members, Associate members and Observers ... The new body would have responsibility for taking forward the definition of a European defence policy, as envisaged in the Treaty on European Union ... It could meet back-to-back with Heads of State and Government meeting in the European Council'. A WEU Council of 18 members would thus include both Norway, which refuses adhesion to the EU, and Turkey, which has little perspective of joining, rendering impossible the eventual fusion with the EU.

7. 'We therefore stand ready to make collective assets of the Alliance available, on the basis of consultations in the North Atlantic Council, for WEU operations undertaken by the European Allies in pursuit of their Common Foreign and Security Policy.' North Atlantic Council Declaration, Press Communiqué, M-1(94)3, para. 6.

8. See the Declaration on the WEU (annex to the Treaty of European Union), which declares: 'States which are members of the European Union are invited to accede to WEU on conditions to be agreed in accordance with Article XI of the modified Brussels Treaty, or to become observers if they so wish. Simultaneously, other European member-states of NATO are invited to become associate members of WEU in a way which will give them the possibility to participate fully in the activities of the WEU'.

9. If a WEU military operation risked being defeated, then the WEU members involved in this operation could use their right, as members of NATO, to call upon US military intervention to defend them, under the provision of Article 5 of the NATO Treaty. This recent interpretation of NATO and WEU membership thus partly contradicts the WEU Declaration cited above, as the criterion to become a member of the WEU is no longer that of EU membership, but membership of both the EU and NATO.

10. The Transatlantic Declaration, signed in Paris on 20 November 1990, states: 'To achieve their common goals, the European Community and its member states and the United States of America will inform and consult each other on important matters of common interest, both politic and economic, with a view to bringing their position as close as possible without prejudice to their respective independence'.

11. See then Foreign Minister Alain Juppé's call for the consideration of a new transatlantic charter in his speech for the twentieth anniversary of the Foreign Ministry's policy planning staff, Paris, 30 January 1995, published as 'Quel Horizon pour la Politique Etrangère Française?', *Politique Etrangère*, no. 1, Spring 1995, pp. 245–59.

12. 'The WEU is henceforth recognised as a component of the defence of the European Union. It should set the objective of making autonomous European military action possible in cases other than those which bring into play the principal guarantee of the North Atlantic Treaty'. See *Livre Blanc sur la Défense* (Paris: La Documentation Française, 1994), p. 53.

13. This is, in fact, what is foreseen in the Petersberg Declaration of 19 June 1992 which defined the missions of the WEU.

Chapter 3
France's New Relationship with NATO

Robert P. Grant

NATO's January 1994 summit meeting in Brussels was a defining event in the evolution of France's post-Cold War relationship with the Alliance. French officials agreed strongly with the US-proposed initiatives that Alliance leaders announced at the summit, including Partnership for Peace (PFP), Combined Joint Task Forces (CJTFs) and a NATO policy framework on how to protect against the threat of nuclear, biological and chemical (NBC) weapons proliferation.[1] The summit, which one French official described as 'the best NATO summit ever, from France's viewpoint', also gave wholehearted backing to two major French policy goals: the development of a European Security and Defence Identity (ESDI) through the European Union (EU) and strengthening the European pillar of the Atlantic Alliance through the Western European Union (WEU).[2] Less than one month after the summit ended, France led the United States into backing a NATO ultimatum designed to break the Serb siege of Sarajevo, the first Western initiative to have a positive, albeit temporary, impact on the fighting in Bosnia.[3] These developments inspired then Foreign Minister Alain Juppé to ask the startling question, 'is not Franco-American entente the Alliance's most visible dynamic element?'.[4] US–French leadership again shaped NATO actions in Bosnia during the summer of 1995, helping to create the conditions that led to the peace agreement signed in December 1995.[5]

The culmination of France's *rapprochement* with NATO – for now, as the process seems likely to continue – came in December 1995, when Foreign Minister Hervé de Charette announced that France would henceforth participate fully in NATO's Military Committee and that the French defence minister would also 'be able to regularly take part in the work of the Alliance, alongside his colleagues'.[6] With the deployment of the Bosnian Peace Implementation Force (IFOR), French ground troops are under direct NATO command for the first time since 1966.

Why has France conducted this *rapprochement* with the Alliance after appearing to want to marginalise NATO's role in European security during the immediate post-Cold War years? To what extent does the *rapprochement* reflect a fundamental change in France's attitude towards NATO? And what will be the main consequences of the new French posture?

Initial Post-Cold War Estrangement

The end of the Cold War did not lead France to abandon the traditional Gaullist critique of NATO military integration.[7] Throughout 1990 and 1991, French leaders reiterated that France would not rejoin NATO's Integrated Military Structure (IMS).[8]

Some French analysts acknowledged that during the Cold War there had been a certain military and political logic behind the IMS because NATO was facing the threat of massive attack with minimal warning time, and Europeans needed the reassurance that US armed forces would be automatically implicated in responding to any such aggression.[9] However, many French defence experts argued that without a Soviet threat, NATO only needed a capability for joint planning, common procedures to ensure interoperability, and joint exercises. Allied countries could accomplish these tasks without the institutionalisation of multinational commands in peacetime.[10]

From the French perspective, a reformed NATO would have these enduring roles: to balance the Soviet Union's (later Russia's) geostrategic mass on the continent; to ensure US involvement in European defence; and to maintain a transatlantic capability to undertake improvised, multinational military operations. Meaningful NATO reform entailed 'returning to the spirit of the 1949 treaty', or significantly weakening the role of the integrated military command.[11] Europeans would exercise much greater responsibility within a radically revised military structure, while alongside this new NATO an emerging West European defence entity would deal with the types of limited conflict likely to arise in Europe.[12]

In short, to France, the end of the Cold War allowed NATO to move towards eliminating the IMS, removed the military need for the United States and NATO to be the central players in West European security, and created a real possibility for Western Europe to construct a serious defence entity. The end of the Cold War greatly renewed France's long-standing ambitions for a European defence entity. Not only did these ambitions seem more achievable, but the need for such an entity had become more compelling. With no Soviet threat, an eventual US disengagement from European security appeared more likely, and the European defence entity would ultimately have to be capable of assuming an increasing share of collective defence responsibilities. German unification also constituted a significant incentive for France to strive for far-reaching European defence cooperation.

French analysis that NATO's integrated military command no longer had any military or political rationale ran contrary to Washington's refusal to countenance any modification to the IMS. Thus the statement by the then French Ambassador to NATO, Gabriel Robin, that 'if we are ready to make enough adjustments in the structures, I personally wouldn't rule out the full participation of France', remained untested.[13] Furthermore, the French saw the Alliance's 1990–91 military reorganisation, creating the essentially all-European Rapid Reaction Corps (ARRC), as providing only a 'façade' of Europeanisation.[14]

These views caused France to resist the US-led efforts to reorganise NATO's force posture and to expand NATO's role beyond the collective defence responsibilities embodied in Article 5 of the North Atlantic Treaty. Paris simultaneously moved to give substance to European defence cooperation. While French leaders never had any illusions that a fully capable European defence entity would take shape overnight, there was an expectation of steady, meaningful progress. The October 1991 initiative to create the Franco-German Eurocorps and the signing of the Maastricht Treaty on European Union in December 1991 seemed to bear out this expectation.

Given these French goals, tensions with the United States were probably inevitable. France's immediate post-Cold War vision of European security autonomy was too radical for Washington and most of the other allies. US anxiety to establish a leading national and NATO role in the new Europe arguably led to an overly rigid attitude in Washington towards France's goal of developing European defence cooperation. The United States sought to undermine French initiatives in this direction even as it was formally acknowledging in NATO declarations that European defence cooperation could reinforce both European security and the Alliance. The Bush administration reacted with particular consternation to France and Germany's October 1991 announcement of the Franco-German Eurocorps, worrying that it would draw German troops away from their NATO commitment.[15] The inflexibility in both US and French positions was mutually reinforcing, and led to open competition between European and transatlantic approaches to security. The setting up in July 1992 of separate WEU and NATO naval task forces in the Adriatic Sea to enforce the embargo against Serbia was a visible manifestation of this competition.

Paris was careful not to let its relations with the US and NATO deteriorate too badly. French forces participated in the 1991 Gulf War under US military command, despite France's great reluctance to go to war against Iraq.[16] France took part in NATO's 1990–91 strategy review, agreed to the Alliance's new

Strategic Concept despite expressing reservations towards some of its elements, and then allowed formal NATO adoption of non-Article 5 missions, such as peacekeeping, at the June 1992 meeting of NATO foreign ministers. The overall tone of the period, however, was one of intense competition between French and US security policies. Although Presidents George Bush and François Mitterrand were able to maintain a close personal relationship, ties between many other US and French officials became increasingly bitter.[17]

France's *Rapprochement* with the Alliance

Given this inauspicious beginning to the post-Cold War relationship between France and NATO, the events of the three-year period from December 1992 to December 1995 are remarkable. In a very significant move, tensions over the Eurocorps ended with the conclusion in December 1992 and the signing on 21 January 1993 of a three-way agreement between France, Germany and NATO. The agreement provided for French forces within the Eurocorps to come under NATO's 'operational command' in time of crisis. Previous agreements concerning NATO's use of French forces had only provided for an eventual yielding of 'operational control' of those forces, and Washington was, according to one report, 'agreeably surprised' that Paris had accepted to place its Eurocorps units under NATO's operational command.[18]

Operational command allows greater flexibility in the use of the forces placed at a commander's disposal, as there is a broader definition of the mission for which the forces are released. French sources claimed that three conditions placed on NATO's use of the Eurocorps made the 'operational command' that Paris had agreed to cede very much resemble the conditions of 'operational control'. The three conditions are: that there be agreement between France and Germany regarding release of the forces; that the corps be used for a mission defined in advance by a plan approved by French political authorities; and that the corps be engaged 'as such'.[19] Eurocorps missions could include peacekeeping as well as collective defence under Article 5.[20] A WEU Assembly report on European forces drew the following conclusion: 'it should be noted that the European Corps is adapted to the structures and procedures of the alliance, thus confirming it as compatible with NATO and as France's contribution (in that context) to the strengthening of the European pillar in NATO'.[21]

In December 1992, Mitterrand also authorised French officers to participate in NATO military staff work preparing for a potential UN mandate to implement a Bosnian peace settlement or to protect safe areas.[22] Then, in April 1993, the head of France's mission to the Military Committee, General Jean-Paul Pélisson, began to participate with a 'deliberative voice' in all Committee meetings dealing with peacekeeping missions. France had withdrawn from the Military Committee in 1966, and its military mission to the Committee had retained only observer status with a 'consultative voice'.[23]

French-inspired competition between NATO and the WEU came to an end, symbolised in June 1993, when the separate NATO and WEU naval task forces operating in the Adriatic combined. The combined task force came under the operational control of NATO's integrated military command, subject to the political authority of both the NATO and WEU Councils. French officials began to state that, if Europeans agreed on the need to intervene in a given crisis, the first step would be consultation with Washington on US participation in the intervention. Only if the United States did not wish to participate would the operation become a strictly European one.[24] The acknowledgement of this priority (NATO first, WEU second) did not come without expressions of regret.[25]

French participation in NATO continued to grow. France played a leading role in developing NATO's counter-proliferation initiative, becoming in 1994 the initial co-chair, with the US, of NATO's Senior Defence Group on Proliferation (DGP). France thus found itself at the head of a NATO defence-planning body dealing with an essentially non-Article 5 mission area.[26] During 1993 and 1994, France established new military missions with the three NATO Major Subordinate Commands that are responsible to the Supreme Allied Commander Europe (SACEUR).[27] Direct contact between the French military and Supreme Headquarters Allied Powers Europe (SHAPE) also expanded in order to achieve better coordination regarding operations in former Yugoslavia.[28] In September 1995, the first NATO exercise was held in France since 1965. Approximately 60 aircraft and 1,000 personnel from seven allied countries took part in the four-day exercise simulating NATO air-strikes in Bosnia.[29]

Yet another significant area of movement in France's NATO relationship concerned the participation of France's top defence officials in NATO meetings. In October 1993, NATO defence ministers met informally at Travemünde, Germany, hoping, without avail, to obtain the participation of French Defence Minister, François Léotard. At the time of the Brussels summit, Paris indicated that its defence minister and armed forces chief of staff would henceforth attend NATO meetings 'if questions concerning French forces are taken up or when the meeting agenda places France in a position to intervene'.[30] Several months later, the new defence *White Paper* confirmed this decision, specifying that France's President and Prime Minister would decide on a case-by-case basis upon the participation of the defence minister and chief of staff in NATO meetings.[31] In September 1994, François Léotard attended an informal gathering of NATO defence ministers in Seville, the first time since 1966 that a French defence minister had participated in a NATO meeting. Thirteen months later, the new French Defence Minister, Charles Millon, went to another informal meeting of NATO defence ministers, while France's Chief of Staff, General Jean-Philippe Douin, attended a meeting of the Military Committee for the first time since 1966.

Hervé de Charette's December 1995 speech to the North Atlantic Council (NAC) was thus the logical culmination of an evolution already under way. In addition to announcing France's full participation in the Military Committee and the 'regular' participation of French defence ministers in Alliance meetings, the Foreign Minister indicated that France would take its place within different bodies under the jurisdiction of the Military Committee. These include the NATO Defence College in Rome, the NATO (SHAPE) School in Oberammergau, and the NATO Situation Centre in Brussels. De Charette stated that France would begin a process designed to improve its working relationship with SHAPE.

Reasons for France's *Rapprochement* with the Alliance

Four successive developments contributed to the substantial improvement in relations between France and NATO. The first was what one American analyst characterised as the 'unravelling' of the French plan for Europe.[32] Europe's failure to do more than contain the conflict in former Yugoslavia; the extreme difficulties in obtaining ratification of the Maastricht Treaty in France as well as in a number of other European countries; and the sharp decline in military spending and manpower in virtually all NATO countries combined to frustrate French hopes that there would be relatively rapid, significant progress on ESDI.[33]

The French drew two conclusions from the setbacks to their European aspirations. First, the US and NATO appeared increasingly necessary not only to maintain Western Europe's collective defence capabilities, but also to meet the challenges of the post-Cold War crises that France initially believed Europe could handle on its own. Thus, Paris began to realise that dealing with Europe's new security needs and establishing France as an important actor on the new security agenda meant more rather than less engagement with the United States and NATO.

Jacques Chirac, then leader of the *Rassemblement pour la République* (RPR), noted bluntly in early 1993 the second conclusion – that France had to draw from the limitations of European security cooperation:

> With respect to Europe, we are forced to note that the substantial reduction in the American military presence has not stimulated any decisive European process, far from it. Several of our partners have even begun considerably to reduce their armed forces and are placing themselves more than ever under American protection, incarnated through NATO.
>
> I conclude that if France wants to play a determining role in the creation of a European defence entity, it must take into account this state of mind of its partners, and reconsider to a large degree the form of its relations with NATO. It is clear, in effect, that the

necessary rebalancing of relations within the Atlantic Alliance, relying on existing European institutions such as the WEU, can only take place from the inside, not against the United States, but in agreement with it.[34]

More recently, a French political commentator neatly summed up the position in which France finds itself with respect to defence: 'in order to be more European tomorrow it is necessary to be more Atlanticist today'.[35]

It is impossible to overestimate the importance of this observation for France's relationship with NATO, given the central nature of European ambitions to France's foreign and security policy. While during the initial post-Cold War period France saw NATO as, at best, irrelevant to the development of ESDI and, at worst, as a major obstacle to it, the French view shifted towards recognising NATO as a necessary instrument in the building of ESDI.

The second fundamental development contributing to France's *rapprochement* with the Alliance was the US reticence to become fully engaged in efforts to resolve the Bosnian conflict, and the accompanying US refusal to contribute US ground forces to peacekeeping operations there. The French were dismayed at US reaction to the Bosnian crisis, and the nature of French anxieties over US policy began to shift.[36] Rather than fearing a continuing US hegemony in Western Europe that the end of the Cold War had rendered unjustifiable, France started to worry more about US disengagement, an outcome that would be all the more alarming in light of the limitations of Europe's intervention in Bosnia.

Apprehension remained limited that an actual US withdrawal from Europe was imminent. As one French parliamentary report put it, 'there is no historical example of a superpower losing interest in the evolution of the world ... the United States has the will to maintain American leadership'. However, the report continued: 'while the United States will clearly remain present or active in places where its interests are directly threatened, it will also possibly seek to escape certain of its responsibilities within the international system'.[37]

The third major development was that when the Clinton administration came to power it had a much greater interest in easing the US defence burden, making it more receptive to arguments in favour of a supportive US approach to ESDI. Apparent US willingness to move beyond the ambivalent lip-service previously paid to European defence cooperation and to provide tangible backing for ESDI had a significant impact in Paris.

Finally, France's *rapprochement* with the Alliance was also accelerated following the election, in early 1993, of a conservative–centrist coalition majority in the *Assemblée Nationale*. By the end of 1992, President Mitterrand had already concluded that NATO would be considerably more important in Europe's post-Cold War security architecture than had originally been anticipated, and he facilitated French participation in NATO planning for peace-support operations as well as in any eventual operations themselves. Mitterrand also approved the different steps that had taken place in French–NATO *rapprochement* during the two years between the 1993 National Assembly elections and the expiration of his presidential term. But Mitterrand took a very cautious approach to France's *rapprochement* with the Alliance and preferred to give it minimum visibility. In April 1994, Mitterrand had blocked his Chief of Staff, Admiral Jacques Lanxade, from attending a Military Committee meeting, reflecting his opposition to the regular participation of France's defence minister and military chief of staff in NATO gatherings.[38] When François Léotard attended the NATO defence ministers' meeting in Spain, French officials stressed that the meeting was an 'informal' one, not expected to take any decisions, thus downplaying the significance of Léotard's attendance.[39]

In contrast to Mitterrand, the leaders of the new French government desired greater openness in French–NATO relations and demonstrated a willingness to shed at least some of the caution that had characterised the president's approach to the issue. In the words of Alain Juppé, 'the time has passed for an attitude of haughty reserve towards [the Alliance]'.[40]

The half-hearted participation in NATO decision-making bodies typical of Mitterrand's approach was counter-productive in terms of promoting French goals within the Alliance. Limiting French participation to meetings that addressed issues relating to the use of French forces meant that France could have little influence over broader questions in which it was highly interested, including the reform of the IMS and Europeanisation of the Alliance.

Moreover, Paris' continued reserve towards NATO decision-making bodies did nothing to attenuate long-standing and deeply rooted suspicions held in Washington and elsewhere regarding French intentions towards the Alliance. It was difficult to understand why an 'informal' notice had to be put on the door before the French defence minister could walk into a NATO meeting. Beyond Paris' desire to participate in discussion of the broader Alliance agenda, the decisions regarding French participation in NATO that de Charette announced in December 1995 also responded to the perceived need to do something about this climate of mistrust surrounding France.

The initiative had been planned for some time. Jacques Chirac declared in his one major foreign-policy address of the 1995 presidential campaign, 'without returning to the integrated structure, our country must participate in all Alliance bodies that are based upon a respect for national sovereignty'.[41] Chirac repeated the same formulation as President in a speech delivered to a meeting of French ambassadors on 31 August 1995, adding that France would take 'initiatives' during the coming months.[42] Chirac's speech thus prefigured de Charette's subsequent statement to the NAC. With the decision to deepen France's participation in NATO essentially taken during summer 1995, the French government then had to work out the specific details of the initiative while waiting for the next meeting of the NAC at ministerial level. Paris viewed a NAC ministerial meeting as the most appropriate venue at which to announce its decision. The fact that the December 1995 meeting included defence as well as foreign ministers, and was about Bosnia, made it all the more appropriate.[43]

NATO's Military Committee and Defence Planning Committee (DPC) are both non-integrated bodies that 'respect' national sovereignty, since they take decisions only by unanimous consent. However, the French defence minister will still not participate fully in the work of the DPC. Clarifications issued after de Charette's speech indicated that France will normally participate in *ad hoc*, formal meetings of NATO defence ministers, but will not automatically attend the DPC's regular biannual gatherings. Nonetheless, France has clearly expanded the parameters of its participation in NATO defence-ministerial meetings.

France continues to have reservations towards the DPC for two reasons. The first is that, since the primary role of the DPC is to manage the IMS, it undertakes activities in which France still has no desire to participate, such as the annual reviews of national defence planning. Along with other integrated activities, France views the DPC management of national defence planning as an infringement of national sovereignty.[44]

The second reason relates more broadly to the issue of political control over the military. Upon returning to power in 1958 and establishing the Fifth Republic, General Charles de Gaulle acted vigorously to restore effective civilian control over the armed forces, which had weakened under previous French political regimes.[45] This legacy of the military's escape from the control of responsible political authority continues to affect national-security decision-making in France insofar as the French take a particularly rigorous view of the subordination of military bodies to political authority.[46]

Given this context, the conviction in Paris that SACEUR and the IMS have not been subject to effective political control represents a serious problem. France's perception has been that the only real civilian control over SACEUR stems from US national political authority, which is not, needless to say, a very satisfying state of affairs for France.[47] A common French argument is that NATO must reduce SACEUR's 'excessive autonomy' and remedy the overly weak control under which he operates by restricting his 'extraordinary privileges in terms of equipment, budget, planning, and above all autonomy of decision'.[48]

One French proposal to strengthen political control over the military command structure is to bring defence ministers into NAC meetings.[49] Chirac himself endorsed the idea during the 1995 presidential election campaign, stating, 'I will also propose to our partners that the Atlantic Council, the supreme authority of the Alliance, be able to meet with both Foreign and Defence Ministers, as is already the case in the WEU'.[50]

According to the critique underlying this proposal, the absence of defence ministers and their representatives from the NAC creates two major problems. First, allied governments have used the DPC as a parallel council, effectively leaving NATO with two, coequal governing bodies.[51] Under NATO's collective defence structure the DPC and the Major NATO Commands (MNCs) have even exercised most of the real power within NATO, despite the NAC's status as the Alliance's supreme decision-making body and the MNCs' subordinate position to the Military Committee.[52] If the NAC is to have the authority it was originally intended to have, it must meet with both foreign and defence ministers. Second, the separation between the NAC and the military implementing bodies of the Alliance deprives political decision-makers of adequate exposure to more technical military issues. The presence of defence ministers would provide the NAC with this missing technical military capacity. NATO would not abolish the DPC, but the latter would assume the purely technical role of managing the IMS and would be clearly subordinate to the NAC. All of these reservations regarding the DPC explain France's reluctance to embrace full participation in it.

Adapting the Alliance's Military Structure

The 1994 Brussels summit established the CJTF concept as the key instrument for updating the Alliance's military structures in order to deal more effectively with non-Article 5 missions and to support ESDI's development. Although the term Combined Joint Task Force denotes a multinational, multiservice task force, the heart of the CJTF concept entails creating in advance a combined headquarters structure with staff, procedures and planning, so that a group of countries responding to a non-Article 5 crisis could use NATO command and control as well as other NATO assets according to the particular need.[53] US defence officials conceived CJTF as a means both to further adapt NATO's military structure to post-Cold War missions and to support ESDI by making NATO assets available to a WEU military operation. CJTF interventions would essentially take place either under NATO command, if the United States were a major participant, or under that of the WEU for distinctly European operations. The concept also provides a mechanism for PFP countries to participate in either a NATO- or WEU-led operation.[54]

However, while the other two summit initiatives (expanding eastwards and countering NBC weapons proliferation) have forged steadily ahead, efforts to implement CJTF have been the object of considerable frustration. France believes that the significant progress achieved on NATO enlargement while reform of NATO structures has stalled is tantamount to 'placing the cart before the horse'. French Defence Minister Charles Millon stated in autumn 1995 that 'it makes little sense for NATO to attempt to integrate new members before the allies have finished their current effort to establish military command mechanisms for crisis response'.[55] France is in favour of NATO expansion, but sees it as a secondary issue after NATO reform, and it was uncomfortable when the United States moved to accelerate the enlargement process in late 1994.[56]

Shortly after the 1994 Brussels summit, significant differences emerged between the United States and France on how to set up both NATO- and WEU-led CJTFs. Whereas the US wanted to use CJTF to give NATO's IMS the flexibility to respond to non-Article 5 missions, the French argued that the IMS is inherently unsuited for those types of missions.

This claim is based upon two considerations. First, the disappearance of the automaticity that would, in principle, have characterised NATO's response to an Article 5-type threat has now disappeared. In dealing with the new types of missions that the West currently confronts, it is impossible to know in advance which allies will participate and what forces they will contribute. For France, the IMS – designed for total war – is too heavy and rigid to respond with sufficient flexibility to the new, limited types of military operations that the West has to undertake. Paris has been particularly insistent that command roles and staffing for a non-Article 5 military operation must largely be a function of the countries that are participating in the operation rather than of a pre-set, integrated command arrangement.[57]

France's second reservation regarding the IMS and non-Article 5 operations relates to the perceived inadequacy of multinational political control over SACEUR. This concern has become far more acute in the case of non-Article 5 missions. In effect, different types of peace-support missions are politically sensitive, and, from a French standpoint, require precise political guidance over the conduct of the operation. Paris would like to see as direct a link as possible between an operational commander and the controlling political authorities.

A clear illustration of French concerns regarding effective multinational political control over the integrated military command occurred during NATO's *Operation Deliberate Force* in Bosnia. US Admiral Leighton Smith, Commander-in-Chief of Allied Forces South (CINCSOUTH), took the politically controversial decision to launch *Cruise*-missile strikes against Bosnian Serb air-defences after requesting and receiving permission to do so from the Pentagon via NATO–SACEUR General George Joulwan. Although French General Bernard Janvier, Commander of UN forces in former Yugoslavia, knew in advance of the planned strikes, there was apparently no advance discussion with French or NATO political authorities regarding this decision.[58]

Because of these views regarding the inflexibility of the IMS, as well as its excessive autonomy from political control, France conceived CJTF implementation as taking place, at least in part, outside the integrated command. Just before the Brussels summit, Léotard stated that 'we are going to take part in what could be, by the end of the process, the birth of a sort of NATO

II'.[59] Washington, on the other hand, stressed that NATO had to preserve the IMS as a single command structure for both Article 5 and non-Article 5 missions. Moreover, Washington began to evoke the possibility that non-Article 5 operations could often have implications for defending NATO territory, and US thinking consequently evolved towards a desire for robust CJTF that would include full command and control for a large-scale military operation. The potential for a threat to NATO territory to arise out of a non-Article 5 operation also required, in the US view, CJTF lines of command to lead back to the MNC responsible for Article 5 collective defence. For France, this meant that the IMS was functioning as usual.

By late 1995, the United States had apparently softened its position regarding the central role that the MNCs had to play in the CJTF chain of command, as well as becoming more open to flexible, modular concepts. Differences still remained over the location of CJTF headquarters. The United States believes that any CJTF headquarters must be based within existing NATO commands, while France would like the flexibility to have national or other multinational commands also provide the headquarters. Situating a CJTF headquarters within a national command could be appropriate if one country is playing a preponderant role in an intervention.[60]

While it has not been easy to resolve the issues surrounding implementation of CJTF within NATO, even greater difficulties emerged over the arrangements for a WEU-led CJTF, an issue intimately linked with the construction of ESDI. The frustrations and setbacks surrounding ESDI have not lessened France's strong commitment to it. Paris views the 1996 Intergovernmental Conference (IGC) to review the Maastricht Treaty as a critical step in the evolution of ESDI, since it will probably determine whether Europe can acquire some degree of credibility in the security area. France's goals for the IGC are twofold with respect to ESDI. First, the IGC must establish a more solid foundation for the EU's Common Foreign and Security Policy (CFSP). This foundation should notably include a crisis-analysis centre for the CFSP, an asset that was sorely lacking when Yugoslavia fell apart.[61] Paris hopes that joint crisis analysis will lead to joint decisions.

France supports a strong enough link between the EU and WEU for the latter to execute decisions resulting from the CFSP process. Paris eventually wants to see the WEU integrated within the EU, but French goals for the IGC are focused on interim arrangements that will make the WEU an instrument of the European Council.[62] There is a strong consensus within the WEU to strengthen the organisation's operational capabilities. The French view the Eurocorps and other new European multinational forces as providing the central military elements for ESDI.[63]

The ability of these forces to use NATO assets is essential if the WEU is to have the operational capability to carry out CFSP decisions. For example, Eurocorps deployment remains dependent upon certain US assets assigned to NATO, in particular, air transport.[64] WEU Secretary-General José Cutileiro has observed that, without access to NATO assets, the WEU would be 'reduced for a very long time to very modest activities'.[65] France accepts that constricting European defence resources largely prohibits WEU duplicating existing NATO assets or structures. Space-based intelligence is the one area for which Paris believes that European assets are necessary, since this capability provides an indispensable basis for independent decision-making.

For France, it is critical that the WEU be able to use other NATO assets in an essentially autonomous fashion. The French believe that it would be anomalous for a WEU operation to be subject to the decisions of a US commander (SACEUR). A WEU Assembly report described the impasse:

> NATO's SACEUR, General Joulwan, has stated that he wants specific authority to approve any operational requirements for a CJTF, but it should be noted that this would leave any European operation without the participation of the transatlantic allies still completely dependent on the decision of a United States commander. It really seems illogical to have an American general as the linchpin of Europe's security and defence identity.[66]

Former NATO Secretary-General Willy Claes argued the American case when asked whether the United States should have a 'right of inspection' over WEU operations using NATO assets:

> It all depends on what one means by right of inspection. Let us suppose that we are members of one and the same alliance, that I am not interested in taking part in an operation that you want to carry out but that I would like to help you with logistics and intelligence, do you think that I would want to do so without knowing what will happen with my intelligence and logistics ... This does not mean that the WEU, for example, cannot have a certain amount of autonomy by acting with the aid of other allies.[67]

Paris obviously recognises that the United States has an 'interest' in what takes place during a WEU military operation using NATO assets, but striking the right balance between this interest and France's desire for European autonomy is very difficult. De Charette told the December 1995 meeting of the NAC that the WEU should be able to use NATO assets 'without debarment and without prohibitive conditions'.[68]

French officials fear that the United States may not approve the political objectives of an operation that Europeans want to undertake.[69] US officials have, in the past, recognised that this question constitutes a 'legitimate European concern', but that these kinds of cases will be 'extraordinarily rare'.[70] Yet, the French point out, this situation almost occurred in Bosnia.[71] The UNPROFOR operation also amply illustrates the transatlantic tensions that can emerge in situations where Europe has deployed ground forces while the United States provides significant support for the operation but no ground presence.

From the French perspective, these 'lessons' of Bosnia reinforce the pre-existing inclination to emphasise the need for autonomy in WEU operations that use NATO assets, as well as for restrictions on NATO's ability to deny the use of those assets in the first instance. This view applies in particular to resources such as planning staff and NATO's command, control and communications (C^3) system, which are NATO common assets rather than US national ones assigned to NATO.

There was a clear hope in Paris that its December 1995 initiative would break the stalemate with the US over CJTF implementation by creating a climate of greater trust between the two countries, thereby making Washington more receptive to French concerns.[72] Many of France's allies seemed to share this hope. Following de Charette's speech, a plethora of attributed and background statements emerged from European sources hoping that the French initiative would allow rapid resolution of the CJTF implementation issue.[73] Despite these expectations, US–French discussions after de Charette's speech did not result in any progress.[74]

What Next?
In his speech to the NAC, de Charette reiterated a familiar theme of French NATO policy, namely that, as NATO reforms, France will consider participating more fully. France will continue to propose and to express support for ideas that promote its threefold objectives for NATO: reforming the integrated military command; strengthening political control over the military structure; and using NATO as one element in the construction of ESDI. Both French and non-French sources have advanced proposals that would move NATO in the direction that France desires.

One approach would be to shift power within NATO from the DPC and MNCs to the NAC, meeting with both defence and foreign ministers, and the Military Committee. The decision-making structure that NATO has been using for its operations in former Yugoslavia already represents a shift from the Cold War pattern. The NAC has taken over as the leading decision-making body and the Military Committee has assumed a more prominent role.[75] The Military Committee has examined all SHAPE plans regarding NATO operations in former Yugoslavia, and made proposals to the NAC on those plans. With France fully participating, since 1993, in Military Committee meetings concerning operations in former Yugoslavia, all NATO decisions in this area have been taken by the 16 members together. The major French military role in these operations obviously created a substantial incentive for NATO to shift its decision-making structure in order to accommodate France.

Paris favours a continued evolution that would systematically move the DPC and the MNCs more into the background, leaving the NAC unequivocally as NATO's only decision-making body, with the Military Committee as its key implementing and advisory organ. In the French view, SACEUR would then be truly answerable to the Military Committee and the NAC. On France's initiative, the December 1995 NAC meeting that approved the implementation plan for the Bosnian peace agreement was held with the joint participation of foreign and defence ministers. Paris has not yet proposed that the NAC meet in this manner on a systematic basis, but French officials clearly expect that the December 1995 meeting will not be the last one of its kind.[76]

The French would also like to see a European 'caucus' develop within NATO. For France, such a caucus should be acceptable to the United States, both because it will always be accompanied by bilateral consultations between individual European capitals and Washington, and because it is the only way to ensure that the European allies express a common security policy within NATO in a manner consistent with how they do so outside the organisation.[77] In mid-1994, the WEU introduced a joint position into NATO regarding WEU use of NATO assets and capabilities.[78] The Clinton administration has not opposed, in principle, the introduction of joint European positions within NATO, and the chief obstacle to progress in this area appears to lie more with the limited ability to agree among themselves that Europeans have demonstrated until now.[79]

US analyst Stanley Sloan has proposed a significant step towards strengthening European responsibilities and identity within NATO. Under this proposal, WEU or EU members would nominate the European officers for the positions of Deputy SACEUR and Deputy Supreme Allied Commander Atlantic (SACLANT), and the NAC would then approve the nominations. In the case of a European-led CJTF, the Deputy SACEUR would take control of the operation and enjoy full access to NATO assets. Sloan further suggests that a French officer should be the first Deputy SACEUR in this new system.[80] French officials have expressed considerable interest in this general idea, with reservations, however, regarding the appointment of a French officer as the first Deputy SACEUR.[81] These reservations, if sustained, would probably make the proposal more difficult to implement, insofar as it is based upon a need for the Deputy SACEUR/Deputy SACLANT officers to come from European countries that are likely to be major contributors to a given non-Article 5 mission. Apart from France and the United Kingdom, credible candidates are currently lacking. If the role of the Deputy SACEUR in controlling a European-led CJTF were less automatic, then the link to the IMS would be proportionately weaker. In any event, if the proposal should become the object of serious discussion within NATO, compromises on these points could hopefully be found.

Finally, SACLANT General John Sheehan has suggested a way to revise NATO's military structure. Under Sheehan's concept, NATO would establish a number of Regional Commands in place of the current eight Major Subordinate Commands. The MNCs would transfer more responsibility and operational latitude to the Regional Commands, and Operational Commands would exist below the Regional Commands. The Operational Commands could contain a CJTF nucleus to help form the core for specified CJTFs as the need arises. Sheehan notes that it could be appropriate for a Regional or Operational Command to communicate directly with the Military Committee at the same time it reports to the MNC. He has reportedly stressed that a revised NATO military structure must be able to provide rapid and clear political guidance to field commanders.[82]

These ideas on streamlining and decentralising the military command structure are very much in line with French thinking on how to begin reforming the IMS, and they have attracted substantial interest in Paris.[83] However, they are very controversial within NATO.[84] Sheehan himself asserts that 'effective change will not happen if NATO's future is left to bureaucracies tied to the legacies of the past, or an administrative process'.[85]

If NATO undertakes meaningful reforms such as those discussed above, it would place the issue of CJTF implementation within an entirely different framework, and would very likely help overcome the current stalemate. The lessons of the IFOR operation are also likely to have a major impact on future discussion of CJTF implementation as well as on consideration of broader NATO restructuring. French officials believe that using the IMS has prevented IFOR from being set up in the most effective manner, notably because there are too many layers between the NAC and the forces deployed in the field. France would have preferred a direct link between IFOR Commander US Admiral Leighton Smith and the NAC.[86] Failing that, France would like Admiral Smith's civilian political adviser to report directly to the NAC. Many other Europeans have reportedly supported the French position in favour of close political control over military actions in the field, since IFOR's operational conduct will clearly have a fundamental impact on the unfolding of subsequent events regarding the implementation of the peace agreement.[87]

Washington Post editorialist Jim Hoagland has argued that, should continued Bosnian peace implementation be necessary once the one-year period for which President Bill Clinton has committed US troops expires, it could be an invaluable opportunity to begin rebalancing NATO into a more equal US–European partnership. European willingness to maintain a residual force after the US departure could start NATO on the road towards giving Europeans more power and responsibility within the Alliance.[88] The need for such a European force to make use of NATO assets and capabilities would also hasten a resolution of the dispute over the terms of transferring NATO assets to a WEU-led CJTF.

For many members of the Washington defence community, the term 'WEU-led CJTF' is an oxymoron. Unless Western Europe can establish some degree of credibility in the security area, the French are unlikely to gain very much in voicing complaints that the United States is finding it difficult to approach Europe on a basis of equal partnership rather than leadership. Europe's Rapid Reaction Force in Bosnia was a modest step in the right direction. Unfortunately, the United States' subsequent seizing of control over the military and diplomatic process in Bosnia served to obscure the contribution that the Force made to the events leading up to the start of peace negotiations.

Continued French doctrinal aversion to NATO military integration[89] must not obscure the fact that France has become highly pragmatic in its approach to the transatlantic security relationship. French air, naval and now ground forces have been serving directly under NATO command in former Yugoslavia. General Bernard Janvier is serving as deputy to Admiral Smith, the overall IFOR commander, while some 150 French officers have been inserted into the NATO chain of command. For now at least, the French are more preoccupied with streamlining and decentralising the IMS to meet non-Article 5 missions than with an ideological rejection of it. As a country that will remain one of the largest troop contributors to crisis-management operations, France has a direct interest in this kind of reform of the IMS. There is even some feeling within the French government that, if NATO were sufficiently Europeanised, and if the IMS became less rigid, France could return to full military participation within the Alliance.[90] Nor should France's traditional concern with political control over the military, due to the country's historical experience, obscure the fact that there may now be plausible, pragmatic reasons to strengthen political control over non-Article 5 military operations.[91] The one traditional French doctrinal prohibition that still retains much practical significance is the refusal to place forces under US command in peacetime or in operations where the United States is not the leading contributor.

The stakes involved in finding a better accommodation on NATO between France and the US are high. The two countries are probable partners in many non-Article 5 military operations, and such an accommodation could improve military cooperation even further. Moreover, as France's former ambassador to the WEU Jean-Marie Guéhenno argues, the current status quo in both the transatlantic security relationship and European security cooperation cannot endure. The two most likely outcomes are either a parallel weakening of transatlantic security ties and of European security cooperation, or a parallel strengthening of both.[92] Needless to say, the second outcome would be better than the first, and the United States should seize upon France's pragmatic new approach to NATO to help ensure that it comes about.

Notes

1. For a summary of a November 1993 exchange of views on these initiatives between US and French officials and experts, see Robert P. Grant, *The Changing Franco-American Security Relationship: New Directions for NATO and European Defense Cooperation* (Arlington, VA: US–CREST, 1993), pp. 1–62.

2. The French official's comment on the summit is cited in David Buchan, 'France Goes on the Defence Offensive', *Financial Times*, 24 January 1994. The summit declaration is published in North Atlantic Treaty Organisation, *NATO Handbook* (Brussels: NATO Office of Information and Press, 1995), pp. 269–75.

3. See Claire Tréan, 'L'Initiative de Paris pour la Levée du Siège de Sarajevo', *Le Monde*, 8 February 1994; and Roger Cohen, 'NATO Near Consensus on Sarajevo Ultimatum', *New York Times*, 9 February 1994.

4. See Alain Juppé, 'Quel Horizon pour la Politique Etrangère de la France?', speech given at a reception celebrating the twentieth anniversary of the Foreign Ministry's policy planning staff, Paris, 30 January 1995, reprinted in *Politique Etrangère*, vol. 60, no. 1, Spring 1995, p. 250. Author's translation.

5. See Alain Frachon and Claire Tréan, 'Un Pari Franco-Américain Pour la Paix', *Le Monde*, 1 September 1995.

6. Hervé de Charette, speech delivered to the North Atlantic Council, 5 December 1995. On 22 January 1996, Gilles Andréani, Director of Policy Planning at the French Foreign Ministry, told a Washington audience that the December 1995 initiative was both a confirmation of past moves and 'an opening into the future'. A transcript of Andréani's talk on France and NATO, as well as his subsequent discussion with US policy analysts and officials, is on the internet at http://www.adetocqueville.com.

7. For a comprehensive discussion of the Gaullist legacy and its influence over subsequent French security policy, see Philip H. Gordon, *A Certain Idea of France: French Security Policy and the Gaullist Legacy* (Princeton, NJ: Princeton University Press, 1993).

8. For examples of these statements, see Philip H. Gordon, *French Security Policy After the Cold War: Continuity, Change, and Implications for the United States*, R-4229-A (Santa Monica, CA: RAND, 1992), pp. 11–14.

9. See, for example, Guillaume Parmentier, *Le Retour de l'Histoire: Stratégie et Relations Internationales Pendant et Après la Guerre Froide* (Paris: Éditions Complexe, 1993), pp. 142–71; and François Bresson, 'La France, l'Europe, l'OTAN, et les Autres', in Groupe X-Défense, *Défense: La France et l'Europe* (Paris: Ministère de la Défense/ Service d'Information et de Relations Publiques des Armées, 1995), p. 31.

10. See, for example, Jérôme Paolini, 'Autonomie Stratégique, Alliances, Communautés et Nations', in *Un Nouveau Débat Stratégique, Actes du Colloque de Paris* (Paris: La Documentation Française, September 1992), pp. 163–66; and Frédéric Bozo, *La France et l'OTAN: De la Guerre Froide au Nouvel Ordre Européen* (Paris: Masson, 1991), pp. 169–73.

11. An expression of RPR defence expert François Fillon in 'Entre l'OTAN et l'Europe des Chimères', *Le Monde*, 19 April 1991. The 1949 North Atlantic Treaty established a traditional military alliance, with the creation of the integrated military command following only in 1950 after North Korea invaded the South.

12. See the critique of NATO's post-Cold War role and evolution in Bozo, *La France et l'OTAN*, pp. 165–94.

13. See the interview with Robin in Theresa Hitchens, 'European Allies Urge France

to Rejoin NATO's Military Command', *Defense News*, 10 December 1995. Robin added, 'but it would probably imply some rather radical changes in the structures'.

14. Bozo, *La France et l'OTAN*, p. 188.

15. For an examination of Franco-American tensions during this period, See Charles G. Cogan, *Oldest Allies, Guarded Friends: The United States and France Since 1940* (Westport, CT: Praeger, 1994), pp. 177–88.

16. Alexandra Schwartzbrod, *Le Président Qui N'aimait Pas la Guerre: Dans les Coulisses du Pouvoir Militaire 1981–1995* (Paris: Plon, 1995), pp. 86–97, contains a leading defence journalist's account of the thinking of French political and military leaders regarding the 1991 Gulf War. For more detailed accounts of French participation in the Gulf War, see François Heisbourg, 'France and the Gulf Crisis', in Nicole Gnesotto and John Roper (eds), *Western Europe and the Gulf* (Paris: The Institute for Security Studies, Western European Union, 1992); and David S. Yost, 'France and the Gulf War of 1990–1991: Political-Military Lessons Learned', *Journal of Strategic Studies*, vol. 16, no. 3, September 1993.

17. One senior US official reportedly referred to France as a 'strategic enemy'. See Martine Jacot, 'La Dernière Rencontre Entre le Président Bush et M. Mitterrand a scellé une Longue Relation de Confiance', *Le Monde*, 5 January 1993.

18. With operational command, a commander has the authority 'to assign missions or tasks to subordinate commanders, to deploy units, to reassign forces, and to retain or delegate operational and/or tactical control as may be deemed necessary'. Under operational control, a commander can only 'direct forces assigned so that the commander may accomplish specific missions or tasks which are usually limited by function, time, or location; to deploy units concerned, and to retain or assign tactical control of those units. It does not include authority to assign separate employment of components of the units concerned'. On 'operational control', see Bozo, *La France et l'OTAN*, pp. 109–13; on Washington's surprise, see Daniel Vernet, 'Nouveau Pas de Paris Vers l'OTAN', *Le Monde*, 12 March 1993.

19. Vernet, 'Nouveau Pas'.

20. For a more detailed discussion of the US, French and German three-way debate over the Eurocorps, see Philip H. Gordon, *France, Germany, and the Western Alliance* (Boulder, CO: Westview Press, 1995), pp. 40–46.

21. A view expressed in the Assembly of Western European Union Defence Committee, *European Armed Forces*, Document 1468 (Paris: Assembly of Western European Union, 12 June 1995), p. 5. The January 1993 Eurocorps agreement was subsequently extended to include Spain and Belgium.

22. Pascal Boniface, 'La France', in Boniface (ed.), *L'Année Stratégique 1995: Les Equilibres Militaires* (Paris: Dunod for the Institut des Relations Internationales et Stratégiques, 1995), p. 12.

23. Jacques Isnard, 'La France Siège Désormais Avec Voix Délibérative au Comité Militaire de l'OTAN', *Le Monde*, 14 May 1993. France's observer status meant that the participation of French officers at Military Committee meetings was limited to answering questions that other national representatives addressed to them. Once France assumed a 'deliberative voice' in its relationship to the Committee, it became a full participant in Committee meetings, albeit only for issues related to peace operations.

24. See, for example, Grant, *The Changing Franco-American Security Relationship*, p. 29.

25. RPR deputy Jacques Baumel, Vice-President of the National Assembly's Defence Commission, declared that 'Western countries must put a halt to the absurd battle pitting NATO against WEU'. He also pleaded, however, that 'the WEU must not become, on the other hand, NATO's poor cousin, which takes the leftovers when NATO does not wish to assume certain missions'. Cited in Grant, *The Changing Franco-American Security Relationship*, p. 33.

26. Although NBC weapons could clearly threaten NATO territory, the primary focus within the DGP has been on how an adversary's possession of these weapons could affect the ability of Western forces to intervene in a regional contingency. For a discussion of the substantial degree of convergence in French and American approaches to counterproliferation related issues, see Robert P. Grant, *Counterproliferation and International Security: The Report of a Franco-American Working Group* (Arlington, VA: US–CREST, June 1995).

27. Commission de Défense, *Une Politique Européenne de Défense*, Document 1445 (Paris: Assembly of Western European Union, 17 November 1994), pp. 17–18.

28. Brooks Tigner, 'Cooperative Efforts Boost France's NATO Image', *Defense News*, 2–8 October 1995.

29. *News from France*, 29 September 1995, p. 3.

30. Interview with Defence Minister François Léotard, in *Les Echos*, 7–8 January 1994, p. 5.

31. Ministère de la Défense, *Livre Blanc sur la Défense*, 1994, p. 37.

32. Chapter title in Steven Philip Kramer, *Does France Still Count?: The French Role in the New Europe* (Westport, CT: Praeger Publishers, 1994), pp. 44–60.

33. See *The Military Balance 1995–96* (Oxford: Oxford University Press for the IISS, 1995), p. 264 for a comparison of NATO country military expenditures and manpower in 1985, 1993 and 1994.

34. Remarks delivered at a reception in honour of Parisian reserve officers, 8 February 1993. Author's translation.

35. Jean-Claude Casanova, 'Dissuasion Concertée', *L'Express*, 28 September 1995, p. 26. Author's translation.

36. In early 1993, the European allies tried to persuade both the United States and Russia to send forces to Bosnia. One high-ranking French military official stated at the time, 'if the Americans would deploy even a single battalion to Sarajevo in the coming days, the situation on the ground would immediately take a completely different political direction'. Quoted in Jacques Isnard, 'Des "Frappes Aériennes Défensives"?', *Le Monde*, 10 May 1993. Author's translation. Nineteen months later, Juppé, clearly targeting Washington, criticised 'governments that want to give us lessons when they have not lifted a little finger to put even one man on the ground'. See Alan Riding, 'French Successfully Bluff Their Allies on Bosnia', *New York Times*, 13 December 1994.

37. Senator Jacques Genton, *Rapport Fait au Nom de la Commission des Affaires Etrangères, de la Défense et des Forces Armées sur le Projet de Loi Relatif à la Programmation Militaire pour les Années 1995–2000* (Paris: Sénat, 8 June 1994), pp. 43–44. Author's translation.

38. Boniface, 'La France', pp. 11–12.

39. Alain Louyot, 'Manœuvres d'Automne', *L'Express*, 22 September 1994, pp. 16–17. Mitterrand's more conservative approach to the France–NATO relationship may

have been due in part to a strong distrust of the United States dating back to his days as a government minister in the 1950s. Mitterrand wrote in 1981, 'I like Americans, not their policy. During the Fourth Republic, I was exasperated by the climate of submission to their smallest desires'. Schwartzbrod, *Le Président Qui N'aimait Pas la Guerre*, pp. 88–89.

40. Juppé, 'Quel Horizon?'. Author's translation.

41. Jacques Chirac, speech, Paris, 16 March 1995. Author's translation.

42. 'Intervention du Président de la République, M. Jacques Chirac, devant la Réunion des Ambassadeurs', reprinted in Ministère des Affaires Etrangères, *Bulletin d'Information*, 1 September 1995 (168/95), p. 7.

43. Interviews, December 1995.

44. It constitutes such an infringement far more in principle than in practice, as countries regularly ignore force planning decisions taken within the NATO framework.

45. Michael M. Harrison, *The Reluctant Ally: France and Atlantic Security* (Baltimore, MD: The Johns Hopkins University Press, 1981), pp. 116–20.

46. Guillaume Parmentier, 'La France et l'OTAN', *Défense*, no. 65, March 1995, p. 44.

47. Other allies do not necessarily share this concern, and are satisfied with NATO procedures to ensure that SACEUR takes allied viewpoints into account.

48. André Dumoulin, 'Quel Rôle Face à la Nouvelle Europe?', in Patrice Buffotot (ed.), *La Défense en Europe* (Paris: La Documentation Française, 1995), p. 199. Author's translation.

49. G. Trangis (pseudonym), 'Ni Splendide Isolement, Ni Réintégration', *Le Monde*, 14 July 1993.

50. Speech of 16 March 1995. Author's translation.

51. Gabriel Robin, 'A Quoi Sert l'OTAN?', *Politique Etrangère*, vol. 60, no. 1, Spring 1995, p. 173. Ironically, the DPC's role greatly expanded as a result of France's withdrawal from the IMS, when the DPC became the forum for taking up defence issues on which France did not desire involvement. See Harrison, *The Reluctant Ally*, pp. 158–63.

52. Observation of a US analyst, cited in Maria Alongi and Robert Grant, *Franco-American Security Cooperation: From Principle to Practice* (Arlington, VA: US-CREST, 1995), p. 44.

53. See Barry, chapter 10.

54. US officials also note that CJTF headquarters can facilitate the formation of *ad hoc* coalitions involving some NATO members with other NATO or non-NATO countries. For example, during summer 1994 both France and the US provided humanitarian assistance to Rwandan refugees; in this line of thinking, the command and control of a CJTF headquarters could have made the operation considerably more efficient. See Alongi and Grant, *Franco-American Security Cooperation*, pp. 34–35.

55. Theresa Hitchens, 'France Ties OK of Larger NATO to Reforms', *Defense News*, 9–15 October 1995, p. 6. As reflected in the article title, Hitchens interpreted Millon's remarks, obtained in an interview, as establishing a link between French approval of NATO expansion and NATO reform of its military structures. However, French officials assert that Paris has not established such a link. Interviews, December 1995.

56. In his interview with *Time*, 11 December 1995, Chirac stated, 'it is evident that the Atlantic Alliance must expand eastward'. For French reservations regarding the

accelerated process, see Alongi and Grant, *Franco-American Security Cooperation*, pp. 15–42. These reservations centred on the relationship between NATO and EU enlargement, as well as on the impact of accelerated enlargement for relations with Russia. The subsequent deceleration of the NATO expansion process by late 1995 was therefore a cause for satisfaction in Paris. In his speech to the NAC of 5 December 1995, de Charette praised NATO's study of the 'why and how' of enlargement as a 'good document', characterising it in particular as having 'the merit of affirming that the enlargement of our Alliance and that of the European Union are supporting parallel and mutually supporting processes'. As Robbin Laird has noted, for the French 'the question of NATO expansion clearly takes second place to the question of the development of the European Union and the issues of EU expansion. Given the central debate about the role of European institutions in shaping French economic and cultural development, the question of the expansion of the EU has become a debate about the future of France itself'. See Robbin Laird, *French Security Policy in Transition: Dynamics of Continuity and Change*, McNair Paper 38 (Washington DC: National Defense University, Institute for National Strategic Studies, March 1995), pp. 9–30.

57. See, for example, Bresson, 'La France, l'Europe', p. 31–32. American analysis stressed that when a CJTF headquarters is activated, 'national approval to allow all assigned personnel to deploy – irrespective of a nation's decision to contribute forces – will be needed to avoid degrading command and staff functions on the brink of deployment'. See Charles L. Barry, 'NATO's Bold New Concept–CJTF', *Joint Force Quarterly*, no. 5, Summer 1994, p. 49. Thus, while US and French positions on this aspect of CJTF implementation are not in total opposition, there is a clear difference in emphasis.

58. Rick Atkinson, 'In Almost Losing Its Resolve, NATO Alliance Found Itself', *Washington Post*, 16 November 1995, p. A32. Also interviews, December 1995.

59. Interview with *Les Echos*, 7–8 January 1994, p. 5. Author's translation.

60. Interviews, December 1995.

61. Interviews, December 1995.

62. Interviews, December 1995.

63. France, Spain and Italy have created EUROFOR, a landforce of up to a division in strength, and EUROMARFOR, a maritime force with aero-naval and amphibious capabilities. Both forces can be used within the framework of NATO as well as the WEU. See Assembly of Western European Union Defence Committee, *European Armed Forces*, pp. 7–10.

64. The Eurocorps has conducted several exercises to test its operational capabilities. These exercises notably included Eurotransitex in May 1995 and Pegasus in November 1995. The former demonstrated the corps' ability to project rapidly a small force for humanitarian missions, while the latter involved a heavy, mechanised force of more than 10,000 soldiers. Following the Eurotransitex exercise, Eurocorps Commander General Helmutt Willmann expressed full satisfaction with the corps' communications capabilities, based on the French Syracuse and Rita systems. Eurocorps logistics are assured by national assets, with each participating country responsible for certain missions, such as Belgium for the supply of food and water and Germany for that of fuel. See *Très, Très Urgent (TTU)*, no. 97, 1 June 1995; and no. 116, 16 November 1995.

65. Cited in Rafael Estrella, *Structure and Functions; European Security and Defence Identity and Combined Joint Task Forces, Draft General Report* (Brussels: North

Atlantic Assembly, October 1995), p. 20.

66. Quoted in *ibid.*, p. 19.

67. *Ibid.*, p. 21.

68. Hervé de Charette, speech delivered to the North Atlantic Council, 5 December 1995.

69. Interviews, December 1995.

70. See, for example, the not-for-attribution statements summarised in Grant, *The Changing Franco-American Security Relationship*, p. 59.

71. Interviews, December 1995.

72. Interviews, December 1995.

73. See, for example, 'A New NATO', *The Economist*, 9 December 1995; and Giovanni de Briganti, 'France Turns to NATO as Vision for Europe Erodes', *Defense News*, 11–17 December 1995.

74. Interviews, December 1995.

75. Comments of a US analyst cited in Alongi and Grant, *Franco-American Security Cooperation*, p. 44–45.

76. Interviews, December 1995.

77. A French official made this argument in Alongi and Grant, *Franco-American Security Cooperation*, p. 43.

78. WEU Council of Ministers, *WEU Contribution to the European Union Intergovernmental Conference of 1996* (Brussels: Western European Union Press and Information Service, 14 November 1995), pp. 7–8.

79. The joint WEU position on the organisation's use of NATO assets was apparently left vague in order to allow a consensus to be reached. Interviews, December 1995. On US acceptance of European positions, see Grant, *The Changing Franco-American Security Relationship*, p. 81.

80. Stanley R. Sloan, *NATO's Future: Beyond Collective Defense* (Washington DC: Congressional Research Service, 15 September 1995), pp. 30–32.

81. Interviews, December 1995.

82. Interviews, December 1995.

83. Interviews, December 1995.

84. See Brooks Tigner, 'Commander Envisions More Regional, Efficient NATO', *Defense News*, 13–19 November 1995, p. 16.

85. Remarks delivered to the Heritage Foundation, Washington DC, 6 June 1995.

86. Interviews, December 1995.

87. See William Drozdiak, 'NATO Votes to Start Bosnia Deployment', *Washington Post*, 2 December 1995, p. A14.

88. Jim Hoagland, 'Into the Future of Europe, Facing Backward', *Washington Post*, 7 December 1995, p. A23.

89. For example, defence expert Guillaume Parmentier, since late 1995 deputy diplomatic adviser to Defence Minister Charles Millon, wrote that the rationale behind France's refusal to integrate 'remains valid since this denationalisation of defence creates an unhealthy dependence on the part of countries bereft of command towards the one exercising it, dependence leading to demoralisation and to the refusal to assume responsibilities'. Parmentier, 'La France et l'OTAN', p. 44. Author's translation.

90. Interviews, December 1995. Also see 'A New NATO', *The Economist*, p. 51: 'France's *rapprochement* with NATO could go further. Some of its diplomats say that,

if the first steps prove successful, it could in time fully rejoin the alliance's military structure'.

91. For example, the late Colonel S. Nelson Drew stated at a US–CREST symposium that the French are right to express the need for strong political oversight 'at all levels' when NATO undertakes non-Article 5 operations, since these types of intervention are inherently political in nature. He added that NATO can achieve the necessary political control within the framework of existing structures, as the problem is more one of national will than of institutional failure. See Alongi and Grant, *Franco-American Security Cooperation*, p. 39.

92. Jean-Marie Guéhenno, 'Sécurité Européenne: L'Impossible Statu Quo', *Politique Etrangère*, vol. 60, no. 1, Spring 1995, pp. 25–31.

Chapter 4
The Masque of Institutions

Philip Zelikow

Allegories

In 1994, while Bosnia was burning, the US government began vigorously calling for the enlargement of the NATO Alliance. In June of that year, President Bill Clinton declared that the question was no longer whether NATO would expand, but how and when. Expectations soared and administration officials defended expansion with increasing ardour. Their ardour was more than matched by the vehemence of the warnings that united practically every political figure and expert in Russia in opposing this plan, seeing it as a defining act of post-Cold War hostility.

But NATO is not about to expand. US officials said that the Alliance would decide on its plan for the 'how' and 'when' of enlargement during 1995, present these views to interested countries, and announce in December how they would proceed. They announced that, during 1996, they would continue their consultations. There is no timetable and no set candidates for what the Allies call the 'steady, measured and transparent progress leading to eventual enlargement'.[1] Any expansion is years away. Any decisions on expansion will be made under circumstances – including developments in Bosnia and Russia – that readers can barely anticipate today.

So why put enlargement at the centre of debate? The 27 ongoing bilateral dialogues with NATO's various 'Partners for Peace' can discuss matters ranging from interoperability of weapons to democratic control of armed forces and the murky doctrines of post-communist communist leaders with or without the headlines. The spotlight is on enlargement because Washington has chosen to become a leading player in a new masque, a 'Masque of Institutions'.

Webster's English Dictionary defines a masque as 'a short allegorical dramatic performance popular as court entertainment in sixteenth- and seventeenth-century Europe, performed by masked actors often themselves members of the court, and consisting of dumb show combined with music, dancing, and sometimes poetry culminating in a ceremonial dance participated in by the spectators'.[2] To an audience in East-Central Europe, the character named NATO in this masque is a vividly costumed figure who is an allegory for 'reassurance'. To the audience in Russia, the same character is an ominous figure who is an allegory for 'exclusion'. In both cases, the allegorical theatre is some distance from reality. Yet both US and Russian politicians have preferred to deliver the allegorical message rather than the real one.

Since 1991, the most important issue of European security has been whether Russia and the states of East-Central Europe will become part of the hierarchy of Western political, economic and military power led by the United States, Germany, the UK and France. Will Russia and its neighbours accept this hierarchy and what it represents, or reject it, seeking a new political, economic and cultural identity out of the very fact of this rejection? The answer to this question is likely to be determined mainly by domestic political and economic developments in Russia and the other new democracies in Europe. The answer will not be determined by whether these countries are or are not members in one or another international institution, with the possible exception of the European Union.

The second most important issue in European security since 1991 has been whether military power will be readied or employed to influence political developments in or near Europe, especially where the interests of the great powers are not fully engaged. This question will be answered by the way the United States and its European allies define and pursue their national interests in the particular disputes that arise. Only governments can legally authorise the use of lethal force, and only governments and their polities are politically and morally accountable for its use.

The masque of institutions is an all-too diverting entertainment. Richard Holbrooke, US Assistant Secretary of State for European Affairs, thought Bosnia was 'the greatest collective security failure of the West since the 1930s' and tried to act accordingly. Yet only weeks before the Western powers abandoned the Srebrenica sanctuary-seekers they had solemnly pledged to defend, Holbrooke felt obliged to give a comprehensive presentation on European security that, as was typical, focused on the 'new interlocking security architecture'.[3] Towards the end of 1995, on the eve of becoming NATO's new Secretary-General, Javier Solana published an essay about 'Europe's security agenda' that did not once mention the Dayton peace agreement or political and military developments in or near Russia. Instead, Solana equated the 'security agenda' entirely with the consideration of possible new institutions.[4] And it is hard to find better evidence for the obscuring power of the masque of institutions than the fact that US Deputy Secretary of State Strobe Talbott devoted his most serious intellectual essay published in 1995 to the question of NATO enlargement, amid the horrifying developments that had just occurred in Bosnia and given all the other possible ways of analysing the security challenge in Europe and Russia.[5]

Instead of dwelling on what German Foreign Minister Klaus Kinkel has candidly called 'the abstract and fruitless argument over NATO's enlargement', NATO leaders could instead centre discussion of non-Balkan topics on how they will cooperate to prevent the leakage of vital nuclear material out of Russia; how the US and Europe can deploy common policies that respond to specific and worrisome events in Russia and on its borders; how to respond to the defence policy recommendations of NATO's Senior Defence Group on Proliferation; how the US and Europe can develop shared policies towards the Persian Gulf region; how Europe and America can find common policies towards China and other problems in East Asia; and how they will relate their experiences with Bosnia to future Euro-Atlantic military structures and planning.[6]

Countries and International Institutions

In the security sphere, where lives are at stake, governments use international institutions to pursue their national interests. Institutions have distinctive capacities and routines, thus the reliance on one or another institution has important policy consequences and that reliance then takes on a life of its own.[7] Nevertheless, especially in the security arena, great powers choose whether to use a given institution, not the other way around. Institutions do not kill people, governments do. NATO is a strong institution because governments have invested in creating some elaborate capacities for coordinating national action, making the Alliance the locus for substantial integration of their security policies.

Unlike the European Union's Commission, however, NATO's international staffs have never become an independent political force in their own right. NATO does not intervene in political disputes; its member-countries use the organisation to facilitate their national decisions to intervene. Although it may be convenient to talk about the 'NATO intervention in Bosnia', such phrases are misleading. No one who walked past a neighbour's house and saw a visiting car parked in the drive would say, 'look dear, a Chevrolet is visiting the Bensons tonight'. NATO may be the vehicle for organising the movement of forces into Bosnia, but NATO is not the driver. Only governments can legally authorise their citizens to kill people and destroy property, and only governments are politically and morally accountable for such choices.

If security institutions should therefore be judged by their usefulness to the powers concerned, what do security institutions need to be able to do in order to be useful? International political and security institutions in the new concert of Europe should ensure rapid and effective consultation on issues of common concern, allow freedom for prompt political action and develop the most effective and legitimising combinations of national military forces.[8]

Consultation is not a problem. European governments already discuss their security requirements and international political objectives in their capitals, in NATO, in the European Council, in the Western European Union, in the Organisation for Security and Cooperation in Europe (OSCE) and in the United Nations. There are so many places to consult that officials now spend a considerable amount of their time just trying to ensure that their diplomats are all saying the same thing.

Yet the European Union's Common Foreign and Security Policy (CFSP) aspires to do more than simply provide a place for consultation, and it has achieved a good deal less. The EU's structures, if taken seriously, would only weaken the power of its member-states, while offering few offsetting compensations. This is no surprise, since the EU's treaty articles on political union were animated by the desire to regulate the individual actions of member-states, not empower them. Brussels wanted to establish its institutional supremacy, limiting the scope for national policy, but was unable to craft any coherent supranational executive capable of credibly wielding the power now supposedly brought within the EU's grasp.

Member-states are urged by the Maastricht accords to formulate policy positions in common. Numerous specific topics, including relations with the former Soviet Union and activities in the United Nations and OSCE, are specifically enumerated as appropriate for joint action. Once the need for joint action is asserted, member-states must first agree unanimously in the Council of Ministers that a policy should be the subject of joint action. They must then agree on the specific scope of the action, the Union's general and specific objectives in carrying it out, and the duration, means, procedures and conditions for implementing the action. Every one of these decisions must be unanimous.

Once those decisions are made, the Council can unanimously agree whether there are some specific matters related to the action which can later be decided by a qualified majority. Member-states are, moreover, asked repeatedly to obey the joint action decisions of the Council. The rotating Council Presidency serves as the executive agent and therefore has the added duty of regularly consulting with the European Parliament to determine whether Members of the European Parliament (MEPs) can also support the Union's CFSP decisions.

The conceptual problem of the Maastricht approach to common foreign policy-making is a confusion between forcing governments to agree upon a common line and coordinating adherence to a line they are already individually willing to uphold. If the Community's foreign policy remains fundamentally inter-governmental in nature, only the latter objective will be workable. The Council and Commission are nominally superimposed atop the member-states, but they cannot dispose of the members' resources.

The new requirements could be worse than useless if member-states obey the rules and are actually inhibited in the use of their power, singly or in small combinations, by the shadow of the apparatus above them. The best outcome, unfortunately, is for European governments simply to discard the Maastricht straitjacket when they address any issue of urgent importance.

This hypothesis can be tested by imagining what would have happened if the Gulf crisis of 1990 had occurred after the European Union procedures agreed at Maastricht were fully in place. Would the European political or military responses have been materially different? It is hard to see how the Union would have adopted more effective policies. Unanimity would still be needed; the European parties would be no more powerful or interested. If anything, European policy-making would have been worse. In the Gulf case, the UK or French governments might have been slower to follow the US diplomatic lead. Indeed, the Maastricht Treaty specifically urges them to seek the unanimous agreement of the Council before they can adopt positions in the United Nations, which presumably would have required broad European consultation at each stage in the various phases of extraordinarily intense negotiations among the five permanent members of the Security Council. It is hard to see how this could have helped matters, and it might have hurt.

No great imagination is needed to test the hypothesis in the Bosnian case. The unhappy result of European policy in Bosnia highlighted the political and military fragility of the Maastricht system.

Maastricht went beyond common foreign policy-making to give the European Union a defence component as well – using the Western European Union (WEU). This innovation could usefully add to the net sum of European power in one of two ways: it could make publics more willing to pay for defences organised under European control; or it could give European governments greater freedom to undertake necessary military action under European auspices than they would feel either in *ad hoc* coalitions or in NATO. These are the two most encouraging presumptions. Unfortunately there is no evidence yet that either of these presumptions are true.

But the WEU innovation carried another benefit, in that it brought French military forces closer to coalition military planning. Practically all forces assigned to possible employment by WEU members are already assigned to NATO's integrated military command and have missions in the Alliance – requiring coordination between the WEU and NATO. The Maastricht Treaty states plainly that WEU decisions will not affect the NATO obligations of the EU's member-states and obliges the WEU to ensure that its judgments are 'compatible with the common security and defence policy established within' the NATO framework. This provision reinforced the agreement of the November 1991 Rome NATO summit that: 'the Alliance is the essential forum for consultation among its members and the venue for agreement on policies bearing on the security and defence commitments of Allies under the Washington Treaty'.[9] France recognised the inevitable centrality of NATO and rejoined the Alliance's Military Committee in December 1995. This significant development means that the WEU may have accomplished its most important transitional function.

The United States has been reasonably supportive of a European Security and Defence Identity (ESDI). The risk posed by this 'identity' was that the views of member-governments in the European Council could clash with those of the overlapping but different member-governments of NATO in disposing of the military forces available in Europe. But this danger was and is small, since the major European powers are all represented in NATO and NATO remains a far more capable institution for organising forces and coalition military planning.

In 1990, several governments hoped that the CSCE (now OSCE) might absorb both military alliances and turn into an effective pan-European security institution. But the time for this quixotic idea, originally intended as a device to overcome East–West division by replacing both NATO and the Warsaw Pact, has already passed. Since the 53-nation organisation is plainly too unwieldy, the agenda for enlivening the OSCE revolved for a time around the creation of an OSCE Security Council that would form an inner directorate of leading countries, following the UN model, to formalise a steering group dominated by the great powers. Russia proposed a ten-nation CSCE Security Council in September 1994 and was rebuffed.

Although the OSCE lacks both the authority and the infrastructure to do more than provide another opportunity for political consultation and support for diplomatic initiatives, this role is actually important. Here the OSCE's broad membership is a real asset. OSCE sponsorship of diplomatic missions in Estonia, Latvia, Georgia, Moldova and the Former Yugoslav Republic of Macedonia have been useful. The Organisation has been involved in a truce supervision mission to Nagorno-Karabakh. The OSCE has several responsibilities in rebuilding Bosnia under the Dayton accords, especially assisting in the supervision of free elections using its Office of Free Elections created as a result of NATO (specifically US) initiatives during 1990. The OSCE's essential role is the same as it has been since its predecessor, the CSCE, was founded in 1975: formulating and refining norms for the appropriate behaviour of governments in Europe.

NATO is in no danger of losing its own political identity. It is an increasingly important institution for considering Eastern Europe's fate, beginning with the July 1990 London Declaration's invitation to former Warsaw Pact adversaries to establish diplomatic liaison missions at NATO, extending to the Rome summit's creation of the US–German-proposed North Atlantic Cooperation Council, and continuing to the January 1994 inauguration of the Partnership for Peace.

NATO is generally in excellent health, and association with NATO provides a surer way for East European governments to discuss their security concerns constantly and informally, inside the organisation they rely upon for marshalling US and other allied military power. NATO has effectively preserved its institutional strength to conduct and implement effective coalition military planning. It demonstrated this capacity under moderate strain during the Gulf crisis. The failures in Bosnia were not NATO's failures; NATO effectively performed the tasks set for it by its member-states in coordinating the operation. These included maintaining the air-exclusion zone, upholding the naval blockade, employing combat aircraft in support of UN forces in Bosnia, supporting the United Nations Protection Force (UNPROFOR) in Croatia and providing contingency planning for more ambitious multinational 'peacekeeping' activities. It is now helping to execute the largest-scale military operation undertaken in concert by its member-states since the Alliance was founded.

NATO has maintained a costly and elaborate infrastructure with the proven ability to integrate diverse forces for action in a crisis. This role is crucial because, despite the ever more exalted institutional pronouncements about European defence entities, the main European partners are increasingly unable to conduct modern *national* military operations. The US military presence in Europe remains solid after the planned cutbacks to a force of about 100,000 soldiers and airmen and women. The forces' capability is high; they are backed by powerful units in the US designed effectively for overseas deployment, and NATO has agreed to support the continued deployment of greatly reduced but still-sizeable arsenals of US nuclear weapons in Europe for the foreseeable future.

The US' NATO allies and the new democracies of East-Central Europe are encountering severe problems in just maintaining their military establishments. There is no new wave of anti-military sentiment in Europe, but publics are sceptical of the need to commit any substantial resources for armed forces that seem to have no immediate vital mission.

As a result, no European country is likely alone to be able to mount a major unilateral conventional military campaign outside its homeland (or, for some countries, even *in* their homeland) capable of defeating an adversary that can conduct modern military operations. European countries must therefore plan to fight a war that might involve such adversaries only as part of a coalition. The coalition must be more than political; it must integrate individually fragile and unbalanced national armed forces into a stronger whole, employing national specialisation and divisions of labour. Without such a coalition, national armies will not only fight less effectively – they may be unable to fight sustained modern battles at all.

Only NATO is currently organised to support such a military coalition within Europe. Hence the Alliance has developed the 'Combined Joint Task

Forces' (CJTF) concept to prepare better-integrated groups of multinational forces in peacetime. NATO is also coordinating more combined military planning to combat the danger presented by weapons of mass destruction deployed in or near Europe.

NATO's work on the functional integration of disparate military forces into combined military planning can be extended – and has been extended in the case of 'peacekeeping' or humanitarian relief operations – to non-member-states participating in the Partnership for Peace programme. These capacities will then wait upon the orders of governments, should they find some common purpose requiring the use of force. Most members, like most non-member Partners, will not find such a united aim unless there is some agreement among the great powers to act. If the great powers do concur, most members, like most non-member Partners, may then join in applying some of the plans developed in peacetime.

NATO Enlargement

NATO enlargement may or may not be a good idea, in principle. It is postured as the solution to three different questions:

- How can a withering NATO be saved?
- How can a renewed Russian threat or a 'security vacuum' be prevented?
- How can democratic governance in East-Central Europe be consolidated?[10]

The first question – how to save NATO – is the simplest one. NATO is not in trouble. It is an organisation that has survived with all its key institutions intact; it has recently attracted France to return to its military organisation; it has been asked to undertake an active role of unprecedented scale in organising the Bosnian intervention; and many of its neighbours are clamouring to join it. If this is an organisation in trouble, it would be interesting to hear how NATO's detractors would define success.

The second issue – filling a security vacuum – is more interesting. Proponents of rapid NATO enlargement tend to argue that the new democracies of East-Central Europe are threatened or feel threatened, and need the reassurance which NATO membership can provide. These assertions are puzzling on the surface, because there are no objective manifestations of any serious external security threat to those states that are knocking loudest on NATO's door.

Poland, perhaps the most obvious candidate for early NATO membership, illustrates this point well. Poland is separated from Russia by Belarus and Ukraine. No significant military formations are being massed by Russia on an axis of advance leading towards Poland. A truly threatening accumulation of equipment would run up against the Conventional Armed Forces in Europe (CFE) Treaty constraints, providing some warning. In fact, Russia has just completed the peaceful withdrawal of all its troops in the former Soviet satellites back to the eighteenth-century frontiers of Peter the Great.

There are no acute areas of political tension between Poland and Russia, other than those created by the NATO enlargement issue itself. Poland and Russia have actually concluded an agreement settling claims from the COMECON era and are collaborating on a pipeline construction deal of great strategic and economic value to both countries. Poland is developing its regional relationships with Ukraine, Belarus and Russia, and Polish friendship is valued by all three of those former Soviet republics as a factor in their more troubled relationships with each other. If the Polish government felt genuinely threatened, it would presumably decide to invest in Poland's defences. Instead, the Polish government plans to cut the term of conscription from 18 months to one year; it is disbanding divisions and reducing the size of its armed forces; and it is buying little or no new military equipment. The Czech Republic and Hungary present similar pictures. Hungary's major acquisition of new military equipment last year was the delivery of MiG-29 aircraft – from Russia. Hungary is also cutting its term of conscription – from 12 months to nine.[11]

One reason why expansion is years away is because, as a practical matter, NATO membership for Poland seems to confer few tangible benefits to Poland or to current NATO members that cannot be achieved through the Partnership for Peace. The United States has never gone to war because of a pre-existing treaty of alliance. Such a treaty would only serve to codify and announce a readiness to shed blood that had already been manifested unmistakably by other deeds. There is no obstacle to taking steps to show a defence commitment to Poland, should that be needed, and Poland already enjoys a *de facto* entrée to the bodies where combined military planning could take place.

However, some Poles, and some Americans, allude ominously to Russia's 'imperial thinking'.[12] The analogical proposition is that, as Russia has expanded westwards before, it will expand westwards again. Even if this oversimplification of Russia's past were accurate, historical analogies are always a dubious substitute for analysing the case at hand. It is possible to reply with even vaguer assertions about security dangers, to wit:

> East-Central Europe is littered with potential mini-Weimar Republics, each capable of inflicting immense violence on the others … Ideological mobilisation alongside a security vacuum is once again proving to be Europe's classic recipe for instability and conflict.[13]

But international policies are not developed to affect the behaviour of abstractions. The loaded metaphor, 'security vacuum', is meant to supply a chain of reasoning that should be made explicit.

There is a well-grounded fear of Russian intentions, compounded by a sense of distance from Western protection, that exists in the Baltic states, throughout the Caucasus region and, to some extent, in Ukraine. Analysis of each of these cases may yield quite different policy prescriptions, none of which seems likely to include extending prompt NATO membership to the endangered countries. In fact, the prospect of NATO expansion to more secure countries could well make the situation of these vulnerable regions significantly more dangerous. The main point is this: specific security policy problems should be considered on their merits. Attention to the masque of institutions does not accomplish that task.

Finally, lacking convincing evidence of overt threats, advocates of quick NATO expansion fall back on the argument that NATO membership will reassure the new democracies and thus allow them to proceed with political development unhindered by their fears. This argument often relies on an analogy to NATO's role in shielding the democratic development of the Federal Republic of Germany (FRG) or other West European states. But the NATO Treaty of 1949 was preceded by rather striking manifestations of a real threat, including the Berlin blockade, the forcible installation of communist rule in Czechoslovakia and the active communist efforts to bring down governments in France and Italy ordered by the Moscow-controlled Cominform. German rearmament and the efforts leading to include the FRG in NATO only began in earnest after the Soviet-sponsored attack on South Korea in 1950. It is difficult to discern just what argument is being made about the relationship between domestic political stability and membership in an alliance.

Such analogies are substitutes for analysing the needs of any particular democracy in Europe today. Citing other analogies, such as 'NATO membership helped stabilise democracy and stem authoritarian backsliding in Portugal, Spain, Greece and Turkey', neither elaborates a chain of logic or applies that reasoning to, say, Poland or Hungary.[14] It is not even clear that the assertion holds up for post-war Portugal, Spain, Greece or Turkey.

Poland undoubtedly faces a struggle to sustain democratic governance and a liberal economic system. It is hard, however, to find any evidence, or specific chain of reasoning, in which NATO membership or non-member partnership is even one of the top five factors that will determine whether Poland's democracy will survive. That will depend on Poles, on the struggle for power among the new domestic élites, and on whether the Polish government can meet the demands being placed upon it by radical change. Poland's relationship to the European Union is more consequential, but the prospects for Polish EU membership in the next decade are remote. It is hard to avoid the impression that NATO membership is valued mainly as an alternative, largely symbolic gesture of inclusion and has become a convenient focal point for restless diplomats and ministers. Inclusion is good, but whatever NATO does, nothing will shake Poland's conviction that it must be aligned with the West politically, culturally, economically and militarily. The same cannot be said of Russian attitudes.

The discussion of enlargement must become practical, not theological. Like the proponents, opponents of NATO enlargement are prone to many exaggerations.[15] The 'threat' of NATO enlargement has been eagerly seized upon by Russian politicians. For nationalist, even xenophobic, Russian politicians, the NATO enlargement issue is a blessing. It is an abstraction about which most people know little, except the vestigial, negative associations from the Soviet era. Russian politicians need not fear being contradicted by government officials or Russian security experts, since the experts too oppose NATO enlargement (for their own reasons) or prefer to remain silent on the subject. The masque also diverts attention away from the real but often intractable problems that burden most Russian citizens.

Russian domestic politics are extremely volatile and strongly influenced by a sense of wounded pride and lost status. Consequently, it is hard to be too complacent about the way international issues might be manipulated by those struggling for power, especially given the long shadow cast over the political scene by the Russian military and its perceptions. Moscow's political and military alignment with the West is not a foregone conclusion, as it is in Poland. Russia is a great power with a vast capacity to endanger vital US interests across Eurasia. If, at the end of the 1990s, Russia has chosen to reject and oppose the concert of great powers led by the United States and its allies, then the United States will have suffered a historic setback. Naturally, those who believe Russia is already predestined to be an adversary of the United States are less concerned about this danger.

Meanwhile, Western European states are devising ever more ingenious variations of the masque of institutions. One of these is to use the Western European Union as a sort of NATO surrogate. Full members of the WEU are bound by a strong collective defence treaty originally signed in 1948, when it was directed at both Germany and the USSR. Greece became the latest full member of the WEU in January 1994. The WEU, trying to align its membership with that of NATO, has moved towards offering 'associate' membership to Iceland, Norway and Turkey.

Like NATO, the WEU has recruited its own coterie of non-member partners, called 'Associate Partners'. These Associate Partners may participate directly in WEU decisions and join in the activities of its 'planning cell'. The Associate Partners' club is more exclusive, including only the new democracies of East-Central Europe and the Baltic republics. Russia and Ukraine are NATO Partners, but are not WEU Associate Partners. Perhaps this anomaly will be seen as a way of opening another back door into NATO's councils for some countries and not others, but by a route so convoluted that it will not give offence. In any case, only the players will understand.

Conclusion

Until recently there was an apparent sense in Europe that ambitious political goals could be sustained without too much attention to old-fashioned military power. This may be true. Issues of economic reform and internal political development are most prominent at the moment, and many domestic conflicts – even bloody ones – may not present a case for active diplomatic or military intervention. There is, however, an unstable international environment in and around Europe. In this environment, it is sensible for the major powers to maintain the evident capacity for strong political action reinforced, if needed, by their military forces.

The current task for these powers and their publics is to consider the depth of their commitment to the principles that they have agreed should regulate future political relations among the nations of Europe. If European states wish to be great powers they must all (not only Germany) become comfortable with a more expansive, global definition of their vital interests linked to the fate of the international system as a whole. They must also look to strengthening or better integrating the aspects of diplomatic and military power – as well as economic might – that go with their shared responsibilities as partners in leadership.

The new concert of Europe can rely upon a set of eclectic, confusing, but ultimately workable structures for political consultation and coordination. Radically new structural designs are not needed. With the new system now in place, NATO will continue to play a key role alongside EU and OSCE structures. The organisations for European foreign policy-making agreed at Maastricht may actually weaken the system and limit, not enhance, European assertiveness.

The masque of institutions has been a diversion from the specific policy issues arising in the eastern half of Europe. It has also been a diversion from direct discussion of the vital interests, regional policies and needed military readiness of the governments in the Euro-Atlantic community.

Notes

1. See Final Communiqué, M-NAC-2(95)118, Ministerial Meeting of the North Atlantic Council, NATO Headquarters, Brussels, 5 December 1995; and Richard C. Holbrooke, 'Europe Must Avoid Being Held a Prisoner By Its History', remarks to the North Atlantic Assembly, Budapest, 29 May 1995.

2. *Webster's Third New International Dictionary of the English Language Unabridged*, vol. 2 (Chicago, IL: Merriam-Webster, 1986), p. 1388.

3. See Richard C. Holbrooke's statement before the Subcommittee on Airland Forces of the Senate Armed Services Committee, 'The Future of NATO and Europe's Changing Security Landscape', 5 April 1995.

4. Javier Solana, 'The European Security Agenda', *NATO Review*, vol. 43, no. 6, November 1995, pp. 11–14.

5. Strobe Talbott, 'Why NATO Should Grow', *New York Review of Books*, 10 August 1995, p. 27

6. For Kinkel, see his statement to the Bundestag, 'German Participation in NATO's Bosnia Mission', Bonn, 6 December 1995. For the work of NATO's Senior Defence Group on Proliferation, see NATO Press Release (95)124, 'NATO's Response to Proliferation of Weapons of Mass Destruction: Facts and Way Ahead', 29 November 1995. On the Persian Gulf issue, see the provocative essay by Shibley Telhami and Michael O'Hanlon, 'Europe's Oil, Our Troops', *New York Times*, 30 December 1995, p. 27. Several of the regional issues within the Alliance are ably presented, despite being placed under an umbrella recommendation for institutional reform, in Ronald D. Asmus, Robert D. Blackwill and F. Stephen Larrabee, 'Can NATO Survive?', *Washington Quarterly*, vol. 19, no. 2, Spring 1996.

7. Hence, despite the title of chapter, it is not possible to underestimate the importance of institutions in explaining state behaviour. Even an inanimate tool can affect the craftsman's approach, and these institutions are far from inanimate. For a useful illustration of the complex synergy between institutional and other causal variables, see Jack S. Levy, 'Organizational Routines and the Causes of War', *International Studies Quarterly*, vol. 30, no. 2, June 1986, pp. 193–222.

8. For the term 'a new concert of Europe', see Philip Zelikow, 'The New Concert of Europe', *Survival*, vol. 19, no. 2, Summer 1992, pp. 12–30.

9. Final Communiqué, S-1(91)86, Meeting of the North Atlantic Council of Heads of State and Governments, Rome, 8 November 1991.

10. Two representative and well-articulated cases for enlargement are Talbott, 'Why NATO Should Grow'; and Ronald D. Asmus, Richard L. Kugler and F. Stephen Larrabee, 'Building a New NATO', *Foreign Affairs*, vol. 72, no. 4, September–October 1993, p. 28.

11. *The Military Balance 1994–95* (London: Brassey's for the IISS, 1994) and *The Military Balance 1995–96* (Oxford: Oxford University Press for the IISS, 1995).

12. Andrzej Olechowski, quoted in Steven Erlanger, 'East Europe Watches the Bear, Warily', *New York Times*, 21 October 1994.

13. Asmus, Kugler and Larrabee, 'Building a New NATO', p. 29.

14. *Ibid.*, p. 30.

15. For a rebuttal of one such exaggeration, the assertion that NATO enlargement was foreclosed by the 1990 negotiations surrounding German unification, see Philip Zelikow, 'NATO Expansion Was Not Ruled Out', *International Herald Tribune*, 10 August 1995.

Part II
NATO Enlargement

Chapter 5
NATO Enlargement: A Framework for Analysis

Ronald D. Asmus, Richard L. Kugler and F. Stephen Larrabee

> As I have said, [NATO expansion] is no longer a question of
> whether, but when and how. And that expansion will not depend on
> the appearance of a new threat in Europe. It will be an instrument
> to advance security and stability for the entire region . . . And now
> what we have to do is to get the NATO partners together and to
> discuss what the next steps should be.
>
> *President Bill Clinton, Warsaw, July 1994*

At the initiative of the Clinton administration, the Atlantic Alliance has
taken the first cautious steps towards eastern expansion. At the January
1994 summit, NATO embraced the goal of expansion and launched the
Partnership for Peace (PFP) initiative. More recently, at the December 1994
ministerial meeting, NATO initiated an internal study, to be concluded
before the end of 1995, defining the road map for an expanded Alliance.

Although the enlargement process has been launched, many tough issues
lie ahead. While there is growing political support for enlargement, Alliance
leaders have not yet agreed upon, or even begun seriously to debate, the core
questions that must be addressed. NATO must define the specifics of
enlargement if it is to consolidate political consensus, set the right direction
for restructuring NATO's militaries and provide appropriate guidance to
candidate members through the PFP process. At the same time, NATO
enlargement must be part of a balanced package designed to increase

cooperation with Russia and Ukraine and incorporate both in a new, all-European security framework.

NATO enlargement will be a complex political and military undertaking. There are both good and bad ways to enlarge. Depending on how it is handled, enlargement could stabilise a new European security order or contribute to either the unravelling of the Alliance, or a new Cold War with Russia. Coming on the ruins of the Alliance's failed policies in Bosnia and in the aftermath of war, genocide and the failure of collective security in the Balkans, NATO enlargement will be the next test of the Alliance's ability to maintain peace and stability in post-Cold War Europe. The stakes are high. Failure could be disastrous, both for the Alliance's future and for European stability.

This chapter presents an analytical framework for how to enlarge NATO. Its purpose is not to lay out any single, fixed blueprint, but to present a framework for thinking about the issues, options and trade-offs that the Alliance faces. Although the Alliance has so far avoided naming the countries to be included in the first tranche of NATO enlargement, it is hardly a secret that the leading candidates are the Visegrad countries (Poland, Hungary, Slovakia and the Czech Republic) in East-Central Europe. The framework presented here, therefore, focuses on how the Alliance should expand to East-Central Europe and develop a policy package *vis-à-vis* both Russia and Ukraine. Other issues – how to deal with the former neutral states, the Baltic countries or the Balkans – are clearly important, but beyond the scope of this chapter.

The basic message is that NATO has flexibility in terms of when and how it expands. Yet it must make a series of decisions on different levels that add up to a coherent political and military package. The Alliance must select a policy path, a defence concept and a military strategy that not only make sense on their own respective merits, but which also fit together. The Alliance needs to know why it is enlarging, what extending new security guarantees entails for both old and new members and what the risks involved are. To craft the right package, the Alliance must weigh its choices carefully, for they touch on important political issues regarding Europe's future security order. How these choices are made will determine the costs and consequences of expanded membership for both old and new members.

Three Paths to NATO Enlargement

This article sets out three alternative paths to NATO enlargement for East-Central Europe. Each path leads to an expanded NATO, but the rationale, assumptions, timetable and criteria of each are different. The key policy question is: which path should the Alliance be on?

The first path is 'Evolutionary Expansion'. This path assumes that the main problems facing East-Central Europe are economic and political. It also assumes that the states of East-Central Europe do not face any immediate security threats and that their own reforms are essentially 'on track'. Therefore, the top priority for East-Central Europe should be its integration into the European Union (EU) as the best means to address these problems. At the same time, an enlarged NATO is important as part of the overall integration of these countries into both the European and Atlantic communities. Membership in NATO, however, is seen as secondary to membership in the EU. While the ultimate goal is congruent membership in both institutions, the EU is seen as the key driving organisation in this process.

Proponents of this path thus see no urgent reason for the Alliance to expand in the immediate future. Instead, they emphasise the importance of moving slowly and of using that time to ease concerns in the West and to diminish the risk of a new confrontation with Moscow over enlargement. By growing in conjunction with the European Union, NATO enlargement prevents so-called 'back-door' commitments from emerging, which could arise if the East-Central Europeans join the Western European Union (WEU) through the EU, but do not join NATO.[1] Because NATO membership is linked to joining the EU, the criteria for new members would be set primarily by the EU. An estimated timetable for East-Central Europeans joining NATO might be ten years, as it is difficult to imagine these countries being ready for EU membership much earlier.

The second path is 'Promote Stability'. In contrast to the first path, proponents of Promote Stability argue that the political situation in Eastern and Central Europe is fragile. The collapse of communism and the unravelling of the former Soviet Union not only liberated Eastern Europe, but created in their wake a new security vacuum between Germany and Russia. This security vacuum threatens to undercut the fragile new democracies in East-Central Europe by rekindling nationalism and reviving old patterns of geopolitical competition and conflict, thereby endangering the historic gains of the end of the Cold War.

Proponents of this school emphasise the linkage between democracy and security. The countries of East-Central Europe, they believe, need a strong security framework to develop into stable democracies. Proponents often draw an analogy with post-war West Germany and note the important role that NATO played in stabilising German democracy.[2] Membership in the European Union is important, but it is not enough. It does not resolve the underlying geopolitical dilemma facing these countries. Moreover, leaving these countries in a strategic 'no-man's land' could not only tempt Russia to try to reassert its influence in the area, but could also create a new strategic dilemma for Germany.

NATO must, therefore, provide the security framework necessary to anchor these countries to the West and stabilise Central Europe as a whole.

Given the risks as well as the consequences of instability in Central Europe for the continent as a whole, proponents of this path argue that NATO cannot wait until the European Union is ready to expand. Poland's security, they insist, should not be made contingent upon whether Warsaw meets the EU's standards on agriculture or social welfare policy. The criteria for NATO membership would be set by the Alliance and reflect its strategic priorities. Concern about instability in the region pushes proponents of Promote Stability to embrace a timetable of three to five years (before the end of the decade), with EU expansion to follow as quickly as possible.

The third path is 'Strategic Response'. In this case, NATO enlargement would not take place unless and until Russia moves in an authoritarian or expansionist direction and again poses a military threat to these countries. Proponents of this path include 'Russia firsters' – those who believe the West's top policy priority should be to stabilise Russia – and those who see the Alliance's primary role as a collective defence organisation for deterring an attack against its members and, if necessary, fighting wars to defend Western interests beyond NATO's borders. The former oppose early expansion because they fear it will provoke Moscow and contribute to the emergence of a new Russian threat, while the latter fear that enlargement would undercut political and military cohesion in the Alliance, saddle it with second-rate militaries in East-Central Europe and divert attention away from the need to prepare the Alliance for new conflicts in areas such as the Persian Gulf.

Figure 1: Alternative Paths to NATO Enlargement

Path	Rationale	Assumptions	Timetable	Criteria	Decides	PFP
Evolutionary Expansion	Part of overall Western integration	• No major security problems • ECE* 'on track' • EU/NATO parallel • Avoid back-door commitments	Along with or after EU membership (ten years)	Political, economic	EU and NATO / ECE	Slow track
Promote Stability	Provide political/security anchor	• Security vacuum • ECE potentially unstable • NATO precedes	Along with or before EU membership (five years)	Political, strategic	NATO / ECE	Fast track
Strategic Response	Respond to Russian threat	Expansion not needed unless Russia goes sour	Situation in Russia is catalyst	Strategic	Events in Russia	Interim step

Note: *ECE East-Central Europe

According to this path, the decision on whether and when to expand would be based purely on strategic criteria and events in Russia. NATO should give Moscow every chance and not do anything to facilitate a turn for the worse in Russia. However, if a new Russian threat emerges, the Alliance must be prepared to enlarge quickly. If no such threat emerges, NATO might never have to expand. Figure 1 presents an overview of these three paths. In short, events in Russia should decide whether and when NATO expands. Partnership for Peace should be seen as an interim step to expand security cooperation with East-Central Europe while the Alliance adopts a 'wait-and-see' attitude towards Russia.

Choosing the Right Enlargement Path

Choosing the right enlargement path is the most important decision the Alliance must take, for it will determine the rationale, timetable and criteria for NATO expansion. These paths represent very different approaches to European security. It is not only a question of different timing. Each represents a very different set of assumptions about European security, an alternative strategic rationale about why the Alliance is expanding, which institutions should take the lead and the time-frame for expansion. Each of these paths has advantages and disadvantages that need to be carefully weighed. The Evolutionary path, for example, assumes that the problems facing these countries are essentially political and economic, puts the EU forward as the central institution for resolving these problems and seeks to harmonise the economic and security integration of these countries, as well as to give the Alliance time to prepare both old and new members for enlarged membership. Moreover, by making the European Union the central institution for integrating these countries into the West, this strategy also places most of the burden on the Europeans. The proponents of this path also insist that by linking EU and NATO enlargement, such a process will be made more palatable and harder to oppose for Moscow.

There are, however, several drawbacks to this approach. It neither addresses current East-Central European security concerns, nor is it clear that the Alliance can afford to wait until the EU expands. By linking NATO's future to the European Union, it possibly allows the Europeans to decide when and where Washington will assume new security commitments, thereby creating a potentially explosive issue in the US Congress. If there is a US consensus on any single issue in this debate, it is that the Alliance needs to avoid the trap of NATO enlargement becoming hostage to the internal workings of the EU, over which Washington has little influence.

The primary advantage of the Promote Stability path is that it provides the East-Central Europeans with the political and security anchor they so desperately want. Moreover, it enables the United States and NATO to determine the criteria for and pace of enlargement and serves as a geopolitical hedge. Although NATO is expanding primarily for political reasons and to project stability to the region, it will also be much better positioned to respond militarily in the future should the need arise. On the other hand, the Promote Stability path also has several disadvantages. It forces the United States to take the lead in this process and, because of its shorter timetable, compels the Alliance to decide sooner rather than later on how to implement new security guarantees. A more rapid enlargement of NATO also forces the Alliance to face the issue of Russian sensitivities as well as what to do about excluding Ukraine and other countries – such as the Baltic states – that may not be included in the first round of enlargement.

The advantage of the Strategic Response path is that it allows the Alliance to adopt a 'wait-and-see attitude' as it awaits the outcome of the political struggle in Moscow. Moreover, under Strategic Response, Western policy is bending over backwards not to take any steps that might adversely affect relations with Moscow unless and until it decides that Moscow again poses a threat to those countries. The disadvantages of this approach are that it does not deal with the current security concerns of the East-Central Europeans; it offers no answer to the problem of potential 'back-door' commitments through WEU expansion when the EU eventually does expand; and it *de facto* allows Russia to determine the Alliance's future. Moreover, it is not clear how the Alliance will decide if and when a new Russian threat has emerged. In some scenarios this may be obvious, but it could also be an issue over which the Alliance might end up badly divided. It is also not clear whether NATO would actually be able to summon the courage to enlarge in the face of a newly emerged Russian threat or whether the West would conclude that such a step was too dangerous and quietly acquiesce to new power realities.

Figure 2: Membership Criteria Depend Upon Choice of Path

	Evolutionary Expansion	Promote Stability	Strategic Response
Strategic Interest	**	***	***
Democratic Rule	***	***	**
Economic Development	***	**	*
Territorial Claims	***	***	*
Human/Minority Rights	***	***	*
Civilian Control of Military	***	**	*
Out-of-Area/Peace-Support Operation	**	**	*
Achievable Compatability of Forces	**	**	*

Notes: *** Very Important, ** Important, * Not Important

Finally, the importance of choosing the appropriate path for NATO enlargement is also reflected in the debate over the kind of criteria that should be applied to new members. Criteria have the advantage of providing the Alliance with a rationale for both inclusion and exclusion. They are also important as incentives to keep the reforms in East-Central Europe on track. Yet, the priority that the Alliance might attach to different criteria will vary considerably, depending upon the enlargement path it embraces.

The left-hand column in Figure 2 summarises the kinds of standards that have been discussed as possible criteria for expanded NATO membership. Many of them are different and more demanding than the criteria used in the past. During the Cold War, the criteria NATO used were largely limited to whether bringing a certain country into the Alliance served the West's strategic interests. Since the end of the Cold War, the Alliance has debated whether to embrace some combination of the much longer list of criteria shown in Figure 2.

Each of the possible paths to enlargement would weigh these criteria differently. Because the Evolutionary path ties NATO enlargement to the EU, those criteria that are crucial for EU membership would be very important for NATO as well. The countries that are most eligible for NATO membership are former neutral countries, such as Finland, Austria or Sweden, who have recently joined the EU – and thus, under the Maastricht Treaty, are eligible to join the WEU at any time and certainly qualify for NATO on all of the listed criteria. The only uncertainty would be whether NATO sees it as in its interests to have a country like Finland, with its 1,200km-long border with Russia, in the Alliance.

In the case of Promote Stability, a country like Poland would be at the top of the list of candidate members, based on a combination of NATO's strategic interest in stabilising Poland and the belief that Alliance membership would facilitate and reinforce Poland's transition to democracy. In the case of Strategic Response, in contrast, the key factor is the need to deter or fight a war against a new Russian threat. In this case, a country like Slovakia, which presumably would not qualify under the Evolutionary path and whose prospects under Promote Stability are also uncertain, would be on NATO's short-list of candidate members due to its strategic location. Bulgaria and Romania would also become potential partners as part of a neo-containment strategy to thwart this new Russian threat.

The NATO enlargement debate has been so complex and, at times, confused because it involves so many diverse and overlapping agendas. It forces the Alliance to confront first-order policy questions on Europe's future political order, over which a clear consensus has not yet emerged. The answers to the following six questions are crucial in determining the enlargement path the Alliance should pursue:

- How important is NATO enlargement for the future stability of Eastern and Central Europe?
- What should be the relationship between EU and NATO enlargement?
- *Quo vadis* Russia? What impact will NATO expansion have on Russia's future? Can the risk of a negative impact be minimised?
- How vulnerable will those states be that are not included in an expanded NATO, such as Ukraine and the Baltic states? How can NATO minimise this vulnerability?

- What should be the future US role in European security? How will expansion affect that role?
- Does NATO need to be revitalised?

These questions give a sense of the many agendas at play in the NATO enlargement debate. They also underscore that NATO enlargement, precisely because it touches on such critical political issues, is the defining issue for the Alliance and Europe in the 1990s. What is at stake is not only reunifying Europe, but also the future role of the United States, Germany and Russia in a new European order.

Extending New Security Guarantees

NATO enlargement will extend security guarantees to new members in East-Central Europe. How these guarantees are implemented is central to the future cohesion of the Alliance. At the same time, it is important to note that Article 5 of the NATO Treaty pledges the Alliance to collective defence, but says nothing about how security guarantees should be implemented. Throughout the history of the Alliance, guarantees have been implemented in different ways at different times, as demonstrated by the very different ways in which NATO has chosen to defend West Germany, Norway, Turkey and Spain.

The Alliance today faces a radically different strategic environment than it did during the Cold War. NATO needs to decide which defence arrangements make sense in the 1990s, both for itself and for East-Central Europe. In addition to choosing the proper enlargement path, NATO must decide what kind of defence concept, military strategy and force goals are appropriate for an expanded Alliance. Enlargement will not only compel the Alliance to consider alternative ways of moving east, but will also force NATO to face up to how the Alliance as a whole should be restructured to carry out new border defence missions.

Three factors will be important in shaping how NATO implements Article 5 guarantees in East-Central Europe. The first, of course, is the threat that these countries face now and, potentially, in the future. The need to balance Russian power is one important factor in this equation, but it is by no means the only one. The armed forces of new members should also be structured to defend their borders against other threats and to participate in the full range of peace-support and crisis-management operations that the Alliance has embraced. Emphasising these other missions underscores that enlargement is currently not a strategic response to a new Russian threat and that these countries will contribute to Alliance objectives throughout Europe.

Second, and equally important, is the political willingness, military needs and indigenous capabilities of the host country. During the Cold War, a NATO ally, such as Norway, relied on a defence concept that did not involve permanently deployed foreign troops on its soil. While Norway faced a Soviet military threat, geography and internal politics led Oslo to opt for a defence relationship that relied on Alliance reinforcements in a crisis. In West Germany, by contrast, the massive Warsaw Pact threat, coupled with geography and domestic political imperatives, made forward defence a political imperative – and with it a massive permanent peacetime presence of NATO combat troops. It was not until the early 1960s, however, that the Alliance felt that it had the political consensus and military capabilities to move its defence lines up to the inter-German border.

The Alliance must explore with candidate members in East-Central Europe what their expectations are over new security guarantees. Do these countries want a West German or a Norwegian-type defence? How are the domestic politics and sovereignty concerns of these countries likely to impact on such issues as a foreign military presence? Some East-Central European countries may want NATO troops on their soil, but others may not. Will a NATO guarantee be credible without a foreign troop presence? And if foreign troops are to be deployed in East-Central Europe, who should supply them? Although a US military presence may be welcome, are the Poles – or the Czechs for that matter – ready to station the *Bundeswehr* on their soil?

The ability of the East-Central Europeans to acquire the kind of defence relationship they want within NATO will also be shaped by what they themselves bring to the table – politically, economically and militarily. It is not only demand but also supply that will determine how much influence and support they enjoy. During the Cold War, for example, it was West Germany's performance on a wide array of issues, as well as its growing political, economic and military clout, that moved the Alliance step-by-step over several decades towards an increasingly robust defence of the inter-German border.

The third crucial factor is what the other members of the Alliance are willing and able to contribute to an expanded Alliance. What kind of division of labour will emerge in an expanded NATO? Which countries will take the lead in assuming crucial roles and missions? Who is willing to do what will also shape decisions on how command structures are reformed and key responsibilities distributed. NATO's traditional rule of thumb that those countries contributing the most also assume major leadership and command roles should be maintained.

Looking towards the future, NATO must build a consensus on how best to implement security guarantees to new members in an expanded Alliance. It is important to start building that consensus now to set the direction and to put into motion the process of restructuring the militaries of both new and old Alliance members, a process that is likely to take considerable time. Such overall direction and guidance is crucial if NATO hopes to use the

PFP process effectively to prepare candidate members for eventual Alliance membership. This, in turn, requires a decision about the 'endgame' that the Alliance wants to achieve. PFP should be structured differently for candidate members than for others. Moreover, how PFP is structured will depend on the defence relations with the new members that the Alliance chooses.

Again, the key message is that the Alliance has both choice and flexibility. What is required is a set of decisions that add up to a coherent conceptual package consisting of a defence policy, a military strategy and conventional force goals. Such a package should be flexible, for the Alliance will certainly evolve over time in response to its own internal needs and Europe's evolving security environment. But what is needed now is a clear sense of where the Alliance wants to go and what it wants to achieve.

Figure 3 suggests a spectrum and typology of alternative defence concepts for defending new NATO members in East-Central Europe. Moving from left to right, this spectrum reflects shifting roles and missions and growing Alliance involvement in implementing new security guarantees. Each of these represent an Article 5 guarantee and has clear advantages and disadvantages. The issue is which one makes the most sense for both East-Central Europe and the rest of the Alliance in the 1990s.

Figure 3: Alternative Defence Concepts Have Different Implications for the Alliance

	Self-Defence Dominant	Functional Division of Labour	Core Group Defence	Full-Scale Multinational Defence
Roles and Missions	• Major responsibility assumed by host country, selective allied support – e.g., C^3I, infrastructure • No or little foreign troop presence	• Defence responsibilities shared by function between indigenous and allied forces – e.g., ground v air/naval • Emphasis on reinforcement, infrastructure • Low foreign-troop presence	• Small core group assumes key roles and missions • Limited joint posture, e.g., some foreign-combat troops	• Collective defence model • Full-joint posture e.g., sizeable foreign-combat troops
Advantages	• Least provocative to Russia • Least demanding on NATO	• Comparative advantage • Modest military requirements fall on small subset • Easier to obtain political consensus?	• Credible political commitment by motivated allies • Military requirements • Easier to obtain political consensus?	• Credible political commitment • Credible defence strategy and posture • High integration/ interoperability
Disadvantages	• Low defence capability • Little interoperability • Uncertain political credibility	• Uncertain defence credibility if indigenous defence capabilities weak • Weak interoperability • Uncertain Alliance cohesion	• Unfair burden-sharing • Uncertain Alliance cohesion – 'opting out' • Provoke Russia? • Reverse multinational integration?	• Overload NATO politically? • Provoke Russia • Costly for ECE • Integrated command upheaval

Starting on the left-hand side of the figure, the first defence concept, Self-Defence Dominant, envisions the host country retaining the major responsibility for its own defence. The rest of the Alliance would provide support in areas like infrastructure, logistics and C³I (command, control, communications and intelligence). There would, therefore, be little or no foreign troop presence in peacetime and no major preparations for combat troops to be committed in wartime.

The second defence concept is the Functional Division of Labour. Here, the Alliance would distribute roles and missions based on a theory of comparative advantage. This would allow the host country to focus its efforts on the missions it is capable of fulfilling (such as providing for its own ground defence), while NATO would concentrate on providing tactical air-power on the assumption that this is where the rest of the Alliance is strong and the countries of East-Central Europe are relatively weak. NATO would broaden the infrastructure provided for new members from mere logistics and C³I to include reception facilities and the capability for significant reinforcement in a crisis. As a result, NATO's presence in the host country would increase, but could still be limited.

The third defence concept is the Core Group Defence. Here, a subset of Alliance members takes the next step in increased engagement in defending a new member and plans the wartime deployment of a full-joint posture, including ground-combat troops, in the host country. Peacetime deployments would be limited to a handful of countries. For example, in addition to the kind of support discussed above, the United States might, along with Germany, deploy a brigade in Poland to underscore NATO's security commitment.

The fourth and final defence concept is Full-Scale Multinational Defence. This would entail the collective defence model of Alliance structures, such as Allied Forces Central Europe (AFCENT), but could conceivably be kept more modest militarily. It would involve wartime force commitments by most, if not all, of AFCENT's members.

This spectrum is illustrative and is designed to lay out the kinds of choices NATO has in deciding which defence concept should be implemented for new members in East-Central Europe. Figure 3 also lists a number of advantages and disadvantages of each concept. While not exhaustive, these nevertheless highlight the need for the Alliance to find a balance and to prioritise between different political and military objectives. As one moves from left to right on Figure 3, the credibility of NATO's security guarantee, as well as the kind and quality of the integration and interoperability of these countries' forces with those of the Alliance, will improve. If NATO's goal is to integrate and Westernise the armed forces of these countries, engage them in serious peacetime training and make them capable of participating in the full range of possible Alliance missions, including both peacekeeping and other non-Article 5 missions, then achieving appropriate levels of integration and interoperability is important.

Such goals, however, have to be balanced by the Russian factor. One of the greatest fears of the Alliance is that expansion could catalyse Russian military counter-moves that will, in turn, pressure NATO into assuming a more robust military presence. The Alliance will, therefore, also want to tailor its defence concept to new members to minimise the risk of such a cycle starting. The desire not to provoke Moscow might lead the Alliance to embrace a less provocative defence concept.

The Alliance will have to debate these factors to reach a consensus. A long series of questions needs to be addressed. Who in the Alliance is willing to go how far along this spectrum and why? How should the Alliance balance the need to maintain the integrity of the integrated command structure, provide credible commitments and yet still remain sensitive to Russian concerns? At what point does NATO's existing command structure cease to make sense? Does AFCENT become Allied Forces Eastern Europe (AFEAST)? Such questions underscore that this debate is as much over reorganising the West as it is about expanding to the East. NATO enlargement will be the catalyst sparking a much broader debate over restructuring the Alliance, one in which different views of the internal requirements of the Alliance will come to the forefront.

The Alliance must also decide what kind of military strategy to employ in conjunction with its new defence concept. Figure 4 suggests a typology of

Figure 4: Choice of Defence Concept Shapes Military Strategy

Alternative Defence Concepts	Self-Defence Dominant	Functional Division of Labour	Core Group Defence	Full-Scale Multinational Defence
Military Strategy	*Power Projection*	*Mixed Power Projection and Forward Presence*	*Forward Presence*	
	• Low threat, long warning time, forward defence not imperative	• Medium threat, medium warning time, forward defence not imperative	• High threat, short warning time, forward defence imperative	
	• No Allied presence in peacetime; reliance on power projection in crisis	• Modest Allied presence in peacetime	• Sizeable forward peace-time deployments of Allied combat forces	
	• Requires strong Allied mobility assets	• Requires strong Allied mobility assets, POMCUS, prepositioned WRS, infrastructure and reception facilities	• Requires strong Allied mobility assets augmented by substantial reinforcement capabilities	

Notes: POMCUS Prepositioning of Material Configured in Unit Sets
WRS War Reserve Stock

alternative military strategies that the Alliance might consider. Should it rely on a power-projection strategy or one emphasising forward presence? Or perhaps a hybrid emphasising infrastructure and some presence?

Forward presence is reassuring to new members, but may be more costly than a power-projection capability. It could be kept limited, barring the re-emergence of a Russian threat. Whether, and how much of, a forward presence is required will be shaped by political and military requirements that will only become clear as the Alliance debates this issue with new members. The Alliance will also have to examine the implications of peacetime training for forward presence. Power projection is probably less costly and is definitely less provocative, but is only adequate if there is sufficient time for deployment. Power projection would also require a major reorientation and restructuring of NATO forces, especially the West Europeans that are currently tied to territorial defence missions. The advantages of a mixed strategy are that it would build the infrastructure needed for power projection and crisis response while not taking the controversial step of stationing large NATO forces in East-Central Europe during peacetime (see Figure 4).

Finally, an enlarged NATO must also decide how to set conventional force goals, which should reflect the Alliance's security objectives, strategy, doctrine and available resources, as well as anticipated threats and contingencies. Clarifying NATO's planned conventional force goals would also enlighten the purpose and objective of enlargement. Are Alliance forces expected to perform border defence missions in East-Central Europe and thus be limited to political reassurance in the absence of any real threat? Or is the goal to prepare NATO armed forces for a lesser regional contingency (LRC) along with crisis-management and peace-support operations? Or, is the Alliance aiming to fight a major regional contingency (MRC) if necessary? An adequate defence posture is critical, but adequacy is a relative concept. Much depends on the force goals the Alliance wants to pursue.

NATO, therefore, has flexibility and choice in implementing new security guarantees. The costs and consequences for the Alliance, including old and new members, will vary, depending on which choices it makes. The pyramid presented in Figure 5 puts the analysis presented here into a framework showing the connection between the choices the Alliance must make at these different levels and how the different pieces of the expansion package might fit together. Above all, it highlights how the different assumptions and rationale for expansion at the political level set the overall strategic direction for how NATO will implement Article 5 guarantees. It is meant to be suggestive, not mechanistic, because a broad array of alternative packages is feasible. For example, if the Alliance shares the relatively benign assumptions underlying Evolutionary Expansion, then it might be prepared to live with a package consisting of the Self-Defence Dominant Defence concept and a military strategy based on power projection. In contrast, if it assumes that there is going to be a new Russian threat, then NATO will be pulled towards the right-hand side of the pyramid, including the more robust Full-Scale Multinational Defence concept and a military strategy emphasising forward presence. If the Alliance embraces the Promote Stability path, it might embrace the Functional Division of Labour or Core Group Defence concepts along with a mixed military strategy to provide reassurance, while avoiding a provocative military posture.

Figure 5: NATO Enlargement Alternatives

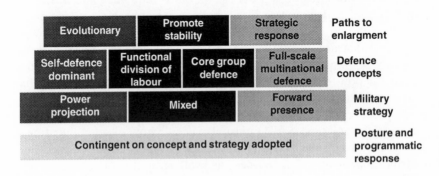

This pyramid highlights some of the tensions inherent in crafting NATO's expansion package and the need to balance conflicting political and military objectives. Different countries may prefer different options, reflecting their own priorities and sense of what NATO membership and credibility should entail. For example, some countries will view a foreign military presence as essential for a credible security guarantee; others, however, will not. The Alliance needs to decide on the package that makes sense in the current climate while retaining the flexibility to move towards a more robust defence posture should the security environment deteriorate.

Above all, this pyramid underscores the Alliance's flexibility. Not only does it have different options, but defence concepts for new members can evolve over time and in response to an evolving strategic environment. One should not forget that the defence of West Germany, for example, was built over years and decades. NATO's defence concept for the Federal Republic changed considerably over time. NATO today has little choice but to start modestly in terms of constructing a defence package for East-Central Europe and to build over time. The key question is how far the Alliance wants and needs to go given Europe's new strategic environment.

The Alliance will also have to re-examine NATO's nuclear strategy in an expanded Alliance. NATO will want to avoid creating a two-tiered Alliance in which some members have a nuclear guarantee and others do not.

However, the degree and extent to which new members will need nuclear reassurance will depend not only on the threat, but also on NATO's political credibility and on how security guarantees are implemented. The issue is whether extending NATO's nuclear umbrella will require any changes in nuclear strategy, doctrine, deployments or hardware. Will expanded NATO membership mean that nuclear weapons must be deployed on the soil of new members or that NATO's nuclear forces should be enlarged or reconfigured?

The list of difficult issues the Alliance needs to face could be continued. Forging a consensus on these issues may be the greatest challenge facing the Alliance, but it must be achieved if NATO is to master the timing and manner of expansion.

Dealing with Russia

In deciding when and how to expand, the Alliance needs to take into consideration the impact on Russia. There are strong reasons why NATO expansion is not contrary to Russia's interests. No one, least of all Moscow, wishes to see Central Europe destabilised by extreme nationalism, geopolitical rivalries and increased political and economic instability. Just as it is beneficial to Russia for Germany to be firmly anchored in NATO, the same logic applies to Poland and other countries in East-Central Europe. A secure Poland is likely to be less anti-Russian and more interested in cooperation and bridge-building than an insecure Poland again caught in the old geopolitical dilemma between Germany and Russia.

While there are a few Russian academics who acknowledge this logic, most members of the Russian élite, including both democrats and nationalists, oppose NATO expansion. Four factors have contributed to this view. First, Moscow is concerned about being isolated and marginalised. Second, Russian democrats are worried that expansion might undermine reform by playing into the hands of the nationalists. Third, the Russian military is concerned about a new 'NATO threat' appearing close to Russia's borders. Fourth, and finally, there is an instinctual feeling among many Russian strategists and politicians that NATO enlargement will inevitably lead to a European security system that neither recognises nor leaves room for Russia's great-power status and influence.

Russia is in a period of national redefinition. A political struggle is taking place between Westernisers, who see Russia's future tied closely to Europe and the West, and the Eurasianists, who emphasise Russia's uniqueness and role as a Eurasian power. At the same time, the centre of political gravity has shifted in a nationalistic direction. A resurgence of geopolitics is taking place in Russian foreign policy. Driven by these new dynamics, even Russian democrats such as Foreign Minister Andrei Kozyrev have adopted both the rhetoric and, in some cases, the substance of the nationalists.

Growing Russian opposition to NATO enlargement is only one example of this trend.

While Moscow could not stop enlargement, it could take steps to damage important Western interests elsewhere. These could include accelerating the reintegration of the Commonwealth of Independent States (CIS) and turning it into a counter-bloc to NATO; increasing pressure on Ukraine and the Baltic states; building up Russia's military presence in forward areas (Belarus, Kaliningrad or Moldova); abrogating arms-control agreements, such as the Conventional Armed Forces in Europe (CFE) Treaty or Strategic Arms Reduction Talks (START II) Treaty; opting out of the PFP; curtailing bilateral defence cooperation with Western countries; and reducing cooperation in the United Nations on an array of issues, ranging from Iraq to Bosnia.

But Russian countermeasures to NATO enlargement would entail serious costs and risks for Russia as well. They would diminish NATO's willingness to provide Moscow with the kinds of equities discussed above and could jeopardise Russia's overall political and economic relationship with the West. Moscow's actions could leave Russia weaker and more isolated. As far as the CIS is concerned, Moscow can ill afford to subsidise the economies of the weaker members and is reluctant to do so, as its recent hesitation in creating a monetary union with Belarus underscores. Not only are some CIS states likely to resist Russian political domination, especially over security, but increased pressure on Ukraine or the Baltic states could exacerbate anti-Russian feelings and drive these countries to seek closer ties with the West. Russia's ability to initiate a military build-up *vis-à-vis* an expanded NATO is also limited. Such a build-up would leave Russia vulnerable to the more serious and real national security threats it faces in the south and east. Hence, even a Russia dominated by nationalists would have to weigh carefully the costs of provoking a major crisis with the West over NATO enlargement.

Different views have emerged in the West over how to deal with Moscow if NATO expands. A handful of commentators have already concluded that Russian foreign policy is becoming expansionist and that the Alliance should adopt a new policy of neo-containment. Such voices are currently a distinct minority. At the other extreme, there are a handful of commentators insisting that Russia and East-Central Europe should join the Alliance simultaneously. This, however, would not only turn NATO into another OSCE, but it would destroy the geopolitical balance in Europe and raise the prospect of Alliance troops, under Article 5, defending the Russo-Chinese border.

Between these two extremes, mainstream thinking revolves around two schools of thought. One argues that Russia is simply too big and different ever to join NATO and that this should be made clear to Moscow. The

Alliance should, however, offer Moscow a strategic partnership to underscore the fact that enlargement is not aimed against Russia, but that the integration of the East-Central Europeans will be balanced by increased cooperation with Russia in a broader all-European context. This view has been most openly articulated by German Defence Minister Volker Rühe, but is widely shared in private throughout the continent.

Another school of thought, however, argues that it should still be possible for Russia eventually to join the Alliance, even though it is unrealistic at the moment. Closing the door now, they insist, would send the political signal that the West is excluding Russia and would, therefore, run the risk of a new division of Europe. Instead, the issue should remain open to ease the plight of Russian President Boris Yeltsin and the Russian democrats. This standpoint has been embraced by the United States.

The issue of Russian membership, however, does not have to be faced now. It is not even clear that Russia wants to be a member of NATO. The real issue is what is, or should be, Russia's place in the new emerging security order. The policy challenge is to include Russia as an active participant in all-European processes while not giving it a veto over either NATO or the EU's future, minimise the negative impact on Russian politics of NATO enlargement and guard against any Russian counter-moves that could damage important Western interests. To do so, the West needs to develop a portfolio of equities and incentives to offer Moscow as inducements for shaping future Russian behaviour and sustaining and, indeed, expanding cooperation while NATO grows.

How should the Alliance craft a strategy for Russia under NATO enlargement? The real issue is less one of how to 'compensate' Moscow, but how the Alliance should structure its relations with Russia based on Western interests. The suggestions contained in Figure 6 should be seen as a menu from which Alliance policy-makers can choose such a package.[3] NATO has to continue to expand political consultations through the Group of Eight (G-8) and parliamentary ties. Both the United States and the European Union need to liberalise trade and expand economic cooperation, while continuing to support assistance for Russia through multilateral institutions like the International Monetary Fund (IMF). The West can also underscore cooperation by continuing and, where possible, expanding both scientific and technological joint ventures in areas such as space. Enhanced political and economic cooperation will counter the accusation that NATO expansion is designed to isolate and threaten Russia.

More controversial and important, however, is the security domain. The Alliance must decide whether, and how far, it is willing to answer Russia's proposals for reform of the OSCE, perhaps adapting them to correspond to NATO's own interests. First, while subordinating NATO to the OSCE is not acceptable, the Alliance might consider strengthening the OSCE to

Figure 6: A Strategy for Russia

Political–economic component
• Intensify G-8 political consultation
• Expand EU–Russian economic cooperation and trade liberalisation
• Increase bilateral/multilateral economic assistance and trade liberalisation
• Expand scientific and technological cooperation
• Strengthen parliamentary ties, such as the North Atlantic Assembly and the Duma

Security component
• OSCE Security Council?
• Regular meetings between Russia and key NATO councils
• Contact Group as a model for informal consultations?
• Regular US–Russian consultations before NATO consensus?
• Amend CFE sublimits?
• Expand PFP programme
• Expand US–Russian bilateral military contacts
• NATO–Russian Treaty?

develop a parallel track in European security. The creation of a Directorate in shaping the emerging European security order and a more permanent 'seat or Security Council within the OSCE would give Moscow a greater voice at the table'. The tough issue will be deciding what rights or responsibilities such a Directorate or Security Council should have. Moreover, many West European countries, especially the smaller ones, are likely to oppose the creation of such a council, since it would diminish their role.

Second, NATO could institutionalise regular meetings between the key Alliance Councils – such as the North Atlantic Council (NAC), Defence Planning Committee (DPC) and the Nuclear Planning Group (NPG) – and Moscow on a regular basis. This would go far towards establishing the type of broader security dialogue that Moscow has long wanted. While such a step would also reinforce the message that NATO is striving for a new, cooperative relationship with Russia, Moscow's priority will not be to establish a relationship at the level of 16+1 (or 20+1) with NATO. By the time NATO has reached a consensus at that level, Moscow will find itself confronted with a painfully crafted position that allows for little negotiating leeway.[4] Russia wants to be consulted before key decisions are made, not afterwards.

Therefore, Moscow will most likely try to use its bilateral ties with key NATO members to influence Alliance thinking before the Alliance reaches a consensus. It will probably want a 'Quad plus 1' relationship with

NATO's key powers (the informal discussions between Washington, London, Paris and Bonn is an attempt to establish a core consensus). The Bosnian Contact Group is *de facto* such an arrangement. Does the Alliance wish to replicate this on other issues or give it a more institutional character? Moscow is likely to seek to gain leverage or control over future NATO actions – either through a UN mandate, a reform of the OSCE or by gaining access to NATO's internal deliberations and decision-making processes. The key issue is whether and how the Alliance will choose to respond to Moscow's desire to have an input into or influence NATO decision-making – and how formal or informal such influence will be.

Third, Russia already wants to see a revision of the CFE Treaty. NATO enlargement may lead Moscow to seek further revisions. NATO has thus far resisted any reopening of the Treaty. However, the CFE Treaty, which was a product of bloc-to-bloc negotiations, may need to be reviewed in any case as a result of enlargement. Indeed, the Alliance may want to see its own revisions of the Treaty, such as changes that might allow the countries of East-Central Europe to become better military partners, especially in future crisis-management and peacekeeping operations.

Fourth, the Alliance can move individually and collectively to expand both the PFP programme and bilateral military contacts to counter the image of a new Russian threat and to make defence cooperation with the West more attractive to the Russian military.[5]

Fifth, the Alliance needs to decide whether it should try to codify this new cooperative relationship through a NATO–Russian Treaty. Such a Treaty would underscore the political desire to build a new cooperative relationship between NATO and Russia and could spell out provisions for expanded military cooperation, including crisis management and peacekeeping.

Finally, how NATO expands to East-Central Europe will not only be important for inter-Alliance dynamics, but also in terms of its relations with Russia. The kind of defence concept and military strategy that NATO employs for new members could influence Russian thinking on a variety of issues, especially its behaviour towards Ukraine and the Baltic states and its future defence spending, military doctrine and force deployments. If and when Moscow decides that NATO is serious about expanding, the modalities of enlargement will become important, especially for the Russian General Staff.

Whether and what kind of forward deployments and military capabilities NATO adopts will be crucial in shaping not only Russian perceptions, but also Moscow's reactions, especially in the military field, to Alliance enlargement. Some in the West will be tempted to discuss the military modalities of NATO enlargement with Moscow in advance in an attempt to underscore cooperation. Some Western politicians have suggested that NATO should consider a special status or arrangement for Poland that might, for example, limit or ban foreign troops, nuclear weapons or integrated command structures in an attempt to enlarge NATO, yet not provoke Moscow. Russia, in turn, may table its own requests for restricting NATO's presence or the scope of its activities.

NATO faced the same issue during the two-plus-four talks on German unification when Moscow, with some support in the West, pushed to create a special status for the former East Germany in the Alliance. NATO was fortunate enough to avoid that pitfall through last-minute negotiations in the West and with Moscow. Such issues could again prove divisive. They underscore the need for the Alliance to deal with such issues with both old and new members. If East-Central Europe were to perceive that Poland's defence was being decided in Moscow, the political impact would be devastating. There may well be temporary or transitional limitations on NATO activities on the territory of new members that make political and military sense. But if there are to be limitations on NATO deployments, these should be the product of a unilateral NATO decision, based on the Alliance's assessment of its strategic needs, and not on negotiations with Moscow.

Many of these steps will cause controversy within the Alliance. They need to be weighed carefully and debated so that NATO can craft a package that gives it the flexibility to react to a changing strategic environment. At the same time, NATO must recognise that it will be the content of its efforts to build a new cooperative relationship with Moscow that will be decisive in sending the right signal and message.

The Ukrainian Factor

NATO also needs to consider the impact of any expansion on Ukraine. While Ukraine is not a candidate for either EU or NATO membership, its independence is a crucial Western interest. Ukraine's future orientation will be a key factor affecting the future balance of power in Central Europe.

There are a variety of future Ukrainian security options. These range from a 'Finlandised' Ukraine that is pro-Western, politically and economically stable, but militarily neutral – like the status that Finland enjoyed *vis-à-vis* the Soviet Union during the Cold War; to a Ukraine that is increasingly reorientating itself economically towards Russia, but which remains militarily neutral (Ukraine 'lite'); to a partitioned Ukraine, with its eastern portions' reintegrated with Russia and an independent western Ukraine; to a Ukraine that is both economically and militarily reintegrated with Russia (Ukraine 'heavy').

The West would prefer to have a Finlandised Ukraine – politically and economically stable and pro-Western, but militarily neutral. The worst outcome from the West's point of view would be if Ukraine is reintegrated with Russia into the CIS – politically, economically and militarily. Ukraine can currently be described as being in a state of Ukraine 'lite'. Kiev is seeking closer economic ties with Moscow, but has not (yet) reoriented itself militarily and has refused to join a CIS collective defence arrangement.

The key question is whether Kiev's economic reorientation towards Moscow and the CIS will eventually lead to greater defence integration. And will NATO enlargement help or exacerbate Ukraine's security dilemma?

While Ukraine's economic ties with Russia may make sense, its military reintegration would alter the balance of power in Central and Eastern Europe. Therefore, Western policy should be designed to bolster Ukrainian independence and prevent Kiev's military integration into the CIS. Unfortunately, a Finlandised Ukraine, while in many ways ideal for NATO, is not at present realistic without significantly greater Western political and economic engagement.

Ukraine's future security orientation will have a critical impact upon NATO enlargement. Ukraine functions as a political buffer for the countries of East-Central Europe, albeit one whose future is somewhat tenuous. For the Alliance, an independent Ukraine provides enhanced strategic depth should a new Russian threat emerge. Should Ukraine be compelled to reintegrate strategically with Russia, this would significantly alter the parameters for NATO defence planning. Ukraine's security orientation will also shape how NATO implements future security guarantees in the new members in East-Central Europe. Should Ukraine become a stable and neutral state, it will significantly lighten the possible defence burden for an expanded NATO. However, should Ukraine be reintegrated with Russia both economically and strategically, opening up the possibility of Russia deploying military forces on Ukrainian soil close to Poland's border, it will increase pressure on NATO to deploy a more robust and credible defence posture, including forward-deployed Western troops, in East-Central Europe.

The key to determining which way Ukraine goes lies in its domestic politics. The greatest threat to Ukraine's independence and sovereignty comes from the lack of a coherent and successful reform programme to stabilise the country. The West, nevertheless, does have an important role to play, both in supporting the internal reform programme that now seems to be progressing and in helping to develop security arrangements in and around Ukraine that preserve its independence. The key policy dilemma, therefore, is where and how NATO enlargement affects these dynamics.

At the moment, there is no clear consensus within the Ukrainian élite about the impact of NATO enlargement. Some leading Ukrainian officials believe that NATO enlargement will enhance Ukraine's security, noting that having the Alliance next door will cast a security shadow over the country and make the West pay greater attention to it. Most, however, are concerned that NATO enlargement will trigger increased Moscow pressure on Kiev to reintegrate and will relegate Ukraine to a Russian sphere of influence, thereby redividing Europe and creating a 'new Yalta'. The latter would only increase the already strong sense of disillusionment with the West in Ukraine and spark either greater nationalism or accommodation with Moscow.

Therefore, part of the NATO enlargement package must also contain a strategy for maintaining Ukrainian independence. The goal of such a strategy must be to avoid a new division of Europe at the Polish–Ukrainian border and to sustain Ukraine's independence, above all militarily. Such a strategy must include stronger political support for Ukrainian independence and an economic stabilisation package. If the West opts to upgrade institutions like the OSCE, Ukraine should be given a prominent role to ensure that it, too, has a seat at the European security table. NATO must also develop the same kind of partnership with Ukraine that it is seeking with Russia – institutionalised contacts, an expanded PFP programme and increased bilateral defence cooperation. The West needs to support closer ties between East-Central Europe and Ukraine so that as the East-Central Europeans are integrated into the West they help pull Ukraine in a westward direction and create a counterbalance to Russia's pull to the East.

Defining the Enlargement Package

The agenda facing NATO is as challenging as the one faced by the West in the late 1940s. The creation of the Atlantic Alliance was not only a response to a Soviet threat, but also part of a larger effort and vision to build a new and stable European order. Western leaders understood that a security framework was needed to stabilise democracy in post-totalitarian Germany and to thwart the return of nationalism and destructive geopolitics in Europe as a whole. With a stable security framework under US leadership in place, Western Europe was able to rebuild, launch European integration and break out of old geopolitical rivalry. The same logic should now be applied to Eastern Europe, which clearly suffers from many of the same problems.

NATO enlargement is a central component of the long-range vision of a unified Europe and Atlantic community. Choosing the right enlargement path is the most important decision facing the Alliance because it will set the rationale, timetable and criteria guiding the process. Making the right decision requires a clear sense of what is at stake for the Alliance. It is a vital US and Western interest that the gains of the end of the Cold War are not squandered and that democracy in East-Central Europe is not allowed to fail or be crushed. While there are certainly costs and potential risks in enlarging NATO, there are also costs and risks in remaining wedded to the status quo.

The Bosnian disaster shows that there is a price to be paid for moving slowly and incrementally to stem new instability and conflict in Europe and that taking half steps may seem politically convenient at the time, but often ends up resolving little, if anything. Although some may argue that in the aftermath of the Bosnian crisis NATO enlargement is too risky, the exact opposite is the case. Enlargement of the Alliance is needed now more than ever to prevent instability and conflict from arising in Central Europe – where two World Wars and the Cold War originated.

While it is the most demanding politically, the Promote Stability path makes the most strategic sense for Western interests. The Evolutionary path is simply too slow and makes East-Central European security a function of EU expansion at a time when the EU's future is increasingly uncertain. Subordinating NATO's future to the vagaries of the politics of the European Union is likely to undercut the US commitment to the Alliance. The Strategic Response path, on the other hand, is reactive and subordinates everything to the transition in Russia, which is likely to remain uncertain for a long time. It is a prescription for political paralysis and strategic impotence and could lead to the slow decay – and ultimate disintegration – of the Alliance and an unstable Europe.

The Promote Stability path is the best way to expand the security framework that will help to stabilise the region and facilitate the political and economic integration of these countries into the European and Atlantic communities. It is the only path that gets Poland and the Visegrad states into NATO fast enough to make a difference. It is essential for addressing Germany's growing vulnerability and concern over new instability in the East. It will anchor not only the East-Central Europeans in the West, but also keep the United States front and centre in European security. If matched with the right policy package towards Moscow and Kiev, it can help to stabilise East-Central Europe and make these countries better partners and more interested in cooperating with Russia and Ukraine.

However, the Promote Stability path also presents Western policy-makers with several difficult policy challenges. The first is the need for an integrated strategy to extend both economic stability and security to East-Central Europe. Saying that NATO should go first does not mean that the European Union does not have a crucial role to play or that the economic integration of these countries into the West is less important. On the contrary, the simultaneous extension of both market access and security commitments holds the greatest promise of stabilising the region and securing the gains of the Cold War. The best policy package for these countries is rapid NATO membership coupled with immediate and improved market access, the latter paving the way for entry into the EU. NATO must drive the process. Otherwise, there is a danger that it will be dragged out a decade or longer.

NATO should set itself the goal of bringing the countries of East-Central Europe into the Alliance and, if possible, the European Union by the end of the decade. Such a strategy would put NATO at the cutting edge of the expansion process, but would also pull the European Union along in the same direction, pressuring it to open its markets to provide the economic stability that these countries require. It would direct US policy towards rapid

EU enlargement and a multi-speed Europe. So long as it is clear that decisions about future US security commitments are being made in NATO and not through the European Union, such a strategy would increase political support for the enlargement of the Alliance on Capitol Hill by proving that the Europeans are assuming a major share of the burden of stabilising the region. By developing both the security and economic components, NATO would also signal that expansion is part of the broader process of European enlargement and not a military move to isolate Russia.

Above all, such a strategy would require the United States to make the extension of stability to East-Central Europe the defining issue of European security in this decade. While issues of defence interoperability and standardisation are important, they should not be allowed to obscure the fact that the main objective behind expansion is political – to secure and integrate these new and fragile democracies in the Atlantic community. The West will have failed if, by the year 2000, the militaries of East-Central Europe are modern and capable, but their countries have nationalist authoritarian regimes and are caught in a strategic vacuum between West and East.

The second policy challenge is to enlarge NATO without destabilising Russia or Ukraine. Ultimately, Russia's reaction will depend on three closely interrelated factors – the modalities of enlargement, the time-frame in which enlargement takes place and the content of the strategic relationship with Moscow. The latter will be extremely important. If the West develops a genuine and robust strategic partnership with Moscow – that is, if Moscow is given a genuine opportunity to shape key decisions affecting the new security order in Europe – Russia is likely to find enlargement more palatable.

However, this will require the West to decide what role it really wants Russia to play in European political, economic and security affairs. The Alliance needs to make some hard choices about where and what it wants to talk about with Moscow. In particular, it means expanding the consultation process with Moscow and discussing important security issues with Russia before key decisions are made, not afterwards, so that Moscow's views and interests are integrated into the Alliance's decision-making process at an early stage. This does not mean giving Moscow a veto over NATO decisions. But it will require the Alliance to develop new mechanisms and approaches to consultations with Russia.

The Alliance should make a serious attempt to reassure Moscow about NATO enlargement, while recognising that Russia's future is uncertain and that the Alliance's role in shaping that future is limited. It is also premature to conclude that NATO enlargement can decisively tip the power balance in Moscow. Although Russian democrats are understandably concerned that nationalists will exploit the issue against them, NATO enlargement is only one small factor in the equation that will determine Russia's future. As it expands, NATO should leave the door open for greater cooperation with Moscow. Whether Russia walks through the door or chooses self-isolation should be its choice, not NATO's.

Finally, how NATO enlarges will be especially important to Kiev. The military modalities of enlargement need to be fine-tuned to take Ukrainian concerns and sensitivities into account. NATO needs to avoid giving Moscow a pretext for seeking to reabsorb Ukraine. If and when the Alliance chooses to discuss the details of NATO enlargement, it needs to make it clear that enlargement cannot be used to justify Russian moves against Ukraine. Such moves by Russia could end up precipitating what Moscow and the Alliance should, in principle, both want to avoid and which is currently not needed, namely a major NATO military build-up in East-Central Europe.

The third great policy challenge is forging a new Alliance consensus on how to implement Article 5 security guarantees to new members. Clearly, expansion must be accompanied by a coherent military programme to ensure that new Article 5 security guarantees are credible. But NATO does not have to recreate an old Cold War-style defence for East-Central Europe for the simple reasons that Europe's new strategic environment is far more advantageous than it was during the Cold War and that the threats and dangers facing the Alliance have been radically reduced. What the Alliance needs is a new approach that is appropriate for the new era.

The Alliance must define the desired military package for an expanded NATO while retaining the flexibility to respond to new developments should Europe's strategic environment deteriorate in the future. What kind of defence concept makes sense for East-Central Europe in the 1990s? The Alliance should avoid creating new members with a special status like France or Spain. Therefore, the Alliance should start with something like a Functional Division of Labour or Core Group Defence concept, building towards Full-Scale Multinational Defence only if this ultimately proves necessary. Similarly, the Alliance could begin with a military strategy based on power projection and could move towards a mixed strategy that places greater emphasis on prepared infrastructure and, perhaps, eventually deploy some forces in East-Central Europe.

The issue of Allied forward presence in East-Central Europe is something for the Alliance as a whole to decide. As matters stand today, there is no military requirement for stationed NATO forces to meet warfighting needs. If there is a requirement for peacetime deployments, it derives from the need for political reassurance and credibility as well as peacetime training to develop interoperability. The requirement for forward presence, however, will be modest. Some and, perhaps, all needs can be met by rotational deployments and exercises. Hence, NATO can expect to rely primarily, if not exclusively, on power projection or a mixed strategy unless and until a major military threat appears on the horizon.

Similarly, the requirements for nuclear deterrence in an expanded NATO will also be radically different and smaller than during the Cold War because the threat is different and because the Alliance can now build a more credible conventional posture. Article 5 involves a political commitment to defence and deterrence, not the deployment of nuclear weapons on foreign soil. During the Cold War, different kinds of nuclear arrangements were sought by and offered to the three front-line states facing the Soviet Union – Norway, Turkey and West Germany. Working out future arrangements with new members should be easier than in the past. Currently, there is little interest in East-Central Europe in deploying NATO nuclear weapons on their soil. Politically, NATO enlargement is currently being considered to extend stability to East-Central Europe, not in response to a new Russian strategic threat.

Militarily, the situation has also been transformed. During the Cold War, NATO was highly dependent upon nuclear weapons to deter the Warsaw Pact. Changed geopolitical circumstances should allow the Alliance to pursue a more credible conventional strategy and a more flexible nuclear strategy and doctrine. NATO has already embraced a more existential form of extended deterrence with nuclear weapons as 'weapons of last resort'. NATO enlargement will not change this. Currently, only seven of the 14 European members of the Alliance participate in nuclear burden-sharing arrangements. NATO members do not require nuclear weapons on their soil to be covered by a NATO security guarantee.

The budgetary costs will, of course, depend upon the defence planning framework and the specifics of the package that is adopted. If the Alliance chooses to rely on a power-projection or mixed strategy and expects new members to contribute strong forces of their own, the costs of enlargement should be moderate. They can be spread out over a number of years and can be paid for by cuts elsewhere in Western European border defence forces. Many of these changes and new programmes to improve Alliance projection capabilities are steps that NATO should take, regardless of whether enlargement occurs, to equip it for crisis-management missions beyond current borders.

Will NATO be able to fulfil its defence commitments to new members? It will find it difficult to do so not because of inadequate forces – even after the currently planned downsizing is complete, NATO will have nearly 30 division equivalents and 1,800 combat aircraft in Northern and Central Europe and an equal number in the Southern region – but, as NATO's defence posture is still focused on its old Cold War missions, because it cannot project sizeable power outwards to East-Central Europe and elsewhere. This can be rectified if NATO acquires the mobile logistic units, transportation assets, C^3I structure and other assets needed to make the Alliance capable of defending new members in East-Central Europe. This programme can be pursued with a fraction of the money that the Alliance plans to spend on defence over the coming decade.

With such improved projection capabilities provided mostly by AFCENT members, NATO could carry out new defence commitments in East-Central Europe. The Alliance will not need to respond militarily unless a new Russian threat emerges. However, even if this happens, Russia is unlikely to regain its military balance for several years. This will provide NATO with time to prepare.

The final question is whether the Alliance could deal with a new Russian military threat – the kind that would require a robust forward-presence strategy and deploying sizeable Allied forces in East-Central Europe. Such a force posture would be expensive. But even here, the costs facing the Alliance must be weighed against the costs to the West of doing nothing. If Russia were to become aggressively expansionist, would NATO be so foolish as not to defend East-Central Europe? Here, too, one should avoid assuming worst-case scenarios. Even a re-armed Russia would not be the military Leviathan the Soviet Union once was. It would have an imposing military force, but probably not a great deal more than that of Iran, Iraq or North Korea – in short, a major regional contingency-sized threat. Defending against such a threat would be very different than against the theatre-wide challenge posed by the Warsaw Pact during the Cold War. Moreover, to pose that kind of threat, Russia would have to mobilise and concentrate its military forces against Europe, leaving its eastern and southern flanks vulnerable. If the United States can defend the Persian Gulf and South Korea from these threats from several thousand miles away, then NATO should be able to defend Poland and other East-Central European states from a distance of several hundred kilometres.

Without making light of the problems and difficulties involved in carrying out new security commitments, as well as the political imperative of avoiding a new Cold War with Russia, NATO enlargement is less a matter of military capability than of political will. The Alliance has the military assets to fulfil new commitments. But has it the political will and strategic foresight to recognise its vital interests and the strategic stakes involved in anchoring East-Central Europe into the West and securing the gains of the end of the Cold War? Or will NATO retreat into a passive role and allow events on the ground to rekindle the geopolitical dynamics that have been the breeding ground for two world wars? The costs to the West of the failure of democracy in East-Central Europe would be much higher than the costs of expanding NATO to ensure that this region does not yet again become a source of instability and conflict.

US leadership will be critical, especially after the débâcle in Bosnia. The US President must be directly and forcefully engaged to forge the necessary consensus, both among the Allies and in Congress, for enlargement. Europe will follow and Russia will acquiesce only if the United States provides the requisite leadership and vision to expand the Atlantic and European communities as part of the broader processes of European enlargement and building a new cooperative relationship with Russia.

Notes

1. A 'back-door' commitment for the United States could arise, for example, if Poland were to join the EU and the WEU, but were not allowed to join NATO. Thus, a country like Germany would extend a security guarantee to Poland under the WEU. Should Poland be involved in a conflict, Germany would be obliged to come to its defence. Such German involvement would invoke Article 5 of the NATO Treaty, thereby involving the United States. The issue may be some years off for the East-Central Europeans, since they will not be joining the European Union or WEU soon. However, it is already a very real one for the former neutral countries that have just joined the EU, such as Austria, Sweden and Finland. Should any of these countries opt for full WEU membership, the issue of 'back-door' commitments will arise.

2. See, for example, German Defence Minister Volker Rühe, 'NATO Oeffnung im deutschen Interesse', *Das Parlament*, vol. 44, no. 3, 21 January 1994, p. 5.

3. The authors would like to thank Robert D. Blackwill for his helpful suggestions on crafting a policy package for Russia.

4. For further details, see Richard L. Kugler, *Commitment to Purpose: How Alliance Partnership Won the Cold War*, MR-198-FF/RC (Santa Monica, CA: RAND, 1993).

5. Some have already drawn an analogy with the US experience in dealing with the European Union, in which Washington quickly discovered that the EU's negotiating position – the result of numerous internal compromises – left it with little room for manoeuvre. Therefore, US policy quickly switched to using both multilateral and bilateral channels to try to influence the internal EU debate before a consensus had been reached.

Chapter 6
The Flawed Logic of NATO Enlargement

Michael E. Brown

There is a strong consensus in the American foreign-policy establishment and, to a lesser extent, in Western Europe that at least one or two Central European states should become full members of NATO in the near future. US President Bill Clinton stated after the January 1994 NATO summit that, 'the question is no longer whether NATO will take on new members, but when and how'.[1] Clinton reaffirmed his commitment to NATO enlargement during his trip to Europe in July.[2] Some German leaders, Defence Minister Volker Rühe in particular, have been outspoken in their support of NATO enlargement.[3] The communiqué issued at the end of the ministerial meeting of the North Atlantic Council (NAC) in December 1994 stated that NATO enlargement was expected and that it would be welcomed.[4] Prominent former US policy-makers – including Henry Kissinger, Zbigniew Brzezinski, Harold Brown and James Baker – support NATO enlargement, as does the Republican leadership of the new US Congress. Many experts on both sides of the Atlantic also support this broad position.[5]

Although many Western policy-makers and analysts believe that NATO should expand, there is a debate over when and how this should take place. There are three main schools of thought. First, some believe that NATO should proceed slowly and bring one or two new states into the Alliance at a time. Poland and the Czech Republic are generally seen as being at the front of the queue, with Hungary and, perhaps, Slovakia leading subsequent waves. This school believes that starting the accession process in three to five years and proceeding incrementally will minimise the possibility of a hostile Russian response.[6] Second, some believe that NATO should move quickly to extend membership to Poland, the Czech Republic, Hungary and Slovakia (the Visegrad Four). Those who advocate this course of action believe that Russian expansionism is either already under way, or inevitable.[7] Third, some believe that NATO enlargement should be closely coordinated with enlargement of the European Union (EU). This, it is said, would minimise the risk of NATO enlargement being seen as threatening to Russia and help prevent the Alliance and the EU's military arm, the Western European Union (WEU), from having conflicting security commitments.[8]

Current US and NATO policy embraces a gradualist approach to enlargement, at least as far as timing is concerned. At the December 1994 NAC meeting, Alliance leaders decided that there would be a study of the issue in 1995 and that the results of these deliberations would be presented to interested parties before the end of the year.[9] US policy-makers hope (although they cannot yet say so publicly) that accession discussions will begin in 1996 and that the Alliance's membership will begin to expand in 1996, 1997 or 1998.[10]

This chapter argues that all three schools of thought are misguided because they all proceed from the premise that NATO enlargement should, without question, take place.[11] Its contention is that all of the arguments most commonly put forward in support of NATO enlargement are flawed and that enlargement is unnecessary given the current strategic and political situation in Europe. Moreover, NATO enlargement could spark a backlash in Russia that could damage European and US security.

NATO enlargement should not be a mechanistic process or tied to a rigid timetable, as many of its supporters suggest.[12] Rather, it should be linked to strategic circumstances: if Russia begins to threaten Eastern and Central Europe militarily, then NATO should offer membership and security guarantees to the Visegrad Four and perhaps other states as well. NATO should declare that it will expand if necessary, but that it will not expand until strategic circumstances demand it.

Adopting this approach would give NATO a nuanced strategy that would maximise the Alliance's chances of developing a stable, peaceful security order in Europe while guarding against the possibility of Russian aggression. Russian leaders interested in cooperation with the West would be in a better position to keep expansionist elements under control and have a powerful incentive to pursue benign policies towards their neighbours in Eastern and Central Europe. US and Western European leaders should nurture this relationship while laying the political and military groundwork for extending new security commitments should NATO enlargement become necessary.

There are risks associated with adopting this approach. NATO leaders would have to decide which Russian actions would prompt enlargement and sustain a consensus on enlargement under difficult geopolitical circumstances.

The risks and potential costs associated with other approaches, however, are greater. Prompt expansion of NATO – bringing the Visegrad Four into the fold quickly – would probably lead to Russian actions in Eastern Europe and in the area of arms control that would weaken, not enhance, European and US security. A new East–West confrontation would probably develop, with much of the responsibility lying with NATO members. Adopting a gradualist approach would reduce, but not eliminate, these risks.

Deciding among these approaches is, therefore, not clear cut. In the end, however, one should have more faith in NATO's ability to act decisively when vital interests are threatened than in Russia's ability to accept provocation without retaliation.

NATO Enlargement is Not Needed

Advocates of NATO enlargement put forward six main strategic and political arguments for widening the Alliance.

First, it is said that NATO enlargement is needed to deter Russian aggression in Eastern and Central Europe. Some commentators are concerned that, because Russia has strengthened its position in Central Asia and the Caucasus over the past year or two and because Moscow has long considered Eastern and Central Europe to be part of its sphere of influence, Russia will try to dominate this region again. Former US National Security Advisor Zbigniew Brzezinski is concerned that Russia's 'imperial impulse remains strong and even appears to be strengthening'.[13] Another former US official, Peter Rodman, maintains that Russia is getting back on its feet and that 'the lengthening shadow of Russian strength' poses a threat to Central European security. 'Russia is a force of nature', he says, and Russian imperialism is 'inevitable'.[14]

NATO is a collective defence organisation designed to deter and, if necessary, defend against direct military threats to member-states. Russia does not at present pose a military threat to Central and Eastern Europe and is not strengthening its conventional military capabilities. The Conventional Forces in Europe (CFE) Treaty obligates Russia to keep much of its firepower east of the Urals. According to authoritative sources, no Russian combat formations currently operate at more than 75% of their authorised manpower levels and roughly 70% of all divisions operate at less than 50% of authorised levels.[15] Moreover, Russia's military leadership is in disarray at both the ministerial and operational levels.[16] The inability of the Russian military to quash a small number of lightly armed insurrectionists in Chechnya testifies to its current operational capabilities. Western defence and intelligence experts believe that the Russian military is incapable of launching a conventional offensive against the West and that it would take Moscow at least a year to field such a capability. Indeed, Brzezinski concedes that 'neither the alliance nor its prospective new members are facing any imminent threat'. Talk of a Russian military threat, he notes, 'is not justified, either by actual circumstances or even by worst-case scenarios for the near future'.[17] NATO leaders will, therefore, have plenty of time to extend membership and security guarantees to states in Central and Eastern Europe if Russia begins to build up its offensive conventional capabilities.

If the Russian military threat were real, or even slight but growing, one would expect states in Eastern and Central Europe to be building up their military forces. This, however, is not the case. Poland, which has powerful historical reasons for fearing Russia, is reducing military conscription from 18 to 12 months. In the past year, the Polish Army disbanded one of its 11 mechanised divisions and converted another into an armoured cavalry division. Hungary is reducing conscription from 12 to ten months. The Czech Army has converted one of its three mechanised divisions into a mechanised brigade and disbanded its infantry division. None of these armies acquired much new equipment in the past year.[18] These are not the actions of states concerned about military threats.

Second, advocates of NATO enlargement maintain that, even if there is no Russian military threat, membership should be offered to Central Europe because this would 'project stability' into the region. Michael Mandelbaum argues that NATO enlargement would extend the Alliance's 'zone of stability' eastwards, while Volker Rühe insists that 'if we do not export stability, we will import instability'.[19] This is one of the most prominent arguments in favour of NATO enlargement.

It is certainly true that there is instability in the eastern half of Europe: there are ethnic problems in Estonia and Latvia; Ukraine has ethnic difficulties in Crimea and severe economic problems; Russian involvement in Moldova has galvanised a secessionist split that also engages Romania; and war rages in the Balkans, which may spread to Macedonia, Albania and Bulgaria.

No one, however, is suggesting that NATO should extend membership to any of these countries in the near future. Those countries at the front of the NATO queue – Poland, the Czech Republic and Hungary – are in fact quite stable. They have few ethnic minorities and ethnic violence is virtually non-existent.[20] The Czech–Slovak divorce stands out as a model of peaceful conflict resolution. Violent border disputes are unlikely and inter-state conflict in general is highly remote.

The case for 'projecting stability' into this part of Central Europe is therefore specious. If one looks at specific cases, instead of treating Eastern Europe as an analytically indistinguishable whole, one finds that these countries and the region they encompass are already quite stable.[21]

This stability is reinforced by the desire Poland, the Czech Republic and Hungary have to join the EU. Because these states are determined to join, and because their chances of doing so are quite good, they have a powerful incentive to treat ethnic minorities well, respect international borders and international norms of behaviour, and conduct their internal and external affairs peacefully.

Even if intra-state or inter-state tensions appear in the region, NATO membership would not be the solution. The Alliance does not have the means to address the political and economic problems that are the cause of many ethnic disputes, nor does it have the political and economic levers needed to contain intra-alliance conflicts. NATO is a collective defence organisation, not a collective security organisation. It was unsuccessful in preventing the Turkish invasion of Cyprus in 1974, and there is no reason to think it would be better at preventing or controlling intra-regional disputes in the Visegrad area should Central European states join the Alliance. The EU is better positioned to address the root causes of ethnic conflict and better equipped to deal with violence when it breaks out because of its leverage over countries anxious to join the Union.

Third, advocates of NATO enlargement maintain that, because it will take many years for former Warsaw Pact states to meet the economic and political standards of the European Union, the West must do something to reassure these states about their prospects of being fully integrated into the West. Since EU membership will not be attained for many years, it is said, NATO membership should be extended to bridge the gap. This will allow the Visegrad states, in particular, to join Europe's most important security organisation while waiting to join its most important economic institution. According to Ronald Asmus, Richard Kugler and Stephen Larrabee, NATO must 'provide the security framework necessary to anchor these countries to the West'.[22]

This is another specious argument. Although there are good reasons for being unsure about Russia's geopolitical orientation in the future – its interest in 'Westernising' has ebbed and flowed since the time of Peter the Great – there is no doubt about Polish, Czech and Hungarian inclinations. These countries are historically, politically, culturally, socially and economically linked with Western Europe. Although these countries would like to become NATO members and will be disappointed if membership is not forthcoming, this will not lead them to turn away from Western Europe. As Vaclav Havel, the President of the Czech Republic and a leading enthusiast of NATO enlargement, observed, 'we have always belonged to the Western sphere of European civilisation'.[23]

Fourth, advocates of NATO enlargement claim that taking steps to bring Visegrad states into the Alliance would help to dampen aggressive nationalism and promote democracy in the region. Robert Zoellick argues that taking firm steps towards enlargement would 'strengthen the hands of democratic reformers in these nations'.[24] Asmus, Kugler and Larrabee maintain that the lack of a Western security commitment to the region 'threatens to undercut democracy and the reform process in these fragile democracies and to rekindle nationalism' in the region.[25]

While extending NATO membership would help to reinforce democratic reforms in the Visegrad area, it will not have a decisive impact on domestic political developments in these countries. Aggressive nationalism is unlikely to develop in this region because there are few ethnic problems. In addition, the prospect of joining the EU is the key to outside influence over domestic political developments in Central Europe. Governments in Central Europe are instituting minority rights safeguards and embracing democracy in part because they want to do so, but also because they must do so if they are to become members of the European Union. They will continue to implement such policies if NATO membership is not forthcoming – even if it is specifically denied – as long as they have a realistic chance of joining the EU. Central Europe might not be happy with the slow pace with which the EU is moving towards accession, but it is highly unlikely that they will deviate from the democratic path as long as membership is a possibility. NATO membership will play a secondary and non-essential role in reinforcing democratic trends in Central Europe as long as these countries are moving towards membership of the EU. Holding back on NATO membership will, therefore, not 'undercut democracy' or 'rekindle nationalism' in the region.

Fifth, advocates of NATO enlargement argue that it is needed to address German concerns about Russia and, more specifically, about the fate of the states to its immediate east. If Russia adopts aggressive policies and if NATO fails to extend security commitments to the Visegrad area, the 'security vacuum' in Central and Eastern Europe could lead Germany to establish bilateral security ties with its Eastern neighbours. This, it is said, could lead to a German–Russian confrontation in Central and Eastern Europe, NATO's demise and the return of balance-of-power politics to Europe. Henry Kissinger has argued that, 'if things turn out badly in Russia, it would lead to a no-man's land between Germany and Russia, a condition that has caused many European wars'.[26] Delaying NATO enlargement, he maintains, 'invites Germany and Russia to fill the vacuum between them either unilaterally or bilaterally – a contingency everyone in Europe, Germany above all, seeks to avoid'.[27]

There is no doubt that a German–Russian security competition in Central and Eastern Europe must be avoided and that German security concerns must be addressed. It does not follow, however, that NATO should now make a commitment to extend membership to states in this region. Russia does not pose a military threat to Central and Eastern Europe at the present time. If Russia becomes more aggressive towards this region in the future, NATO will have sufficient time to respond before Moscow poses a military danger to its Western neighbours. A German–Russian security competition need not ensue.

Germany is naturally and rightly concerned about the possibility of Russian aggression and instability in Poland and the Czech Republic. Significantly, however, the German government is not pushing for the rapid expansion of

NATO. In the run-up to the December 1994 ministerial meeting of the North Atlantic Council, Germany played a leading role in modifying a US proposal for a six-to-eight-month study of enlargement. Germany, along with France, argued successfully in favour of a longer study.[28] Germany's main concern was that moving quickly to expand NATO would trigger a backlash in Russia that would endanger European security. As German Foreign Minister Klaus Kinkel argued: 'We cannot risk reviving East–West strategic rivalry. It would be tragic if, in reassuring some countries, we alarmed others'.[29] If Germany were worried about Russian aggression or the dangers posed by a security vacuum to its east, it would be urging the United States to move faster – not slower – towards NATO enlargement.

Given that Russia does not now pose a military threat to Eastern and Central Europe and that Germany is urging caution on enlargement, it is hard to argue that there is a looming security vacuum in Central Europe or that NATO foot-dragging is pushing Germany to renationalise its security policy.

A sixth and final argument made by advocates of NATO enlargement is that it is important for all members of the WEU to join NATO as well. Although all current WEU members belong to NATO, this may not be so in the future if the European Union takes on new members, some or all of whom might join the WEU as well. Should this happen, Finland or Poland, for example, might have security guarantees from Germany and France through the WEU, but not through NATO. This, it is said, could 'destroy the Atlantic Alliance' and, through 'back-door' security commitments, 'draw the United States into a conflict over which it had little if any control'.[30]

This is a danger only if Russia poses a military threat to its Western neighbours and only if the expansion of the Alliance is tied to a mechanistic timetable or to the attainment of a high level of interoperability between NATO and Central European military forces, as some suggest. The danger is that WEU security commitments could be extended to non-NATO states that are exposed to Russian aggression. This could indeed strain the Atlantic Alliance and draw the United States into a conflict it was not formally obligated to fight.

This problem disappears, however, if NATO membership is tied to strategic circumstances – the emergence of a Russian military threat. In the absence of such a threat, it makes little difference if some states have only WEU security commitments: intra-regional disputes involving WEU members are unlikely to escalate enough for either the United States to be drawn in or for NATO to be thrown into particular disrepute. If there is a Russian military threat, NATO membership should be extended to all WEU, and perhaps several non-WEU, members.

NATO Enlargement would be Counter-productive

In addition to serving no compelling strategic or political purpose, extending NATO membership and security guarantees to states in Central and Eastern

Europe could have profound and unfortunate consequences for European and US security. It would undoubtedly have reverberations in Russian domestic politics and could lead Moscow to adopt foreign and defence policies that would diminish, not enhance, European and US security.

Diminished security for the West is probable if the four Visegrad states are rapidly incorporated into NATO. This is also likely even if NATO adopts a gradualist approach to enlargement, moving slowly to bring in one or two states at a time, perhaps in conjunction with moves to expand the European Union and the WEU.

NATO enlargement has three potentially harmful consequences for European and American security.

First, enlargement would strengthen the hands of radical nationalists and political opportunists in Russia, who will use NATO's action to discredit the current leadership and its pro-Western line. This would improve the opposition's chances of seizing power, either through the electoral process or through unconstitutional means. Many of Russia's leading nationalist figures and some of its military leaders do not have a deep and abiding commitment to democratic rule. A return to authoritarianism would consequently be more likely.

The prospects for the democratic reform process in Russia are uncertain at best. Given Russia's long history of authoritarian rule, it would not be wise to assume that democracy will take hold. There is a chance, however, that it will succeed. The fate of the reform process will, of course, be determined largely by domestic developments, but external actions could play a role as well. NATO enlargement, which would be characterised by radical nationalists and opportunists as a devastating blow to Russian national security and yet another humiliation of a once-great power, could play an important role in the struggle for power in Moscow. In the absence of a military threat, it would be foolhardy for NATO to take steps that will hurt democracy's chances in Russia.

Second, NATO enlargement will probably lead Russia to adopt a more aggressive policy in Eastern Europe. If President Boris Yeltsin or another reformer is still in office, he will have to adopt a tougher line to maintain his hold on power. Most Russian policy-makers, even those supporting democratic and economic reform, have strong nationalist inclinations; they would not have to be pushed hard to adopt more assertive foreign and defence policies. If NATO enlargement brings radical nationalists to power, they will by definition adopt a more confrontational stance towards the West.

In either case, Russian leaders would characterise NATO enlargement as an attempt to shift the European balance of power in the West's favour and as a delineation of spheres of influence in Central and Eastern Europe. The West, they would conclude, had unilaterally defined its sphere of influence; Russia, they would argue, should take steps to secure a buffer of its own and establish greater control over non-NATO areas. Extending NATO membership to some states in Central and Eastern Europe would draw a line in the region between areas protected by the Alliance and areas over which Russia would probably seek to exert greater control.

In current discussions about NATO expansion, only four states – Poland, Hungary, the Czech Republic and Slovakia – are mentioned as near-term candidates for admission. If NATO brings these four states into the fold, twice that number – Estonia, Latvia, Lithuania, Belarus, Ukraine, Moldova, Romania and Bulgaria – might find themselves subjected to mounting Russian pressure. Belarus, Ukraine and Moldova, for example, might be pressured to join the Russian Federation or participate in the transformation of the Commonwealth of Independent States (CIS) into a federal entity. Many, perhaps most, of the states left out of NATO will be drawn into Russia's orbit in ways that might otherwise be avoidable.

It is thus entirely possible that Russian aggression in Eastern Europe will be encouraged, not discouraged, by NATO enlargement. The threat that NATO deployments were meant to address could be triggered by NATO actions, once again dividing Europe into two blocs. European security as a whole – Central and Eastern European security in particular – would be diminished, not enhanced.

Third, if the foregoing analysis of Russian domestic politics is correct, policy-makers in Moscow – reformers and radical nationalists – will characterise NATO enlargement as a change in the balance of power. Military leaders will see NATO enlargement as both a strategic threat and a bureaucratic opportunity: it will allow them to make a politically powerful case for reviving Russia's moribund military forces.

NATO enlargement could, for example, lead Russia to pull out of the conventional and nuclear arms-control agreements that currently structure Moscow's military relations with the West. Even now, Moscow feels that the flank limitations of the CFE Treaty unfairly impinge on Russian national security. NATO enlargement would undoubtedly lead many in Russia's political and military circles to argue that the Treaty as a whole should be abandoned. Similarly, many in Moscow object to some of the provisions of the second Strategic Arms Reduction Talks Treaty (START II). NATO enlargement would probably lead Moscow to push harder for the renegotiation of these provisions. Moscow's interest in additional nuclear arms-reduction agreements – which radical nationalists would characterise as disarmament in the face of aggression – would undoubtedly be dampened. Moscow's willingness to allow Western inspectors to monitor its denuclearisation efforts – which radical nationalists would characterise as espionage – would probably diminish. Russian withdrawal from the cooperative denuclearisation process now under way could not be ruled out.[31]

Unfortunately, it is not entirely implausible that NATO enlargement would drive the Russian leadership to call for a military build-up designed to strengthen Russia's military and international position. This would undoubtedly appeal to many Russian politicians, military leaders and citizens. It is certainly true that Russia does not have the economic wherewithal to begin a rapid military build-up, but it does have a military–industrial base, however withered, on which to build. It would take time for Russia to rebuild its conventional arsenal and restore the offensive conventional capabilities it once had, but its ability to do so should not be doubted. Although Russia's economy and military are currently weak, the same was true of Germany's in January 1933.[32]

Bringing all four Visegrad states into the Alliance quickly would push Russian reformers to adopt a tougher foreign policy and strengthen the hands of Russian politicians opposed to cooperation with the West. Whether radical nationalists would be able to use this as a springboard to power is impossible to say, but there is no denying that rapid NATO enlargement involves significant risks. The Alliance should pursue this course only if its leaders believe that Russian aggression in Central and Eastern Europe is inevitable and if NATO is only interested in or capable of protecting Poland, Hungary, the Czech Republic and, perhaps, Slovakia.

Advocates of NATO enlargement have proposed three main ways of minimising these risks. First, some argue that NATO should extend membership to all four Visegrad states, but with two caveats: that these states would not join NATO's integrated military command structure; and, more importantly, that Alliance forces would not be deployed on their territory. Henry Kissinger has argued that this kind of 'qualified' NATO membership would extend defensive guarantees without exacerbating Russian security concerns.[33]

There are two problems with this argument. First, many if not most Russian leaders will nonetheless view NATO enlargement as an aggressive act. No matter how NATO expansion is packaged, it will involve US nuclear and military guarantees to states in Central Europe. It will be seen in Moscow as a change in the balance of power and an extension of Washington's – and Bonn's – sphere of influence. Many Russian leaders will argue that direct action must be taken to safeguard the country's national security interests. Second, extending qualified membership would not sidestep the problems created by drawing a new line in Eastern Europe. Extending qualified NATO membership to some states in the region will probably lead Moscow to adopt more aggressive policies towards others. Many in Russia will see NATO enlargement in any form as the delineation of Central and Eastern Europe into two spheres of influence.

Many advocates of NATO enlargement propose a second course to minimise such risks: moving slowly and extending membership to only one or two new states at a time. This, it is said, would give Western leaders time to convince Russian leaders that NATO's intentions were benign. Bringing in only one or two states at a time would reinforce this impression.[34]

This approach faces the same basic problems as the first. Russian leaders will see any form of NATO enlargement, even if it is incremental, as a change in the balance of power and an extension of Washington's and Bonn's sphere of influence. NATO efforts at 'spin control' will fail in the face of these overriding geostrategic concerns. In addition, this approach will not sidestep the problem of drawing a new line in Eastern Europe: it will simply draw a bad line. Only one or two states would be brought into NATO and a very large number would be left out, perhaps to face a resurgent or strident Russia.

Some advocates of NATO enlargement therefore propose a third course of action: extending membership to new states only as they are brought into the European Union and the WEU. This, it is said, will minimise the risk of NATO enlargement being perceived by Moscow as threatening and help keep Alliance and WEU security commitments from going in different directions.[35]

The main problem with this approach is that many Russian leaders will challenge the contention that this is not an aggressive act. They will agree that enlarging the European Union is for economic and political reasons and that enlarging the WEU is to 'project stability' into the region, but they will have difficulty viewing NATO enlargement, US security commitments and US nuclear guarantees in the same benign terms. Because NATO is first and foremost a collective defence organisation, Russian leaders will quite rightly see its enlargement as having an anti-Russian dimension – regardless of how it is presented or packaged.

A second problem with this option is the linking of NATO enlargement to European Union and WEU enlargement. There are instances in which the two should not be linked. For example, if Russia embarked on an expansionist course, it would not be wise to wait until Poland was ready to join the EU before bringing it into NATO. Conversely, Finland is set to join the European Union at the end of 1995; its highly capable military makes it a suitable candidate for membership of the WEU, but it is far from clear that NATO membership should follow. The EU and NATO have distinct, but complementary roles to play in European affairs.

Proposals for minimising the risks associated with NATO enlargement cannot eliminate them completely. Given the nationalist inclinations of most Russian policy-makers, the hypersensitivity in Russia to national security issues and Moscow's treatment in international affairs, the strong showing of radical nationalists in recent elections and the volatile state of Russian domestic politics, it is hard to anticipate Russian reactions to NATO actions. Although the development of a kinder, gentler Russia is far from certain, it is not in the interests of the United States or Europe to take steps that would make Russian authoritarianism or belligerence more likely.

NATO Enlargement and European Security

To keep great-power conflict from breaking out in Central and Eastern Europe, two interrelated security problems need to be addressed. First, Russian aggression in Eastern and Central Europe must be discouraged. Second, instability in Eastern and Central Europe must be kept to a minimum. In each area, NATO and the EU have indispensable, complementary roles to play. Western strategy for dealing with these security problems should be based on an understanding of this complementarity and the development of this partnership for peace.

Western Strategy and Russia

The West must not be sanguine about Russia's imperialistic past, its aggressive policies in parts of the former Soviet Union or the prospects for democracy and market reform in Russia. It is entirely possible that Moscow will embark on an expansionist course in Eastern Europe in the future.

Over the past year or two, Russian leaders have pursued a more assertive policy towards other former members of the Soviet Union. Moscow has re-established control over parts of Central Asia and the Caucasus and put considerable political and economic pressure on Ukraine.[36] If Russia were to regain control of Ukraine, it might try to re-establish a sphere of influence in Central and Eastern Europe.

NATO leaders should state in clear and unequivocal terms that it will extend Alliance membership and full security guarantees to Central and Eastern European states if Russian actions merit this response. NATO leaders should state, furthermore, that one of the purposes of the Partnership for Peace (PFP) programme is the development of closer military ties with the states of Central and Eastern Europe and preparing the military foundation for expansion and new defence arrangements in the region should Russian behaviour call for such steps.

Russian actions that should trigger NATO enlargement into Central and Eastern Europe fall into four broad categories. First, NATO should expand if Russia builds up its conventional military forces near neighbouring states in the West in violation of the CFE Treaty. This would constitute a direct military threat to Central and Eastern Europe. Second, NATO should expand if Moscow violates its pledges to respect international borders in general and Ukrainian sovereignty in particular. This would indicate that Russia's expansionist impulses had prevailed over its public commitments to honour the international status quo. Third, NATO should expand if Moscow absorbs Ukraine or Belarus into the Russian Federation or transforms the CIS into a federal entity. This would represent a change in the European balance of power and would indicate that Russia was once again pursuing an imperialist agenda. Fourth, NATO should expand if Moscow withdraws from either of the strategic arms reduction treaties (START I and II) or discontinues the denuclearisation process to which it has committed itself. This would indicate that Russian military policy was moving in a more confrontational direction.

NATO leaders should make it clear, however, that although the Alliance will enlarge if it is needed, enlargement will not take place until it is needed.

This would give Moscow's leaders a powerful incentive to live up to the international commitments they have made. NATO would position itself to deter and defend against Russian aggression in Eastern and Central Europe, but it would not stimulate Russia's nationalistic impulses.

The European Union also has a role to play in discouraging and protecting Eastern and Central Europe from Russian aggression. If Moscow tries to re-establish a sphere of influence in Eastern and Central Europe, it is quite possible, and perhaps probable, that Russia will rely on economic and political instruments of leverage: blatant military aggression would ruin its relations with the West and precipitate the same sort of military confrontation that drove it into bankruptcy during the Cold War. NATO membership will not insulate Central and Eastern European states from Russian economic and political machinations. Should Russia embark on this course, the key to safeguarding these states will be integrating them into the Western European economic system and the EU: this would reduce their economic and political vulnerability. This should be done as a preventive measure, and it can be done without provoking a hostile Russian reaction.

At the same time, the West should make a concerted effort to develop a stable, peaceful relationship with Moscow and to bolster Russia's democratic and economic reforms. Washington should continue to treat Moscow as a valued and respected partner. NATO, as Zbigniew Brzezinski has suggested, should propose signing a formal treaty with Russia that would reassure Moscow about the Alliance's benign intentions, reinforce Russia's non-aggression pledges and strengthen the consultative and planning mechanisms embodied in the North Atlantic Cooperation Council (NACC) and the PFP programme. This would also reassure Russia about its role and stature in international affairs.[37]

The European Union, for its part, should develop closer political and economic ties with Moscow. Lowering trade barriers would be a particularly constructive step in the near term. This would bolster Russia's democratic and market reforms, which have experienced initial problems. In the long term, the goal should be the development of a Russia that would be fully integrated politically and economically into European affairs and would, therefore, be eligible for membership of the EU. This is decades away and, indeed, may never happen, but is nonetheless a worthwhile long-term objective.

Western Strategy and Central and Eastern Europe
Russian expansionism and the renationalisation of Western European defence policies can best be prevented by minimising turmoil and conflict in Central and Eastern Europe. Instability in the region will present Moscow with geostrategic opportunities that, if history is any guide, it will find hard to resist. Instability in this region is of special concern for Germany because of its proximity. If problems here are not addressed by the European Union

or NATO, Germany will be inclined to undertake initiatives of its own. Problems in Central and Eastern Europe could trigger a German–Russian security competition and the renationalisation of Western European foreign and defence policies that Europe would do well to avoid.

It does not follow, however, that extending NATO membership to states in Central and Eastern Europe will address the problems that this region faces. Once again, both NATO and the EU have essential roles to play.

NATO is a collective defence organisation, not a collective security organisation. Its contribution to Central and Eastern European security should be the extension of full membership and security commitments if Russia takes steps that merit these actions. The Alliance should continue, through bilateral partnerships and multilateral exercises, to develop closer security relationships with Central and Eastern European states and to make the military forces of NATO and non-NATO Europe more interoperable. If Russia embarks on an aggressive or expansionist course, NATO must be ready to extend full membership and defence commitments quickly.

The EU has an essential role to play in Central and Eastern Europe. It, more than NATO, is the key to dampening intra-state and intra-regional conflicts that do not involve Russia. NATO cannot address the political and economic roots of ethnic conflicts, nor does it have the political and economic levers to contain intra-regional conflicts. The EU is better positioned in both respects. By lowering trade barriers and extending more economic assistance, the EU could stimulate economic development, thereby dampening ethnic tensions in Eastern Europe. By outlining a course for bringing Central and Eastern European states into the fold, the European Union would give potential members powerful incentives to protect minority rights, embrace democracy and meet international norms of behaviour. This would maximise the EU's leverage in the short run and the prospects for stability in Central and Eastern Europe in the long run.

NATO is the ultimate guarantor of Central and Eastern European security against external threats – for example, Russian aggression. The European Union is the key to promoting stability within the region. NATO should expand if circumstances demand, but the EU should expand as quickly as it can.

The United States has to accept that NATO and the EU have complementary roles to play in European security. There are countless references to this complementarity in official communiqués, but it is only in the past year or two that there has been an acceptance of this principle in US thinking. The Clinton administration deserves credit for its enthusiastic, seemingly genuine, endorsement of a European security and defence identity and the development of a common European foreign and security policy.[38] It is possible that the EU's role in security policy will grow, especially in Central and Eastern Europe. This does not necessarily mean, however, that NATO is being eclipsed or that US involvement in European security is no longer needed. This is not a zero-sum game, in which one organisation's gain is necessarily another's loss. Developing a better appreciation of this at an official level and communicating it effectively to the American people will be one of the challenges that Washington will have to face.

Weighing Risks

The strategy outlined above can be criticised on three main grounds. First, critics will say that President Yeltsin is simply trying to use the West's fear of radical Russian nationalists to prevent NATO enlargement. It would be a mistake, they will argue, to allow Yeltsin's gambit to succeed. There is no doubt that Yeltsin is indeed playing the 'nationalist card' in his negotiations with the West over NATO enlargement. However, the West should not worry about radical Russian nationalists because Yeltsin says they are dangerous; the West should worry about Russian nationalism because its analysis of Russian domestic politics suggests that it has the potential to be dangerous.

Second, critics will point out that it will be difficult to identify the Russian actions that will trigger NATO enlargement. There is no doubt that this is a challenging problem; the criteria for enlargement outlined in this chapter constitute only a first effort. Nevertheless, some Russian actions – building up military forces in the west in violation of the CFE Treaty – would clearly constitute grounds for NATO enlargement. Expanding and refining this list of criteria should be within the capabilities of the Western strategic-studies community.

Third, critics will argue that NATO should enlarge now, when there is only a minor threat from Moscow and when most of Europe is peaceful. If NATO waits until Moscow becomes more aggressive, they will say, the Alliance will fail to act because Russian actions might not constitute clear threats to European security, NATO leaders might disagree about what to do or Alliance leaders might worry that enlargement will lead to a further deterioration in relations with Moscow. The Alliance will lack either the clarity, consensus or will to act decisively at the crucial moment. As a result, states that could have been brought under NATO's umbrella will be lost.

This argument cannot be dismissed lightly. But the difficulty in deciding whether to expand in the face of Russian aggression can be minimised if concrete steps are taken to develop and sustain a consensus within the Alliance while relations with Moscow are on a constructive footing. The key will be agreeing that Russian actions that change the balance of power or have military implications demand a military response from the West – enlarging the NATO Alliance.

Alliance support for NATO enlargement will be hard to mobilise because the current strategic case for enlargement is weak: why should NATO members bear the costs and run the risks associated with enlargement when Russia does not pose a military threat to Central Europe? Alliance support for NATO enlargement will be easier to mobilise if and when Russia poses a clear and present danger to Central and Western European security. Critics of the strategy outlined in this article underestimate the problems associated with enlargement in a low-threat environment and overestimate the problems associated with enlargement in a high-threat environment.

In addition to laying the political groundwork for expansion, the Alliance will have to lay the military groundwork for possible enlargement. Fortunately, this process is already under way both multilaterally (through NACC consultations) and bilaterally (through the PFP programme). The latter, launched in January 1994, involves Central and Eastern European states (and others) in joint planning activities and joint training exercises. The expectation is that over time these partnerships will close the gap that currently exists between NATO and non-NATO forces in virtually every aspect of military policy, including doctrine, forces, organisation and training. In many cases, close working relationships will develop and a foundation for joint military operations will be created. Military obstacles to NATO enlargement will gradually disappear. These cooperative efforts must be continued.

There are risks and costs associated with all of the positions on NATO enlargement discussed in this article. Prompt enlargement of NATO – bringing the Visegrad Four into the Alliance quickly – will, in all probability, cause a backlash in Russian domestic politics that will weaken whatever chances the democratic reform movement has. This could easily lead to actions in Europe and arms-control policy that will have a significant, adverse impact on European and US security. An East–West confrontation could well ensue. If those who favour this course of action are wrong about Russia's imperialistic impulses, NATO members will have only themselves to blame for bringing about this sorry state of affairs.

Those who favour gradualist approaches can reduce, but not eliminate these risks. Given the volatile and unpredictable state of Russian domestic politics, one should be wary of confidently predicting that Russia will quietly accept NATO enlargement in Central and Eastern Europe. It seems far more likely that Russian leaders will seize on NATO enlargement – which will involve a US military commitment and nuclear guarantee – to push an expansionist agenda of their own.

On balance, the risks and costs associated with near-term enlargement of the NATO Alliance are greater than those associated with linking enlargement to strategic circumstances.

Notes

1. Quoted in 'Clinton Hints NATO Would Defend East From Attack', *International Herald Tribune*, 13 January 1994.

2. See the White House, *A National Security Strategy of Engagement and Enlargement* (Washington DC: US Government Printing Office, July 1994), p. 22.

3. See 'Bonn Wants East in Updated NATO', *International Herald Tribune*, 3 October 1993; and Quentin Peel, 'Rühe Call for Partnership with Moscow', *Financial Times*, 8 October 1993.

4. See Final Communiqué, Ministerial Meeting of the North Atlantic Council, M-NAC-2(94)116, Brussels, 1 December 1994.

5. See Henry Kissinger, 'Not This Partnership', *Washington Post*, 24 November 1993; Kissinger, 'It's an Alliance, Not a Relic', *Washington Post*, 16 August 1994; Kissinger, 'Expand NATO Now', *Washington Post*, 19 December 1994; Zbigniew Brzezinski, 'A Plan for Europe', *Foreign Affairs*, vol. 74, no. 1, January–February 1995, pp. 26–42; Brzezinski, 'NATO – Expand or Die?', *New York Times*, 28 December 1994; Brzezinski, 'The Premature Partnership', *Foreign Affairs*, vol. 73, no. 2, March–April 1994, pp. 67–82; Harold Brown, 'Europe: A Sound US Policy of Initiative and Insurance', *International Herald Tribune*, 27–28 August 1994; and former US Secretary of State James Baker quoted in Michael Kramer, 'The Case for a Bigger NATO', *Time*, 10 January 1994. See also Ronald D. Asmus, Richard L. Kugler and F. Stephen Larrabee, 'Building a New NATO', *Foreign Affairs*, vol. 72, no. 4, September–October 1993, pp. 28–40; William E. Odom, 'Strategic Realignment in Europe: NATO's Obligation to the East', in *NATO: The Case for Enlargement* (London: Institute for European Defence and Strategic Studies, 1993); Robert B. Zoellick, 'Set Criteria for NATO Membership Soon', *International Herald Tribune*, 7 January 1994; Michael Mandelbaum, 'NATO: Open Up the Ranks to the East European Democracies', *International Herald Tribune*, 8 September 1993; Peter Corterier, 'Let NATO Stretch Its Arms', *Defense News*, 20–23 December 1993; Michael Clarke, 'NATO Must Upset Russia or Do Nothing and Die', *Sunday Telegraph*, 7 November 1993; and Peter W. Rodman, '4 More for NATO', *Washington Post*, 13 December 1994. See also Proposed Republican Legislation, 'NATO Revitalization and Expansion Act of 1995', 23 September 1994.

6. See A. M. Rosenthal, 'An Expanded NATO is Worth Waiting For', *International Herald Tribune*, 8–9 January 1994; Zoellick, 'Set Criteria for NATO Membership'; Baker's comments in Kramer, 'The Case for a Bigger NATO'; and Asmus *et al.*, chapter 5. See also Harold Brown's endorsement of the Clinton administration's gradualist policy in Brown, 'Europe'.

7. See Odom, 'Strategic Realignment in Europe'; and Rodman, '4 More for NATO'. See also Henry Kissinger's critique of the Clinton administration's Partnership for Peace programme in Kissinger, 'Not This Partnership'.

8. See Brzezinski, 'A Plan for Europe'; Craig R. Whitney, 'Adversarial Allies: Sparring over Bosnia and NATO Membership', *New York Times*, 2 December 1994; and William H. Taft IV, 'An American Perspective on New European Security Challenges', in Charles L. Barry (ed.), *The Search for Peace in Europe* (Washington DC: National Defense University Press, 1993), pp. 267–81.

9. See Final Communiqué, Ministerial Meeting of the North Atlantic Council, M-NAC-2(94)116.

10. Interviews with US National Security Council, State Department and Defense Department officials in December 1994. The Republican leadership of the new US Congress has proposed that Poland, the Czech Republic, Hungary and Slovakia should be invited to become NATO members by January 1999 at the latest. See Proposed Republican Legislation, 'NATO Revitalisation and Expansion Act of 1995'.

11. A small but growing group of people question the wisdom of NATO enlargement. See Gunther Hellmann and Reinhard Wolf, 'Don't Build on a Shaky Foundation',

International Herald Tribunal, 18–19 September 1993; Charles William Maynes, 'No, Expansion Eastward Isn't What NATO Needs', *International Herald Tribune*, 21 September 1993; Charles A. Kupchan, 'Expand NATO – And Split Europe', *New York Times*, 27 November 1994; Maynes, 'For NATO, Expansion Could Prove Fatal', *New York Times*, 2 January 1995; and Fred C. Iklé, 'How to Ruin NATO', *New York Times*, 11 January 1995.

12. James Baker favours the establishment of 'a mechanistic process. It shows the Russians that we're not acting hastily, that we're pursuing our interests in a careful, calibrated way'. Quoted in Kramer, 'The Case for a Bigger NATO'.

13. Brzezinski, 'Premature Partnership', p. 72.

14. Rodman, '4 More for NATO'.

15. *The Military Balance 1994–1995* (London: Brassey's for the IISS, October 1994), pp. 109–10.

16. See 'The Military Mess in Russia', *The Economist*, 17 December 1994, p. 50.

17. See Brzezinski, 'NATO – Expand or Die?'.

18. *The Military Balance 1994–1995*, p. 77.

19. See Mandelbaum, 'NATO'. See also Clarke, 'NATO Must Upset Russia'; and Asmus *et al.*, chapter 5. Rühe is quoted in James O. Jackson, 'Trying to Enlist in NATO', *Time*, 8 November 1993, p. 52.

20. The largest ethnic minorities in this part of Central Europe are the Hungarian minorities in Slovakia and Romania. There have been no recent flare-ups in either case, and the Hungarian government has generally taken a non-confrontational stance in addressing problems encountered by the Hungarian diaspora.

21. Slovakia is potentially unsettled, given the possible return of Vladimir Meciar to power. This, however, is precisely why Slovakia is seen by many in NATO as a weak candidate for early accession. For an overview of recent developments, see 'Slovakia: Wrong Turning', *The Economist*, 12 November 1994, pp. 69–70.

22. See Asmus *et al.*, chapter 5, p. 95.

23. Vaclav Havel, 'We Really Are Part of the NATO Family', *International Herald Tribune*, 20 October 1993.

24. Zoellick, 'Set Criteria for NATO Membership'. See also Mandelbaum, 'NATO: Open Up the Ranks'.

25. See Asmus *et al.*, chapter 5, p. 95.

26. Kissinger, 'Not This Partnership'.

27. Kissinger, 'It's an Alliance'. See also Asmus *et al.*, chapter 5.

28. See Elaine Sciolino, 'US and NATO Say Dispute on Bosnia War is Resolved', *New York Times*, 2 December 1994; Rowland Evans and Robert Novak, 'Yeltsin Victorious', *Washington Post*, 12 December 1994; and Whitney, 'Adversarial Allies'.

29. Klaus Kinkel, 'NATO Requires a Bold But Balanced Response to the East', *International Herald Tribune*, 21 October 1993.

30. Asmus, Kugler and Larrabee, 'Building a New NATO', p. 35.

31. Russian withdrawal from START II, in particular, would undoubtedly be influenced by the status of Ukrainian denuclearisation efforts: if Ukraine still retained nuclear forces on its territory and if Russian influence over Kiev was limited, Moscow would have an incentive to keep the denuclearisation process on track. Alternatively, if Ukraine had already fulfilled its START I pledges and denuclearised, Russia would be less worried about the repercussions of withdrawing from START II.

32. This is Steve Miller's observation.

33. See Kissinger, 'Not This Partnership'.

34. See Rosenthal, 'An Expanded NATO is Worth Waiting For'; Zoellick, 'Set Criteria for NATO Membership'; Baker's comments in Kramer, 'The Case for a Bigger NATO'; and Asmus *et al.*, chapter 5. See also Harold Brown's endorsement of the Clinton administration's gradualist policy in Brown, 'Europe'.

35. See Whitney, 'Adversarial Allies'; and Taft, 'An American Perspective on New European Security Challenges'.

36. See Fiona Hill and Pamela Jewett, *Back in the USSR: Russia's Intervention in the Internal Affairs of the Former Soviet Republics and the Implications for United States Policy Toward Russia*, Strengthening Democratic Institutions Project (Cambridge, MA: John F. Kennedy School of Government, January 1994); and Bruce D. Porter and Carol R. Saivetz, 'The Once and Future Empire: Russia and the "Near Abroad"', *Washington Quarterly*, vol. 17, no. 3, Summer 1994, pp. 75–90.

37. Brzezinski, 'The Way Forward'.

38. See, in particular, President Clinton's remarks on the eve of the January 1994 NATO summit in Brussels in 'Excerpts From Speech: Binding Broader Europe', *New York Times*, 10 January 1994.

Chapter 7
Can Containment Work Again?

Dana H. Allin

It is hardly a promising moment to consider expanding the Western Alliance. Member-governments are weaker and more confused than at any time in a generation. Opposition parties are, for the most part, also in disarray, lacking coherent alternative visions for their societies. Electorates are preoccupied with domestic concerns. These fitful, inward-looking societies are further demoralised by having fumbled, in former Yugoslavia, the overriding moral challenge of the immediate post-Cold War era. The very concept of the 'West' has been blurred beyond recognition by the collapse of the monolithic 'East'.

None of this is particularly surprising. One need not be nostalgic about the Cold War to recognise that the Soviet threat helped to focus the Western mind, providing a not altogether natural unity of purpose. Now, that purpose is gone, and old fractures and quarrels have resurfaced and regained their relative importance.

Under these predictable circumstances, it might have been wise to accept the limits of the idea of the 'West', to have avoided giving false hope to the Bosnians and others who were too dependent on an Alliance that no longer existed as a clear community of interests and to have avoided overburdening the Alliance's principal institution.[1] Rather than seeking a magic formula for the regeneration of NATO, the real task, in this pessimistic analysis, was to manage the Alliance's inevitable political decline and to preserve as much of it as possible as a hedge against future threats.

But policy is never made in perfect circumstances, and policy analysis must take some account of the real choices facing politicians. A commitment has been made to NATO enlargement, albeit with much vagueness and mumbling. All along, NATO members have hoped to square a difficult circle:

how to extend some kind of Western security umbrella to at least the most western of Moscow's former dominions without further feeding Russia's already considerable sense of beleaguerment. The first, equivocal attempt was the establishment of a North Atlantic Cooperation Council (NACC) that embraced the entire former Warsaw Pact. Second, NATO put forward a US-designed Partnership for Peace (PFP) programme that combined immediate military cooperation with the prospect of eventual membership of the Alliance. But the circle could not, in fact, be squared: any scheme that failed to differentiate between the presumed potential threat and its presumed potential victims was unlikely to inspire great confidence. In response to these concerns, a series of statements, including US President Bill Clinton's famous '[not] whether, but when and how' promise in Warsaw in July 1994, have added up to a Western commitment to enlargement.[2] In theory, of course, the promise to expand does not need to be kept, but to go back on it now would constitute another débâcle in a string of embarrassments that the West can ill afford.

This chapter argues that NATO should offer membership to Poland, Hungary, the Czech Republic and, probably, Slovenia and Slovakia. But the benefits of membership should not be exaggerated. A realistic assessment of the risks and rewards of enlargement requires a re-examination of some first principles of European security. How did NATO provide political stability and military security during the Cold War, and how might that success be replicated? And what, precisely, are the East-Central Europeans afraid of?

This last question may seem wilfully obtuse after the December 1993 Russian parliamentary elections, in which the Liberal Democratic Party of nationalist demagogue Vladimir Zhirinovsky received a greater share of the popular vote than Adolf Hitler's Nazi Party in 1930.[3] In the subsequent months after these elections, even ostensibly moderate currents in Russian politics have moved towards a more assertive definition of Russian interests; President Boris Yeltsin and Foreign Minister Andrei Kozyrev have adopted a hard line against Central European accession to NATO; and various pressures, from economic to military intervention, have been applied to break-away Soviet republics, leading to a partial reconsolidation of the Russian empire. Moscow remains mired in its own problems and bitter divisions, but a consensus does appear to be developing that a natural Russian sphere of influence extends, at least, to Poland's borders.[4]

Under such circumstances, the answer to the second question may seem obvious – the East-Central Europeans are afraid of a Russian attack. More concretely, they are afraid that Russia's continuing anguish may turn pathological: with socioeconomic collapse unleashing demons that future tyrants might seek to direct outwards.

Yet, while an aggressive Russian revanchism cannot be ruled out, Eastern Europe's leaders concede that this extreme scenario is not their primary concern. Their immediate anxieties are more subtle and diffuse. As the former Polish

Defence Minister, Janusz Onyszkiewicz, has said, it is 'not to defend against a Russian attack' that Poland seeks NATO membership:

> We see that [attack] as a virtual impossibility. The key reason we want to be in NATO is to secure our own democracies. We need to keep down in our country the very same kind of nationalists Yeltsin is contending with, the same kind that have destroyed Yugoslavia.[5]

More broadly, the East-Central Europeans do not want to be left out in the cold. They look to NATO for psychological shelter, to relieve them of excessive military preoccupations and to generate the climate of confidence in which they can pursue their difficult economic and political reforms.[6]

The Containment Analogy

If this story sounds familiar, it is. A very similar analysis was used to describe the predicament of Western European societies at the outset of the Cold War. Even at the height of post-Second World War tensions – as the Soviets confronted the Western allies for control of Berlin and police terror descended upon the hapless Eastern Europeans – the more sober assessments of a Soviet threat to Western Europe discounted the likelihood of a military invasion.[7] The real danger was seen to be the Soviet potential to exploit the psychological and material fragility of war-torn Western European societies – several of which had to contend with powerful national communist parties of their own.

The years immediately after the Second World War were marked by crises on a different scale to the current situation in East-Central Europe. The European winter of 1947 was fiercely cold, and the year before had been fiercely dry. Industry was demolished; fuel and food were scarce. 'By early 1946', Daniel Yergin reminds us, 'more than 125 million Europeans were subsisting on no more than 2,000 calories a day, many of those millions on no more than 1,000 – in grim contrast to the 3,300 calories that was the average in the United States'.[8] In Poland and the eastern zone of occupied Germany, the Soviets rapidly set about imposing Stalinist regimes. In Greece, communists and conservatives were fighting a savage civil war. Most ominously for Western Europe, perhaps, was the 1948 Czech coup, which installed a Stalinist dictatorship, despite the fact that there were only about 500 Soviet troops in the entire country.[9] But the communists were relatively popular in Czechoslovakia, having won 37% of the vote in free elections in 1947. And they supplemented their popularity with ruthless organisation and tactics, outmanoeuvering non-communist ministers in the government until they had enough authority to begin arrests, show trials and executions. Soviet power in the background helped, but it was not necessary to use it.

The Prague coup was a chilling object-lesson for those countries west of the River Elbe. In France and Italy, especially, large communist parties looked as formidable as their Czech comrades. Prestige was high due to the communists' prominent role in the anti-fascist resistance. Indeed, it is important to remember that communism in general and Stalin's regime in particular were not only militarily victorious in the Second World War, but were also victorious in terms of morale. Notwithstanding the brutal face it showed in Prague, Berlin, Warsaw and Budapest, Soviet communism was viewed as a serious alternative vision of the future. As late as the early 1960s, US President John F. Kennedy was unable to dismiss as empty bluster Soviet premier Nikita Khrushchev's claim that communism's superior economic, diplomatic and technological achievements would 'bury' the West.[10]

The perceived threat, then, was as much economic, political, psychological and moral as it was military, and it derived as much from Western Europe's post-war disarray as it did from Soviet communism's (somewhat illusory) power.

In the view of such post-war planners as George F. Kennan, this political–economic threat mainly required political–economic measures to contain it. Thus, Kennan argued that US Marshall Aid was a more important measure of containment than US military protection. In fact, Kennan viewed a large US military presence and the creation of NATO with West Germany among its members as *detrimental* to Western European reconstruction. Such a 'militarisation' of containment would only divert resources and attention away from more pressing social needs, solidify the division of Europe and lead to a Soviet feeling, justified or not, of encirclement.[11] Similar arguments, of course, are being employed today by opponents of a NATO enlargement eastwards.[12]

Having noted the historical similarity, it must be recognised that the 'militarisation' of containment does not appear to have damaged Western Europe's security – even in Kennan's more subtle political–psychological and socioeconomic terms. As Sir Michael Howard argued a decade ago, it was above all the US military presence – and especially its nuclear umbrella – that provided the 'reassurance' that Europe needed to undertake ambitious physical reconstruction and social renewal.[13]

Despite the presence of the Soviet Army, offensively armed and positioned on the inner German border, Western Europeans were able to conduct their political lives without any great concern for Soviet blackmail. Even in the midst of critical domestic crises – such as France in 1958, 1961 and 1968; Portugal in 1973; and Italy from 1972 until 1979 – the prospect of a Soviet intervention did not weigh much, if at all, in politicians' calculations.[14]

This reassuring function of nuclear terror became ever more palpable as the war scares ended. The Berlin Wall played a pacifying, albeit brutal, role in this process, helping to remove the central unsettled conflict from East–West relations and clarifying the superpowers' respective spheres of vital interest. By the mid-1960s, it was probably a misnomer to speak of a 'Cold War' in the sense of an incipient military conflict that might turn hot at any moment. A nuclear confrontation continued, but this 'existential' threat constituted such a powerful deterrent as to eliminate the plausibility of superpower war.

This left another form of struggle to be waged. What was really going on, in the second half of the Cold War, was a largely peaceful, albeit bitter, contest between two different models of society.[15] Kennan, as early as 1948, was confident about how the contest would be resolved:

> [If] economic recovery could be brought about and public confidence restored in Western Europe – if Western Europe, in other words, could be made the home of a vigorous, prosperous and forward-looking civilisation – the Communist regime in Eastern Europe ... would never be able to stand the comparison, and the spectacle of a happier and more successful life just across the fence ... would be bound in the end to have a disintegrating and eroding effect on the Communist world.[16]

Four decades later, a 'mellowed' communism collapsed and a restored Western civilisation triumphed, much as Kennan had predicted.

The Post-Communist Malaise

Can the success of this strategy of containment teach us anything about dealing with the predicaments of present-day East-Central Europe?

A close look at the region's post-communist history shows some similarities between the current situation and the Cold War era, but many more important differences. A strategy of 'containment II', in the sense of using a military–political alliance to promote political stability, might be worth pursuing. But the fundamental differences between 1949 and 1995 suggest that NATO's role this time will be far more limited.

One thing that is clear from reading Kennan is his conviction that to contain Soviet power it was necessary to quell Western societies' panic and to cure their general malaise. National morale or, as he put it, 'public confidence' and 'forward-looking civilisation' was the basic material of containment.

Judging by recent elections, this elusive quality of forward-looking confidence has gone somewhat sour in East-Central Europe. Former communists have regained power in Hungary, Poland, Slovakia and Slovenia – four of the five most probable candidates for early NATO membership. Some members of the recently displaced governments suggest that this post-communist revival constitutes the first fruit of the West's general diffidence about providing the region with a coherent and forthcoming programme for integration into the European Union (EU) and NATO.[17] Among the many disappointments of the five years since the region was swept by peaceful revolutions, one of the biggest has been the tepid quality of Western support.

But the political reaction in these countries should be kept in perspective. The first reforming governments were probably doomed from the start, no matter what they or their Western well-wishers did. Expectations were great and disillusionment inevitable – particularly as countries like Hungary and

Poland had been living beyond their means on heavy foreign borrowing in the years leading up to 1989. In general, moreover, the present, post-communist governments are neither reactionary, nor even particularly hostile to capitalist reforms. They have no viable alternatives and they do not pretend otherwise. Unlike the early Cold War, there is not at present a confrontation between capitalist democracy and another, ostensibly rational, model of society. To be sure, there are plenty of irrational alternatives, such as the ethno-nationalist delusions being pursued just a few hundred kilometres away in Belgrade and Pale. But the recent electoral choices of East-Central Europe, whatever mistakes they may entail, also confirm a rejection of these delusions.

Hungary is the most important example in this regard, circumstances being such that its nationalist temptation is potentially among the more potent in the region. Hungarians do remember that their nation lost two-thirds of its territory to Austria, Czechoslovakia, Romania and Yugoslavia in the 1920 Treaty of Trianon. Some three million ethnic Hungarians are scattered in neighbouring countries; their treatment in Slovakia and Romania is the subject of much resentment; and in Serbia, the behaviour of the Belgrade government towards ethnic minorities in general does not inspire long-term confidence.

Genuine concerns about compatriots stranded abroad can be hijacked by demagogues. For four years after the first free elections in 1990, the national conservative government, which was dominated by the Hungarian National Forum (MDF), tolerated and sometimes seemed to court anti-Semites and proto-fascists, most notoriously in the case of the right-wing demagogue István Csurka. Csurka had a considerable following in the government, despite his claims of an international Jewish conspiracy. Mainstream conservatives no doubt found this rhetoric abhorrent, but the leadership under the late Prime Minister, Jozsef Antall, took a long time to expel the more outspoken anti-Semites.[18] This attitude rendered the government's propaganda of old-world Hungarian patriotism somewhat ominous. Again, concern for the rights of ethnic Hungarians in neighbouring countries may be a compelling and legitimate national interest, but for obvious reasons of geography and history it needs to be handled wisely.

The Hungarian Socialist Party (former communists) was, therefore, probably wise to de-emphasise the issue of ethnic Hungarians, and in this respect it is reassuring that the electorate rewarded them with one-third of the popular vote and an outright majority of parliamentary seats. The Socialists ran a campaign in part against the Conservatives' nostalgic Hungarian romanticism.[19] They portrayed themselves as the professionals, the technocratic experts and the modernisers, and there was some credibility to their claims. Gyula Horn, the new Prime Minister, was Foreign Minister in the last communist government, which ostentatiously opened its own Iron Curtain and, by allowing East Germans free exit to Austria, effectively destroyed the Berlin Wall. Other former communists also played important roles in the transformation process that, by 1989, had dismantled Hungarian totalitarianism from within.

Many and perhaps most of the former communists, no doubt, have less honourable personal histories, and there is abundant anecdotal evidence of socialists who, once reinstalled at various levels of authority, betray an unforgotten instinct for authoritarianism.[20] Yet even the most trenchant liberal critics of the socialists concede that they do not pose a threat to democracy, as such, but rather to the kind of open competition in economic and professional relations that liberals are striving for. Hungary has a tradition, which some socialists find agreeable, of clientalistic, corporatist deal-making at many levels of the economy, bureaucracy, academia and culture. The threat is of Hungary becoming more like Austria and Italy and less like the United States.[21] This, needless to say, is a threat that EU membership could only effect in the long run, and NATO membership not at all.

This illustrates an important aspect of the communist come-back in East-Central Europe, namely, that the communists never went away. The phenomenon of '*nomenklatura* privatisation' – the allegation that in the economic transformation process, old communist élites have been in a position to reap most of the benefits and take control of a large share of the denationalised assets – has been widely discussed in the region. As Louisa Vinton has noted, this lament is hard to test empirically. It is very much a 'politicised phrase' expressing the conviction 'that communist privileges endure today, in a "propertied" form'.[22] Indeed, travelling in the region one senses a promiscuous tendency to affix the label of 'old communist' to anyone holding opinions or positions that the speaker thinks he or she should not have.

But, however exaggerated it may be in some people's minds, the phenomenon of *nomenklatura* privatisation underscores two reassuring generalisations that can be made about the current situation. First, the continued hold of former communists on various levers of power and influence was largely inherent to the peaceful revolutions of 1989. The old regimes were not so much overthrown as undermined; as their authority collapsed, they handed it over rather than reasserted it by force. In the process, deals were made, as in the roundtable talks in Poland and Hungary, and various assets, such as important newspapers, were never relinquished. Second, what these 'post-communist' parties now represent is not so much an ideology as a set of interests. These are partly the interests of those who have lost from economic change, but are also the interests of the old party élite, who are not all losers and who would not necessarily gain if the revolutions could somehow be reversed.

Adam Michnik, the former dissident intellectual and current Editor of *Gazeta Wyborcza*, Poland's largest daily newspaper, emphasised this last point soon after the September 1993 elections that ended the era of Solidarity governments and brought in a coalition of the Democratic Left Alliance (SLD) and the

Polish Peasant Party (PSL). (The SLD was heir to the old Communist Party, while PSL had been the communists' agrarian partner under the old regime.) For Michnik, the SLD was neither a communist, nor a social democratic party, but rather a coalition of the *ancien régime*, united by the comparable personal histories of its members. It posed some danger of recentralising power, thereby damaging the development of civil society and the success of economic reform. And, since the SLD and the PSL together held a parliamentary, but not popular, majority, Michnik could imagine conflict with President Lech Walesa leading to a 'Yeltsin variant' of authoritarian government, as social instability and doubts about the effectiveness of democratic institutions led to a popular acceptance of non-democratic measures. However, Michnik did not blame the former communists in particular for this prospect and was inclined to believe that the 'logic of democracy' would prevail in Poland.[23]

As for the logic of Western alignment, there is little evidence to contradict the initial assessment of former Polish Foreign Minister, Krzysztof Skubiszewski, who argued that the Left's 1993 victory would not 'entail any changes in [Poland's] foreign policy', which had been 'determined by Poland's basic national interests, the country's *raison d'état* that was accepted in 1989, and not by some party preferences of occasional electoral winners'.[24] In the ensuing year, there has certainly been no significant change in the formal positions of these countries in East-Central Europe *vis-à-vis* EU and NATO membership. To be sure, some critics of the new governments do detect hints of diminished ardour. As it won power in Poland, the SLD was talking about NATO membership in ambiguous and somewhat contradictory tones, with one prominent Party member speaking of a willingness to join a 'changed' NATO that was part of 'a new European political and military system that would cover the entire area of the [then] CSCE ... including Russia as well'.[25] In Hungary, many pro-NATO security experts were dismayed when the new government, citing costs, postponed the joint manoeuvers that had been planned under the auspices of PFP.[26] But Prime Minister Horn remains unreservedly pro-NATO and the socialist government is considerably 'more for than against' NATO membership, as is conceded by the otherwise highly critical Jozsef Szajer, Vice-President and parliamentary caucus chief of the Young Democrats (FIDESZ).[27]

In Szajer's view, the real threat to East-Central Europe's pro-Western orientation comes not from former communists, but from the West itself, which can do considerable harm if it hesitates much longer. 'The whole political class has been basing its legitimacy on joining the West', and at some point this posture must be seen to pay off or it will lose its domestic political appeal.[28] Szajer sees a window of opportunity that has been open for five years but could close in another five, as a fluid moment in Central European history freezes again. Central Europe belongs, historically and culturally, to the West, but there are other alternatives, even if their shape cannot yet be discerned.

NATO's Limited Role

Examined in this general perspective, the relative importance of NATO membership diminishes. The overriding challenge is to make Central Europe's 'Western' vocation more profitable. Although it has important political and moral dimensions, the disillusionment in post-communist Europe stems mainly from the trauma of an uncertain economic transformation; the form of Western integration that can do most to alleviate this trauma, therefore, is the opening of Western markets to East-Central Europeans and the realistic prospect of EU membership – on terms that are generous enough to avoid further disillusionment.

NATO membership could also play a positive, but limited, role in promoting political stability. Cross-border transparency, joint manoeuvers and cooperation could help to professionalise post-communist armies, and further educate them in Western notions of democracy and subordination to civilian control.[29] (It must be added, however, that PFP could probably accomplish these goals on its own.) Common membership in NATO might also help to pacify regional conflicts involving national minorities, although this commonly cited argument seems to be based more on hope than experience.[30] The long-term effect of Greece and Turkey sharing a common alliance has not been entirely clear. Nor is there much evidence that NATO membership has helped to pacify Greece's belligerent nationalism towards Macedonia and Albania. Most recently, the irredentist rhetoric of neo-fascists in Italy's governing coalition played a central role in the Slovenian government crisis that drove the Christian Democratic Foreign Minister from power, leaving former communists in charge.[31]

Much discussion of the political, rather than military, role of NATO enlargement seems to assume an unreal distinction between the two. If one accepts Michael Howard's interpretation of how containment functioned in the Cold War, the credibility of military – in this case, nuclear – protection was critical. It was critical not so much for the potential aggressor who may or may not have been inclined to attack, but for the potential victims, who required reassurance. How credible and reassuring is the likely NATO protection of East-Central Europe?

Here again, the experience of the Cold War is instructive. The security of West Germany, for example, was never seen to rely exclusively upon the declaration that an attack on one NATO member would be considered as an attack on them all. As important was the five American divisions on the central front, which would presumably have become involved in a European war regardless of the vagaries of US public opinion. And, of course, these divisions were backed by a panoply of nuclear weapons, whose use was designed to be nearly automatic if the conventional battle appeared to be lost. Even under these circumstances, there was a long-running debate about the credibility of the US commitment – the stability of transatlantic 'coupling'. Today, it is difficult to imagine a comparable commitment of troops and hardware east of the River Oder. Without this degree of physical coupling, a stark and brutal uncertainty emerges: are the US and Western Europe ready to send troops, much less risk nuclear war, to defend Polish independence?

The answer may not be a self-evident 'no'. And optimists might argue that a somewhat less credible guarantee is fully adequate against a somewhat nebulous threat. But such optimists must be ready to address a whole string of troubling questions. What would be the effect of an Alliance guarantee of somewhat lesser credibility on the dynamics of a future crisis? Would such a commitment be better than no guarantee at all? Or would it invite, rather than forestall, dangerous miscalculation? If NATO members fear antagonising the Russians now, when revanchist elements are still submerged or just bubbling to the surface, will they not be even less willing to provoke Moscow in that hypothetical future in which extreme nationalists actually control Russian policy? Is it not the logic of the situation that the East-Central Europeans will be able to count on NATO's protection only if the passage of years demonstrates that such protection is unnecessary? Most fundamentally, how much reassurance can all of these calculations provide to boost public confidence in East-Central Europe?

The tragedy of Bosnia, and the Alliance's failure to protect it, naturally sharpen all of these dilemmas. For the West, there are, to be sure, extenuating circumstances: the Balkan war is complicated; all combatant parties in former Yugoslavia share some guilt for intransigence and atrocities; and the prospects for successful foreign intervention in a civil war are always uncertain. All of these excuses are valid, insofar as they are all true. It is difficult, however, to imagine that future Eastern European conflicts will be less complicated, will be less fierce or will be more amenable to Western intervention.

The Alliance record over recent years in the Balkans has damaged the credibility of any ambiguous or implicit security guarantees for East-Central Europe. The West's failure to protect Bosnia suggests that future guarantees will need to be all that more explicit.

Conclusion

The present problems of East-Central Europe are fundamentally different from those that afflicted Europe in the first years after the Second World War. First, there is no obvious military threat: Russia's attention, strategic interests and ethnic entanglements are concentrated for the foreseeable future on its 'near abroad'. Second, there is no ideological threat – while democratic capitalism has disappointed and even traumatised many, it has no serious rivals. Under these very different circumstances, the notion that NATO would automatically foster the same sort of political stability that it helped to bring to Western Europe during the Cold War cannot be taken for granted. Its role, both political and military, might well be positive, but would certainly be limited – for the reasons outlined above.

And yet, in the final analysis, the costs of not extending the Western Alliance would exceed the costs of doing so. East-Central Europe's political élite – and this includes the former communists – have staked their legitimacy on their countries' gradual but steady adherence to the West. Rightly or wrongly, this is understood to have essentially two institutional meanings: the European Union, and NATO. The Americans and Western Europeans, perhaps inadvertently, have encouraged this understanding. To turn back now, to close the doors of either or both institutions, would very likely delegitimise that Western orientation among large segments of these societies. No one can be certain that the consequences would be catastrophic, but it is easy to imagine them as intolerable.

The irony, of course, is that the experience of the past few years has raised the possibility that the 'West' no longer exists in any meaningful form. Yet that same experience – barbarism in South-eastern Europe and the outside world's helpless reaction – constitutes convincing evidence of the West's need to reinvent itself.

In doing so, as it better defines itself, the West may tend to make itself more exclusive. This raises the delicate prospect of Russia's exclusion – a central problem of the NATO enlargement debate, which this chapter has only glossed over. Yet, in the absence of any certainty about the Russian reaction, it is probably wisest to fall back on another Kennanesque principle: deal with Moscow not with platitudes, but on the basis of a firm and realistic understanding of respective interests. If this is enough to shatter cooperative relations, then there was little basis for cooperation in the first place. In the long run, Russia should find a self-confident and predictable Western Alliance to be a more reassuring partner than the confused and fitful coalition of today.

Embracing the new democracies on its doorstep is the obvious first step for an Alliance that needs to stand for something in order to reconstruct itself. Betraying the hopes of East-Central Europe would be another stage in the West's own tragic deconstruction.

Notes

1. See Owen Harries, 'The Collapse of the West', *Foreign Affairs*, vol. 72, no. 4, September–October, pp. 41–53.

2. Transcript of address to the Polish parliament, 7 July 1994, in *US Policy Information and Texts*, no. 67, 8 July 1994, p. 2.

3. In Russia's December 1993 parliamentary elections, Vladimir Zhirinovsky's Liberal Democratic Party won 23% of the popular vote, along with a lesser share of seats in the new parliament – 66 out of 450, or 14.7%. In Germany's 1930 Reichstag elections, the Nazis won a popular vote of 18.3% and a comparable share of seats, 107 of 595. See 'Weimar on the Volga', *The Economist*, 18 December 1993, p. 25; and Heinrick Pleticha, *Deutsche Geschichte*, vol. 11 (Guertersloh: Bertelsmann Verlagsgruppe, 1984), p. 99.

4. See the opening chapter by Robert D. Blackwill and Sergei A. Karaganov, in Blackwill and Karaganov (eds), *Damage Limitation or Crisis: Russia and the Outside World* (Washington DC: Brassey's, 1994), pp. 1–23.

5. Michael Kramer, 'The Case for a Bigger NATO', *Time*, 10 January 1994, p. 21.

6. Analysis of East-Central European perspectives in this chapter is based partly on interviews conducted in Budapest, Bratislava and Slovenia in November 1994 and in Warsaw in December 1993.

7. See, for example, *George F. Kennan, Memoirs: 1950–1963* (New York: Pantheon Books, 1972), pp. 90–91.

8. Daniel Yergin, *Shattered Peace: The Origins of the Cold War and the National Security State* (Boston, MA: Houghton Mifflin, 1978), p. 305.

9. *Ibid.*, pp. 348–49.

10. On Kennedy's assessment, see Richard Reeves, *President Kennedy: Profile of Power* (New York: Simon and Schuster, 1993), pp. 37, 40–41, 86–87, 98–99 and *passim*.

11. Kennan had scorned the notion that Stalinist hostility derived from a real fear that Russian security was threatened. But that did not mean that the Soviet Union had *no* legitimate security interests. On the contrary, watching the Cold War develop from his post as Ambassador to Moscow, Kennan had viewed with alarm many of NATO's military preparations, deeming them provocative to a degree that the United States would never have tolerated. 'Surely as one moves one's bases and military facilities towards the Soviet frontiers there comes a point where they tend to create the very thing they were designed to avoid. It is not for us to assume that there are no limits to Soviet patience in the face of encirclement by American bases. Quite aside from political considerations, no great country, peaceful or aggressive, rational or irrational, could sit by and witness with indifference the progressive studding of its own frontiers with the military installations of a great-power competitor'. See Dispatch from Ambassador Kennan (Moscow) to Department of State (Washington), 8 September 1952, reprinted in Kennan, *Memoirs*, p. 354.

12. See, for example, Charles A. Kupchan, 'Extending NATO Eastward Would Be a Grave Error', *International Herald Tribune*, 30 November 1994, p. 4; Editorial, 'Bipartisan Foreign Policy', *New York Times*, 2 January 1994, p. 22; and Brown, chapter 6.

13. Michael Howard, 'Reassurance and Deterrence: Western Defense in the 1980s', *Foreign Affairs*, vol. 61, no. 2, Winter 1982–83, pp. 309–23.

14. The Italian example is perhaps the most illuminating one. In June 1976, in the midst of an economic collapse, with extremists on the Right and Left conducting well-organised terrorist campaigns, many Italians viewing civil war to be imminent and the already strong Italian Communist Party about to score impressive electoral results, Communist Party leader Enrico Berlinguer actually endorsed NATO as a shield to protect Italian socialism against Soviet intervention. 'I want Italy not to quit the Atlantic Pact also for this reason, and not only because our exit would upset the international balance. I feel more secure remaining here'. See Berlinguer interview by Giampola Pansa, in *Corriera della Sera*, 15 June 1976, p. 2.

15. For an extended treatment of this argument, see Dana H. Allin, *Cold War Illusions: America, Europe and Soviet Power, 1969–1989* (New York: St Martin's Press, 1995).

16. George F. Kennan, lecture, at Joint Orientation Conference, The Pentagon, Washington DC, 8 November 1948, quoted in John Lewis Gaddis, *Strategies of*

Containment: A Critical Appraisal of Postwar American National Security Policy (New York: Oxford University Press, 1982), p. 45.

17. Interview with Ivan Baba, former Hungarian Deputy State Secretary for Foreign Affairs, Budapest, 16 November 1994; and conversation with former Polish Labour Minister, Michael Boni, in Bled, Slovenia, November 1994.

18. See István Deák, 'Post-Post-Communist Hungary', *New York Review of Books*, vol. 41, no. 14, 11 August 1994, p. 34.

19. *Ibid.*, and interviews in Budapest, November 1994. After three months in office, the new Prime Minister, Gyula Horn, spoke with some evident pride about his government's de-emphasis of the minorities issue. See Michael Frank's interview with Horn in 'Ein NATO–Ungarn Wäre Keine Bedrohung Rußlands', *Süddeutsche Zeitung*, 30 November 1994, p. 12.

20. Deák recounts such stories as that of a 'former Communist law professor who said to a candidate, a spokesman for the Young Democrats: "Do not imagine that now you will be able to pass your bar exam", or ... the office supervisor, an old Communist bureaucrat, who wrote on the vacation application of an employee who was involved in Conservative politics: "I do not authorise her travel abroad"'. See 'Post-Post-Communist Hungary', p. 38.

21. Interviews in Budapest, November 1994.

22. See Louisa Vinton, 'Poland's New Government: Continuity or Reversal?', *Radio Free Europe/Radio Liberty Research Report*, vol. 2, no. 46, 19 November 1993, p. 2.

23. Basil Kerski und Steffen Sachs, *Die Deutsch-Polnischen Beziehungen als Modell Fuer das Zusammenwachsen von Ost- und Westeuropa*, Report of the Aspen Institute Conference, Warsaw, 15–17 December 1993 (Berlin: Aspen Institute Berlin, 1994), pp. 11–12.

24. Cited in Jan B. de Weydenthal, 'Polish Foreign Policy after the Elections', *RFE/ RL Research Report*, vol. 2, no. 41, 15 October 1993, p. 17.

25. Jerzy Wiatr interview in, *Rzeczpospolita*, 24 September 1993, cited in *ibid.*, p. 18.

26. Interviews in Budapest, November 1994.

27. Horn interview in 'Ein NATO-Ungarn Wäre Keine Bedrohung Rußlands'.

28. Interview with Jozsef Szajer, Budapest, 17 November 1994.

29. Civilian control is not only a 'difficult concept for a military establishment that never had it', but also a matter of developing a civilian establishment with the knowledge and competence to take control, as István Gyarmati, Director of Security Policy in the Hungarian Ministry for Foreign Affairs, emphasises, 'we just don't have many civilian experts on military affairs'. From an interview in Budapest, 17 November 1994.

30. See István Szönyi, 'Minorities and NATO, The Twin Emphases of Hungarian Foreign Policy', *Südost Europa*, vol. 42, nos 11–12, 1993, p. 675.

31. Conversations with former Slovenian Foreign Minister, Lojze Peterle, and Finance Minister, Mitja Gaspari in Bled, Slovenia, 10 November 1994.

Chapter 8
NATO Enlargement and the Baltic States

Ronald D. Asmus and Robert C. Nurick

How to deal with the Baltic states in the context of NATO enlargement is one of the most delicate questions facing the Alliance. It is hardly a secret that NATO is preparing to take initial decisions on the 'who and when' of enlargement in early 1997. And it is also true that while no official 'short list' of primary candidates as yet exists, the Baltic states, for reasons detailed below, are unlikely to be in the first tranche of new Alliance members.

The improbability of near-term Baltic membership in NATO underscores the need for the Alliance to develop a strategy for strengthening Baltic independence and anchoring these states in the West. Baltic leaders fear that NATO enlargement to East-Central Europe will leave them in a kind of grey zone, exposed (as in the past) to Russian pressure and possible neo-imperial ambitions.

NATO has repeatedly pledged that enlargement will enhance the security of Europe as a whole and not produce new dividing lines. Few issues are more likely to test this proposition than the question of where the Baltic states fit into overall Western strategy. The issue of NATO enlargement and the Baltic states will also have an important echo in the domestic politics of Russia and the United States, as well as in the Nordic and other European countries. It is likely to become a high-profile policy issue within the Alliance and in the West's relations with Russia.

History has shown that events in the Baltics often have repercussions well beyond the region. If mishandled, the Baltic issue has the potential to derail

NATO enlargement, redraw the security map in North-eastern Europe and provoke a crisis between the West and Russia.

For all these reasons, NATO is unlikely to be able to implement enlargement successfully without a credible and coherent strategy for dealing with the Baltic states. Developing such a strategy should be a central part of NATO's self-proclaimed 'pre-accession strategy' which the Alliance has pledged to develop and which is designed to prepare the Alliance for successful enlargement. If the purpose of such a pre-accession strategy is to identify and to mitigate potential problems in the enlargement process, then forging a strategy towards the Baltic states should be a top priority.

This chapter defines the building blocks for such a strategy. Its point of departure is the assumption that in early 1997 NATO will officially decide to enlarge to Poland, the Czech Republic and Hungary around the end of the decade. It is in this political and strategic context that the Alliance will also have to define its strategy regarding the Baltic states. The Alliance's ability to craft such a strategy successfully will be crucial in determining the success of NATO enlargement.

NATO Enlargement: Why not the Baltic States?

The liberation of the Baltic states from Soviet rule is certainly one of the more remarkable chapters of the collapse of communism and the unravelling of the USSR.[1] Whereas many of the Soviet successor states had independence thrust upon them in 1991, the Baltic states broke away before the dissolution of the USSR; indeed, the Baltic striving for independence was a catalyst in the dismantling of the Soviet empire.

The Baltic states have experienced a tumultuous history in a region where Russia and key European powers have competed for strategic and ideological influence. Over the centuries the Baltic region has been occupied – often more than once – by Russia, Sweden, Poland and Germany. At the same time, the Baltic peoples have sustained a strong national identity under austere circumstances, an identity that is clearly tied to Europe and the West. Balts do not consider themselves to be part of the Slavic world; they refuse to be categorised as part of Russia's so-called 'near abroad'. They want to be viewed and treated as part of a Central Europe which was artificially cut off from the West by events beyond their control before, during and after the Second World War – on a par with countries such as Poland or the Czech Republic which are now seeking to 'rejoin' Europe.

At the same time, the Baltic states are still wrestling with the legacy of some five decades of integration in the former USSR. Nowhere is this more apparent than in the field of security and defence policy. Not only have the Baltic states had to create new security policies and a defence establishment from the ground up, but a whole host of unresolved issues from the Soviet era – such as the Russophone minorities, border issues, transit rights to

Kaliningrad – have created a unique set of security issues for these countries to grapple with.

As small states in a volatile region, the Baltic states also realise that they cannot fully guarantee their own security. Although they acknowledge the important political and economic components of security in contemporary Europe, their own history and concerns about real or imagined Russian ambitions have left them with limited faith in the promises of collective or 'soft' security.[2] Thus, while acknowledging the importance of regional cooperation and of maintaining friendly relations with Russia, the Baltic states have unambiguously stated that their goal is to become full members of the European Union and NATO – the two organisations they believe can anchor them to the West and provide real security – as soon as possible.

Neutrality or non-alignment as a foreign-policy option is widely and firmly rejected. Baltic diplomacy has taken important steps towards bringing these countries closer to European institutions. In mid-1994, the Baltic states signed free trade agreements with the EU and became associate-partners in the Western Economic Union (WEU). They signed 'Europe Agreements' with the EU in mid-1995 and now enjoy the same official associate-member status as the other six East-Central European states. The Baltic states have repeatedly stated their desire to become full NATO members and were among the first countries to sign up for NATO's Partnership for Peace (PFP) programme in early 1994. Despite a widespread view that the Visegrad countries (the Czech Republic, Hungary, Poland and Slovakia) are the leading candidates for NATO membership, the Baltic states have tried to avoid being isolated from or treated differently from the other Central European candidates.[3]

Why, then, will the Baltic states not be included in the first tranche of NATO enlargement? Some might argue that it is precisely the Baltic states that face a real security problem in today's Europe, a problem that is much more pronounced than, for example, those facing East-Central European countries that are unofficially considered the prime candidates for NATO membership. Comments in Russia's nationalist press openly call for revisionist policies aimed at subjugating or even annexing the Baltic states. While not numerous, such demands reinforce the impression within the Baltic states that they are exposed to a more pressing and real security danger than are other countries in Central Europe.

The current political reality, however, is that the Baltic states are unlikely to be included in the first tranche of NATO enlargement for one basic reason: insufficient political support for their candidacy. Simply put, they do not have the votes. While Poland today probably could muster sufficient support, Baltic membership in NATO is less popular.

Apart from Denmark, which has championed the Baltic cause in Alliance circles, it may well be the United States that has signalled the most public support and sympathy for Baltic concerns and aspirations. Even US support, however, has been limited. What the Baltic states most lack is the active support of the strongest European powers in the Alliance – Germany, France and the United Kingdom. Germany, perhaps the country with the greatest stake in NATO enlargement, has for historical and strategic reasons been reluctant to support Baltic membership publicly in the Alliance. Although the UK has traditionally been active in Northern European security, it was originally sceptical about enlargement and has not supported Baltic aspirations *vis-à-vis* the Alliance. France, while defending the principle that all members of the EU should also join the WEU, has also shown little enthusiasm for full Baltic membership in the WEU or the extension of the explicit security guarantee this would entail.

The reasons why there is such limited support for Baltic membership in NATO are fairly straightforward. They include:

• *Strategic Interest.* Whereas Poland's future is widely considered to be vital to the security and stability of Europe as a whole, many in the West – rightly or wrongly – do not see the Baltic states as an area of vital Western strategic interest. When many NATO members ask themselves whether the Alliance would and should be willing to go to war to defend the Baltic states against foreign aggression, the answer is often muted and unclear, and sometimes simply negative.

• *Russian Sensitivities.* Current Western conventional wisdom assumes that most Russians have accepted the 'loss' and independence of the Baltic states (in contrast to Ukraine, whose loss many Russians seemingly have not accepted). Nevertheless, incorporating a former part of the USSR into NATO would undoubtedly touch a very sensitive political nerve in Moscow. The Baltic states occupy a strategically important part of the Baltic littoral, potentially checking access to Saint Petersburg and separating the Russian enclave of Kaliningrad from the main body of the Russian federation. Baltic independence also deprived Russia of several key naval ports and air-defence radar facilities. Some Russian commentators have categorically stated that Moscow will not accept Baltic membership in NATO and that it would take countermeasures to prevent it. Few in the West are eager to challenge Moscow on this issue.

• *Minority Issues and Border Disputes.* While the Alliance is reluctant to take in any new members with minority problems or border disputes, the issue is especially sensitive with the Baltic states since these minority disputes involve Russians and Russia. Even if they can be resolved, it is difficult for some in the West to imagine a NATO member-state with a Russian minority – especially since Russian national security doctrine makes the protection of Russian minorities beyond Russia's current borders a priority.

- *Defensibility.* Geography, the small size and populations of the Baltic states, and the proximity of Russian military power underscores the problems that would be involved in extending a credible security guarantee to the Baltic states. Defensibility is obviously subject to interpretation and deterrence can come in different forms. Proponents of NATO enlargement to the Baltic states argue that deterrence can exist at different levels and that the Baltic states may be no less defensible, for example, than Denmark was at the height of the Cold War. Nevertheless, this dilemma clearly reinforces Western reluctance about, if not opposition to, Baltic membership in NATO, especially among military leaders.

- *Kaliningrad.* Kaliningrad and the Russian military presence there only reinforce these concerns. The former East Prussia was incorporated into the USSR under Joseph Stalin at the end of the Second World War. It is now a strategic military outpost, albeit one of uncertain long-term value. Troops from the former Soviet Union withdrawn from both the Baltic states and Eastern Europe have been stationed there. The issue of transit rights for the Russian military through Lithuania evokes memories of past corridor arrangements in the region that proved to be the source of subsequent conflict. NATO enlargement to the Baltic states would, in effect, encircle a piece of Russian territory, one that continues to host a major concentration of Russian military power.

These negative factors are not meant to suggest that the Baltic states should not or never will join NATO. But the Baltics' unique circumstances make them a special case. These points simply stress that the hurdles for Baltic membership in NATO are high – considerably higher than for many other countries.

The Imperatives of a Baltic Strategy

The fact that the Baltic states are unlikely to be in the first tranche of NATO enlargement only magnifies the need for a credible Western strategy aimed at sustaining their independence and security. Such a strategy must address five political and strategic imperatives.

First, the West needs to reassure the Baltic states and guard against the 'Korean syndrome' – the fear among many in the region that a NATO enlargement policy that excluded the Baltic states might be read by a hardline regime in Moscow as an invitation to take coercive action against those countries. Such concern assumes that pressure on the Baltic states might be one of the few instruments available for Moscow to demonstrate its displeasure with NATO, thus turning the region into a new confrontation zone. Alternatively, NATO enlargement could simply provide the pretence for action by a future nationalist or revanchist Russian government already intent on re-establishing its influence over the Baltic states. The issue is not only that of a direct Russian military move to reconquer the Baltic states but rather attempts to use political and economic pressure as well as military intimidation to force the Baltic states to be more deferential to Moscow. If NATO enlargement stabilises East-Central Europe but destabilises the Baltic region, it will hardly be deemed a success.

A second and related imperative is for Western leaders to consider the potential impact of enlargement on regional security in North-eastern Europe, and specifically on countries such as Finland and Sweden. Since the end of the Cold War, Nordic strategists have argued that the collapse of communism and the former USSR did not have as dramatic an impact on the Northern balance as it did, for example, in Central Europe. In Central Europe Soviet military power was withdrawn nearly 1,000 kilometres eastward, creating a double zone of newly independent states separating the Alliance from Russia. In Northern Europe, however, there were no shifts of a similar magnitude in the regional military balance.[4]

The geopolitical shift that has most improved Nordic security – in addition to the changed nature of the regime in Moscow – has been Baltic independence. In strategic terms, Baltic independence is to Finland and Sweden what the liberation of East-Central Europe has been to Germany. And just as Germany has made integrating the new democracies into organisations like the EU and NATO a main priority, the Nordic states see it as their top priority to preserve that gain in security and strategic depth as well.

Although Sweden and Finland are not in NATO, the Alliance cannot ignore the overall impact of enlargement on security in North-eastern Europe. Stockholm and Helsinki are concerned that NATO will enlarge to East-Central Europe, the Baltic states will be left in a vulnerable position, the Russians will react harshly, and that their own security will be eroded as a result. For this reason, some Swedish and Finnish commentary has oscillated between ongoing scepticism about NATO enlargement, and insistence that, if it is to occur, it also include the Baltic states in the first tranche.[5]

Nordic nervousness about NATO enlargement is further reinforced by the growing realisation that enlargement to East-Central Europe could fuel their own debates over security policy and their own relations with NATO. Old notions of neutrality have been undermined by several trends. In the Finnish case, after the end of the Cold War, Helsinki moved to renegotiate its bilateral treaty with Moscow, thereby effectively ending a status widely referred to in the West as 'Finlandisation'. Finland and Sweden have joined the EU, become observers in the WEU, joined NATO's PFP, and are currently participating in the Bosnian Peace Implementation Force (IFOR) under NATO – and US – command.

For the time being, Helsinki has chosen to rely on what one observer has termed security through 'osmosis' – a close security relationship in and with the West but one that does not include seeking or receiving formal security guarantees.[6] Finnish officials claim that they are satisfied with the status quo, that they do not suffer from any security deficit and that they are not seeking any additional security guarantees – while also carefully noting that they could reconsider their stance on NATO membership if circumstances change.[7]

A situation in which Swedish or Finnish leaders were to express doubts or even opposition to NATO enlargement would be awkward for the Alliance. At a minimum, these countries can be expected to make the question of how the Alliance plans to deal with the Baltic states a public – and possibly high-profile – issue. Equally important, NATO enlargement to East-Central Europe could also force the question of the desirability of possible northern enlargement of the Alliance onto the public agenda, especially in Finland. NATO enlargement is thus likely to make currently low-key Swedish and Finnish debates more public and raise new questions.

If post-Cold War Finland has truly opted to join 'the West', why should Helsinki not take the final step and become a full member in collective Western defence? Above all, what will Finland do if NATO enlarges, Western relations with Russia deteriorate and tension in North-eastern Europe increases? Would it return to its old policy of neutrality or seek to obtain a formal Western security guarantee? If Finland were to seek to join the Alliance, would NATO be open to taking it in – or would Helsinki suddenly find the door closed? In that case, might it not be preferable for Helsinki to pre-empt the problem by seeking to join prior to a deterioration in the security environment?

Such questions are already being considered not only in Helsinki; trends in the region raise a similar set of questions for Sweden as well, where neutrality and scepticism about NATO are much more deeply entrenched. Stockholm also has the added luxury of having Finland as a buffer between itself and Russia. At the same time, traditional Swedish foreign and defence policy is also being reshaped by factors as disparate as Swedish membership in the EU and deep defence cuts forced by the need for budgetary austerity. While the notion of Swedish membership in NATO remains heresy for many Swedish officials, especially in the current government, there is a growing number of Swedish voices in the media and elsewhere that are raising the issues of eventual Swedish membership in NATO. A Finnish debate over moves towards NATO would inevitably force the same set of issues to the fore in Stockholm.

The third imperative is that a Baltic strategy satisfy the internal political needs of other NATO states. The Baltic issue, for example, has always had a disproportionate impact on US political life. The US never recognised the incorporation of the Baltic states into the USSR during the Cold War. The Baltic-American community remains a well-organised and effective political force in US politics. No US President can run the risk of appearing to have 'sold out' the Baltic states and to have contributed to a 'new Yalta' in the context of enlargement.[8] It is therefore likely to be politically impossible for a US President to enlarge NATO to East-Central Europe without a credible strategy on the Baltic issue.

This political imperative is even more true for NATO allies such as Denmark, whose vital interests are directly affected by developments around the Baltic littoral. The Danish government has repeatedly emphasised its support for full Baltic membership in both the EU and NATO. In the words of Danish Prime Minister Poul Nyrup, 'there should be no first or second division with regard to membership in the EU and NATO'.[9] A Danish Prime Minister and parliament would also find it difficult to support NATO membership for East-Central Europe if they saw it as damaging to the Baltic region's security. More broadly, the Baltic issue will be seen as a critical test of the success of NATO's oft-repeated pledge that enlargement will enhance stability in Europe as a whole, not only for those states to which Alliance membership will be extended. In short, any Baltic strategy must satisfy NATO's own internal political requirements and consensus-building processes.

The fourth imperative is to facilitate EU enlargement to the Baltic states by helping to defuse security issues. To be sure, the key policy dilemmas in the EU enlargement debate have to do with burden-sharing among EU members and political and economic reform in candidate countries. But EU officials admit that it will be impossible to enlarge the EU to any countries in the East without clarifying the security and defence implications of enlargement. This is especially true in the case of Baltic membership. Security is seen in some EU countries as a major stumbling block – reportedly a significant reason why some key EU members believe the Baltic states should not be considered for early EU enlargement.[10]

The issue of Western security commitments (or the lack thereof) is thus already on the agenda. But the political reality is that the EU is unlikely to enlarge to include any of the Baltic states until and unless there is a coordinated strategy with NATO on how to handle Baltic security.

Finally, a Baltic strategy must take into account the question of Russia's relations with the West. The Baltic issue will be one of the most delicate in NATO's future relations with Russia, as well as in US–Russian relations. In the heady days of the collapse of the USSR, Boris Yeltsin and Russian democrats argued that Russia would be better off allowing Baltic independence and that the Balts could serve as a useful source of Western ideas and capital for a reforming Russia. Most Russian officials and commentators still insist that they are not opposed to the prospect of Baltic membership in the EU. They have, however, warned that Moscow will not accept Baltic membership in NATO, and some have said that, if NATO enlarges, they will take countermeasures to ensure that the Baltic states are not included. As Russian rhetoric against NATO enlargement has increased, Russian commentary on the Baltic issue has become more hardline as well.[11]

As Russian criticism of NATO's motives becomes even more pronounced during the 1996 presidential election campaign, the Baltic issue is likely to become a major issue in Russian domestic politics. This intensification, in turn, has increased Baltic nervousness about Russian intentions. Given the political sensitivity surrounding this issue in both Russian and US domestic politics, it has the potential to damage US–Russian relations and to undercut efforts to create a 'privileged partnership' between NATO and Russia.

These factors underscore the stakes involved and the need for NATO to develop a credible strategy on the Baltic issue – and the consequences if it does not. The question, therefore, is what should such a strategy look like?

The Building Blocks

To satisfy the sometimes competing imperatives just discussed, an Alliance strategy for the Baltic states must be based on multiple and complementary building blocks involving all the key regional actors. Properly coordinated, the sum of these building blocks should be greater than the sum of the individual parts. The critical components are:

• *Encouraging Political and Economic Reform.* One of the most important keys to future Baltic independence and security lies in the internal reform process in these countries. Successful political and economic reform is the precondition for Baltic independence, for Western integration, and for Western political support for Baltic foreign-policy objectives. The more successful the Baltic states are in terms of internal political and economic reform, the more likely they will be to receive Western support. Not only will it be easier to integrate them into Western institutions, but it will underline their independence and increase the distance these countries can put between themselves and their Soviet past. On the other hand, the potential faltering of that reform process still constitutes perhaps the greatest risk to the successful integration of these countries into the West. Although the progress the Baltic states have made thus far is impressive, they still clearly have some way to go in both political and economic terms.

One area that will be closely watched by both the West and Russia, and where progress is essential if the Baltic states are to enjoy continued Western support, is the treatment of the Russophone minority. The Russian-speaking minority in the Baltic states, largely concentrated in Estonia and Latvia, mushroomed under Soviet occupation as a consequence of successive large-scale migrations driven by the labour requirements of Moscow's industrialisation policies.[12] The scale of this influx, coupled with strong local memories of the deportations of large numbers of Balts during and immediately after the Second World War, left a legacy of resentment and distrust. For many Latvians and Estonians, the Russians are less immigrants than colonisers, imposed by Moscow, whose loyalties to the new state are at best uncertain and whose presence in such large numbers threatens Baltic political independence and cultural identity. The fact that the former Soviet military and security establishment is also well represented in this population has reinforced Baltic fears that some members of the Russophone community could be susceptible to appeals by revanchist political forces in Moscow that might seek to mobilise the community as a potential fifth column.

These attitudes and fears have been reflected in Estonian and Latvian policies which, especially in the immediate post-1991 years, many outside observers judged to be excessively harsh. In Estonia, the great majority of the Russophone community was not granted automatic citizenship, and the requirements spelled out in the 1992 Law on Citizenship appeared to make naturalisation a long and difficult process. In Latvia, no relevant legislation was enacted at all until 1994: until then Russian-speakers were left in a stateless limbo; they have since been subject to stringent quotas on naturalisation. Not surprisingly, these and related policies have been much resented by the Russians in the region, many of whom have few remaining ties to Russia proper, feel little responsibility for the policies of the USSR, and have voiced support for the sovereignty of the new Baltic states.[13]

Baltic policies have evolved over time. Successive Estonian governments have submitted their legislation to outside review, and have been responsive to Western advice. Latvian legislation, too, has come under broader scrutiny, and at least to a degree has been softened as a result.[14] Both Estonia and Latvia argue that their current legislation now conforms to general European norms. Most outside observers concur. But while the situation confronting the Russian-speaking minorities situation is not as bad as some politicians in Moscow allege, unfortunately it is also not as invulnerable to criticism as Baltic officials sometimes claim. The laws themselves remain very stringent, and – perhaps more important – there still appear to be real problems with implementation.[15]

In any case, the minority issue for the Baltics is not primarily a legal one. Resolving the minority issue is not only a precondition for Western political support and assistance; it is a key to the internal stability of these states. The Baltic states cannot achieve true internal stability if they house a large and potentially embittered Russian minority. The best way to secure the future loyalty of this minority is to insure that they, too, have a stake in Baltic independence and the reform process.

• *Baltic Defence Cooperation.* Defence and security cooperation must also be an important component in any strategy designed to strengthen Baltic independence. Baltic security needs to start with the Baltic states themselves. These countries are still in the process of creating and building their national defence establishments. Even though a Russian attack against the Baltic states is currently unlikely, it is not implausible, especially if relations with Russia deteriorate and a nationalistic revanchist regime comes to power in Moscow.

Against this backdrop, the Alliance should encourage the Baltic countries to expand their existing security and military cooperation arrangements.

Although the Baltic states themselves are at times divided on the desirability of a defence union expanded cooperation should be encouraged as a stepping-stone towards a more effective regional security and defence arrangement.[16] Joint defence efforts would be more efficient as well as make the Baltic states more serious partners for cooperation with NATO, regardless of whether they eventually become members. Finally, in political terms it is important for the Baltic states to show that they are seriously committed to defence and that they are not 'free riders'.

Some commentators suggest that geography, the small populations of the Baltic states and Russia's overwhelming power mean that the Baltic states are 'indefensible'. They argue that military capabilities can, therefore, hardly play an important role in their national security policies since resisting a Russian attack would be futile if such a move were to occur. Security in Europe, however, is much more than a game of simple force balances. Deterrence comes in many forms. One can also conceive of attempts at political intimidation or limited conflict short of a massive and deliberate aggression in which modest military capabilities can be important.

The objective of Baltic national defence can thus be something less than the ability to defeat an attack by overwhelming force. Their national defence doctrine should aim to create a national defence system that could, within modest funding constraints, significantly raise the price that a potential aggressor would have to pay and deny it the option of a quick or painless military victory. Such a development would in itself complicate the military calculus of an aggressive Russia contemplating an attack on the Baltic states, could provide additional warning time to the West; it would also create an important element of deterrence. It is for these reasons that the Baltic and Nordic states expressed such strong concern over a revision of the northern-flank issue on Conventional Armed Forces in Europe (CFE).[17]

The most promising model for Baltic defence, at least in the interim, is a version of the Finnish national defence system. Such a defence system should be created so that it can be integrated into and contribute to broader regional and international cooperative security efforts. By participating in broader efforts, such as IFOR, the Baltic states prove that they are both 'producers' as well as 'consumers' of security. The successful experience of the Baltic battalion (BALTBAT), for example, should be expanded in the years ahead. Baltic airspace should be integrated with that of the West in a fashion akin to the Central European Regional Airspace Initiative. The Initiative is designed to integrate those countries into Europe's wider civilian air-traffic control system; this would also facilitate the development of a regional air-defence communications capability.

Such steps should lead to a situation in which the Baltic states approach the defence status currently enjoyed by countries like Sweden or Finland: countries possessing modern militaries with a heavy emphasis on a national self-sufficiency doctrine; but also countries that have very close relations with NATO and are capable of being integrated into NATO at short notice, if and when that political decision is taken. Creating such a system will undoubtedly take time, perhaps a decade. What is important is establishing the proper direction for the Baltic states and generating the momentum for the needed steps along this path, a process that can then be actively supported by the West.

• *Nordic–Baltic Cooperation.* The ability of the Baltic states to reform themselves politically, economically and militarily will also depend on expanded cooperation with the Nordic states. The Nordic states are a diverse group. Their roles and interests regarding the Baltic states vary. They are nevertheless the main conduit for Western ideas and know-how, economic aid and investment, as well as security and military assistance.

In the area of security assistance, Denmark has assumed a leading role in setting up military cooperation agreements with the five countries around the Baltic rim – Poland, the three Baltic states and Russia. Within Alliance councils, it has championed the cause of NATO enlargement to the Baltic states. Military cooperation with the Baltic states has included advice and material support in establishing a defence resource management system, training for Baltic officers, legal and budgetary expertise, expanded staff exercises and the development of a Combined Baltic Naval Training group. Perhaps most important, it has been a key force behind BALTBAT, the joint peacekeeping battalion. In addition to the Baltic states, the project involves the Nordic countries, the UK, the US, Germany, France and the Netherlands. The supporting countries, notably the Nordic countries and the UK, assist with training BALTBAT soldiers and by donating equipment, weapons and ammunition. Baltic platoons have also been trained by Denmark and then fully integrated into the Danish peacekeeping battalion in Croatia; they were included under Danish auspices in the Nordic brigade in IFOR, thus giving them practical, on-the-job training.[18]

In contrast, Norway has adopted a low profile within NATO and within the Nordic Council. Outside the Alliance, Finland has sustained a low-key public role while quietly and pragmatically helping to train the Baltic militaries. Although the current Swedish Social Democratic-led government has not associated itself with some of the more forceful statements made by Carl Bildt when he was Prime Minister regarding Swedish interests in the Baltic states, in practical terms Stockholm has remained active in promoting security cooperation. Sweden and Finland have been heavily involved in helping the Baltic states with internal security as well.

The Nordic countries are currently not willing or able to extend a formal security guarantee to the Baltic states – and the strategy proposed here does not call on them to do so. Nonetheless, an essential building block of any

Alliance strategy to safeguard the Baltic states must be to encourage the Nordic countries to further their own political, economic and military involvement in, and cooperation with, the Baltic states. The Nordic countries are reluctant to expand their role much beyond what they are doing at present for both economic and political reasons. In Denmark there is a quiet debate about how high a profile Copenhagen should have on Baltic issues. Although Finland has shed 'Finlandisation', caution and a careful balancing act remain the hallmarks of Finnish diplomacy. Sweden today faces major cuts in defence expenditures as Stockholm moves to cut its budget deficits.

Many commentators in these countries suggest that they are already providing significant amounts of assistance and can hardly be expected to do more. But the Baltic issue is arguably the key national security issue facing these countries in the years ahead. Preserving that gain in security and strategic depth must logically be a top national security priority for these countries, and resource decisions should be restructured accordingly. Against this background, it should be possible for them to find additional resources, especially if they concentrate and coordinate their efforts.

The current constraints on the willingness of the Nordics to provide more assistance are not only economic, however. They are also political. These countries fear that more active involvement in the Baltic states will at some point provoke a Russian reaction to their efforts aimed both at the Baltic states and at themselves. They are especially concerned that such efforts – unless they are backed up by the support of the US and the major European powers – could leave them dangerously isolated in a future disagreement with Moscow.

The risk of an undesirable Russian reaction to Western security assistance would nevertheless clearly be much greater if, for example, non-Nordic countries and leading NATO powers such as the US or Germany assumed this role. The Nordic countries are the obvious partners because their presence in the region is more natural and more easily acceptable to Moscow and because it is the Nordic countries' defence doctrine and system that Western strategy should encourage the Baltic states to emulate.

Finally, the Nordic connection offers another opportunity to bring the Baltic states closer to NATO. Denmark has clearly taken the lead in this regard, but Finland and Sweden are also expanding their ties with NATO countries. Each is actively involved in PFP as well as in peace-support activities. Expanded cooperation between the Nordic countries and the Baltic states thereby brings the latter closer to NATO. Through this link, Sweden, Finland and the Baltic countries are all working closely with NATO forces in Bosnia, helping to create the broader web of ties and cooperation that contributes to security and deterrence around the Baltic littoral.

• *EU Enlargement to the Baltic States.* EU enlargement is a central, and perhaps *the* central building block of this strategy. In an ideal world, the three

Baltic countries would be brought into the EU together – and soon. Certainly, accession negotiations with the three (as well as with the other EU candidate members) should commence at the same time. But the three Baltic states are not equally close to meeting the EU's requirements for membership: at present, it appears that Estonia could qualify for the first tranche of EU enlargement, but Latvia and Lithuania probably could not. Under such circumstances, the difficult choice will be between waiting – perhaps for some time – until all three are ready, or moving ahead with the strongest candidate as soon as possible.

It is not any easy choice, but on balance the latter course seems preferable, so as to maximise the prospects that at least one Baltic country would be included in the first tranche of new EU members.

Such a move would set the important precedent of making at least one Baltic state part of 'the West'. It would *de facto* extend an element of deterrence since any Russian intervention – or threat of intervention – in an EU member-state would have serious consequences for its relations with Europe as a whole. Thus a form of linkage between Russian behaviour towards the Baltic states and the EU's overall relationship with Russia would be established. Ultimately, the three Baltic states would all be better off if at least one of them is included in the first tranche of EU enlargement.

The EU would need to work out an understanding with Estonia that it would not opt for full WEU membership. The Baltic states themselves would have to realise that any attempt to blackmail or shame the West into giving a security guarantee which it is not yet prepared to give will only backfire. Instead, the agreement would be that WEU and NATO membership for the Baltic states would come, if at all, as a package. This would help ease Western concerns about prematurely extending a security guarantee and lower many of the inhibitions in EU countries about bringing even a single Baltic country in as part of the first tranche.

Given their small size, the Baltic states would not pose an enormous economic burden on EU members. While the Nordic EU members favour bringing all three Baltic states into the EU, some officials have suggested in private that the EU might adopt an initial balanced enlargement package including Cyprus and Malta in the south, the Czech Republic, Hungary and Poland in East-Central Europe; and perhaps one Baltic state in Northern Europe as an interim step.

The prospects for early Estonian membership in the EU will hinge upon creating a sufficiently strong coalition of countries in the EU willing to make it a top priority. Apart from the Nordic countries, the country whose vote will be essential if Estonia is to be included in the first tranche of EU enlargement is Germany. If Germany commits itself to this goal, France is likely to follow and British opposition will be mitigated.

And, lest the institutional burden of integrating the Baltic states into the West fall almost exclusively on NATO, it is also a basic US and Alliance interest that EU enlargement into the region proceed expeditiously. Washington should therefore encourage Bonn and its other European allies to take this step.

Although NATO and the EU have carefully avoided linking their respective enlargement processes, the political reality is that prospects for the two are intertwined. For example, if the prospects for EU enlargement to East-Central Europe falter, it will make it harder for NATO to enlarge as well. On the other hand, a carefully coordinated orchestration and harmonisation of EU and NATO enlargement would reinforce the shared political and strategic goal of extending stability to the region. For the Baltic states, the equation is different because NATO membership is currently not likely. At the same time, the political reality is that the EU is unlikely to enlarge to the Baltic states unless there is an accepted overall Western strategy on how to handle the security issue. Since NATO has a strong interest in seeing the EU enlarge to the Baltic region, it must coordinate its strategy with that of the EU.

Ideally, the EU would extend membership to Estonia at the same time as NATO enlarges to Poland. Such a development no longer seems possible as the EU timetable increasingly slips beyond the turn of the decade. If the EU cannot match NATO's timetable, it is crucial that it make clear its intent to enlarge to the Baltic states as soon as is feasible, in order to demonstrate that enlargement is a political *fait accompli*. Such an attitude depends on the EU's ability to work out a compromise on a number of issues at the 1996 Inter-governmental Conference that would open the door for enlargement.

• *An 'Open Door' Strategy on NATO Membership.* Keeping the NATO door open for eventual Baltic membership is another key building block in this strategy. Although some have suggested that the Alliance should explicitly rule out Baltic membership in this context in order to ease Russian anxieties, not to leave the door open on the NATO membership issue could have a strong negative political impact in the Baltic states and undermine the reform process. It might also be interpreted by some political forces in Moscow as a green light for political and/or military pressure against the Baltic states. And, as mentioned earlier, it will be politically difficult for the United States and some European NATO allies to implement NATO enlargement to East-Central Europe if it is perceived as 'selling out' the Baltic states.

Therefore, at the same time that the Alliance announces its intent to enlarge to East-Central Europe, it should publicly confirm that the door remains open for eventual membership in NATO for the Baltic republics. Alliance officials in Washington and key European capitals should make it clear that this is not just a passive and rhetorical commitment, but that the US and its allies are committed to creating the conditions that will eventually make Baltic membership in NATO possible. In parallel to these steps, NATO should announce an expanded programme of PFP activities in the Baltic region. This programme would expand cooperation between NATO and non-NATO members such as Sweden, Finland and the Baltic republics – and include Russia. It must be in place and functioning well before NATO actually enlarges towards the end of the decade. The goal should be to cast a cloak of cooperation around the Baltic states to provide an additional element of deterrence.

NATO can also contribute to new patterns of cooperation among key regional actors in creative ways. In the current IFOR set-up in Bosnia, for example, NATO created a situation in which the Nordic brigade – comprising NATO Danish and Norwegian troops, non-NATO Swedish, Finnish and Polish forces as well as contingents from the Baltic states – operates next to Russian troops, all under US command and Alliance auspices. Thus, nearly all the key players in Baltic security find themselves cooperating on the ground in Bosnia under an Alliance umbrella – something that would currently be almost inconceivable if attempted in the Baltic region. Although a modest step, this underscores how the Alliance helps bridge a variety of existing fault-lines and brings together countries in unprecedented patterns of defence cooperation.

At the same time, key Alliance members should start to develop a strategy aimed at chipping away or mitigating the obstacles to eventual Baltic membership in NATO outlined above. This effort must acknowledge that the Baltic states cannot resolve many of these issues on their own, and that both NATO countries and non-NATO countries such as Sweden and Finland must play a central and credible role in addressing these issues and developing specific strategies on each of the obstacles listed earlier.

Finally, the Alliance must also allow for the broader dynamics under way in Northern Europe, above all the issue of possible enlargement in the region. This will require the Alliance first to clarify its own interests and priorities. Although Danish – and some German – leaders speak about the desirability of NATO eventually enlarging to the North, many in the Alliance might be sceptical about, if not opposed to, the prospect of Finland in NATO, given its 1,200-km border with Russia. Others, however, would support the entry of Finland, Sweden and the Baltic states as a Northern package – but only an appropriate future date. In any case, eventual Baltic membership in the Alliance is far from likely to occur, at all, in combination with a Northern enlargement of NATO.

Meanwhile, the political reality is that over the next 12 months NATO will make decisions in three areas which will affect Baltic and Nordic security for the next decade. These three areas include decisions about who will be included in the first tranche of an enlarged NATO; likely attempts to reach an understanding with Russia to mitigate the feared negative consequences that NATO enlargement could have on relations with Moscow; and agreement on NATO structural reform, above all future military command structures. Will the Alliance, for example, build into its new command structures a door that could subsequently be opened to facilitate enlargement to North-eastern Europe?

These linkages are not well understood at present; they are certainly not part of the public debate. Many officials in Northern Europe still see decisions on NATO enlargement either as distant or as something that will not directly affect them. Others are simply in denial that enlargement will take place at all. But these attitudes are likely to change as the reality of NATO enlargement becomes more concrete and its potential ramifications become more apparent. In the final analysis, the Baltic issue should be embedded where it belongs – in a broader reassessment of NATO's strategy in Northern Europe.

• *Dealing with Moscow.* The Alliance strategy outlined here seeks to enmesh the Baltic countries into a web of bilateral, multilateral and institutional ties with the West, without provoking a Russian reaction that increases the security threats to those states or seriously undermines other Western policy objectives towards Russia. This will not be easy to achieve, especially as long as NATO enlargement remains so contentious in Russia's relations with the West, and when the security alignments of the Baltic states have themselves become a highly sensitive issue in Russian domestic politics. Moscow can be expected to resent any strategy that it views as further marginalising its role in Europe or as indifferent to its legitimate security concerns there; it will react especially harshly to a strategy that it perceives as a stepping-stone to Baltic membership in NATO.

In past months, the Russian press has carried a number of ominous warnings against the prospect of Baltic membership in NATO. Although they sometimes imply that Moscow may not be able to halt the accession of East-Central European countries into NATO, such commentaries have suggested that Moscow draw a line to prevent a second round of accession that could include the Baltic states. One study went so far as to claim that such a move would give Moscow the political and moral right to invade these countries.[19] Another apparently laid out specific scenarios for a Russian reoccupation of the Baltic states, potentially as early as 1996 or 1997.[20]

Even Western-oriented and reformist Russian governments are likely to press for official or unofficial assurances from Western countries that Baltic accession to NATO will not occur, and to warn of the consequences both for Russia's domestic transformation and for East–West relations if their pleas are ignored. Some officials will continue to threaten to take steps to prevent it, and a future nationalistic government might conceivably act on such threats. The potential costs for Russian–Western relations are therefore considerable. A key task for NATO will be to minimise those costs as much as possible.

First, it will be especially important to keep the Organisation for Security and Cooperation in Europe (OSCE) – and other relevant Western institutions fully engaged in monitoring the situation – to demonstrate that the West is not indifferent to legitimate Russian grievances, to work with the Nordic countries in pressing the Baltic states where necessary to take further initiatives and dampen the risks of real conflict, to document the real progress that has been achieved and to make it more difficult for Russian political forces to exaggerate and exploit the issue for their own purposes.

Second, where possible the West should seek to address the stark military disparities in the region that heighten the Baltic states' sense of insecurity. On CFE, the West should be flexible in accepting arrangements necessary to ease the real Russian burdens which resulted from the withdrawal of their forces from Eastern Europe, or designed to accommodate reasonable force requirements stemming from the new security threats emerging in and to Russia's south. What should be avoided, however, are permanent arrangements which allow for increased Russian force levels in the north – as if the West accepted the notion that Russia faces new security threats from the Baltic region as well.

Dealing with the heavy concentration of Russian military forces in the Kaliningrad *oblast* may prove an even more difficult problem, at least in the short term. Over the longer term, however, the Russian military may find the alleged strategic benefits of its Kaliningrad 'bastion' to be a distinctly waning asset; some officers are already beginning to question whether its value is worth the cost. Local pressures for economic liberalisation – and thus demilitarisation – may also grow. Evident Western readiness to invest in the area could help encourage such developments, although lingering Russian suspicions of US and especially German intentions in the Kaliningrad region may make it advisable for other countries to take the lead.

Third, as noted above, Russia should be included in the emerging web of multilateral security cooperation wherever possible and the West should look for ways to encourage constructive Russian–Baltic interactions in the security field. For understandable historical reasons, the Baltic states may resist such initiatives. Russia may resist them as well. But precisely because both Baltic and Russian wariness on these matters is so deep-seated, it is in the West's interest to begin to break down old reflexes on both sides. The routine scheduling of joint Russian/Baltic participation in PFP exercises is one obvious vehicle. More difficult, but perhaps equally important in political terms, would be to find ways to enable Russian participation in broader cooperative security arrangements specifically designed for the Baltic area, such as the standing Baltic Sea Force proposed in December 1995 by the WEU Assembly.

It will also be important for the West to develop its multilateral institutions in a way which demonstrates to Russia that the integration of the Baltic states into the EU need not unduly or unfairly complicate Russia's own dealings with it. The reason for this is simple – the belief among some Russians that the ingrained hostility of Baltic governments will inevitably rub off on those Western institutions. Russia does not now officially object to Baltic accession to the European Union; a hardening of its position in this regard could complicate any Baltic security strategy which relies heavily, as this one does, on the EU role.

Squaring this circle will be difficult. It may not be possible. But it must be attempted. Managing these competing demands will require some forbearance by both NATO and the Baltic states themselves – many obstacles will have to be overcome and will often require low-key and quiet diplomacy. It will also require a consistent and clear message to Moscow that Russian policies and behaviour towards the Baltic states will affect its overall relations with the West, for better or worse. In the final analysis, the West's real source of leverage in its relations with Russia derives from the ties between continued political, economic and financial relations with Moscow and Russia's attitude towards the Baltic states.

Benefits, Risks and Requirements

If successfully implemented, the strategy outlined here promises several important benefits. First, by elevating Estonia to a status similar to that currently enjoyed by Sweden and Finland – full membership in the EU, partial membership in the WEU, and expanded cooperation with NATO under PFP – it would provide an institutional manifestation of the West's commitments to and engagement in the Baltic region. This, in turn, would help stabilise the area as a whole, and create incentives for Latvia and Lithuania to accelerate their own reforms in order to obtain similar institutional benefits for themselves. At the same time, the strategy deliberately sidesteps the 'back door' security guarantee issue which full WEU membership would raise. This should make it easier for the EU to accept these states, easier for Russian governments to acquiesce to EU membership for them, and easier for NATO countries to support the overall process.

To be sure, the strategy proposed here does not correspond to the long-term aspirations of the Baltic states. But it should suffice as a compromise and as an interim step. This policy buys time for the Baltic countries to try to build political support for their own objectives, for the West to develop a better sense of its own objectives, and for Russia to continue to adjust to the new political and strategic situation in Europe. At the same time, this strategy candidly acknowledges the real obstacles to eventual Baltic membership in the Alliance and tries to develop strategies to alleviate them.

Second, the strategy is designed to share the burdens within the West. It thus mitigates both Swedish and Finnish apprehensions that they will be left to cope with the regional aftermath of NATO enlargement on their own, and it eases concerns in many NATO countries that Stockholm and Helsinki will not 'pull their own weight' in contributing to security around the Baltic Sea. It acknowledges, however, that an active NATO role will be critical. NATO – and only NATO – can create the overall security framework which will make it easier for the EU to enlarge to the Baltic states and easier for non-NATO countries to become more involved as well.

Finally, the strategy seeks to acknowledge Russian sensitivities while avoiding 'deals' that would compromise the principles NATO has embraced as the basis for future European security and which would be difficult to sustain politically. How Moscow will view such a strategy is, of course, a key question. Despite the increasingly harsh rhetoric that can be found in some Russian commentaries on the Baltic states, there are also other, more measured voices as well. Russia's long-standing Ambassador to Helsinki, Yuri Deryabin, for example, has suggested that the Baltic states strive for a security status similar to that of Finland and Sweden, noting that Russia would not object if a country like Estonia were to cooperate on security matters with Finland.[21] If such a policy approach were to prevail in Moscow, the Baltic states, Russia and the West could perhaps agree on this as a compromise intermediate step while agreeing to disagree on what a longer-term resolution might look like.

Implementing this strategy will not be easy. It requires overcoming the impediments to early Estonian accession to the EU. It assumes that an understanding can be reached with Estonia that it, like Sweden, will not press for full WEU membership when it joins the EU. And it depends upon the readiness of both the Nordic countries and NATO members to assume some new burdens and costs. Such a strategy will require a degree of coordination and harmonisation of policies among diverse actors that will only take place if this issue is made a high policy priority and if an effective policy coordination mechanism is established.

Notes

1. For further details see Anatol Lieven, *The Baltic Revolution* (New Haven, CT: Yale University Press, 1993).

2. For a useful overview of Baltic attitudes on security and defence issues, see Eitvydas Bajarunas, Mare Haab and Ilmars Viksne, 'The Baltic States: Security and Defence After Independence', *Chaillot Papers*, no. 19 (Paris: Institute for Security Studies of the Western European Union, June 1995).

3. Estonian President Lennart Meri has gone so far as to insist that any attempt by NATO to differentiate between the Baltic states and other East-Central European countries would be tantamount to a new form of 'appeasement'. See 'Estland besteht auf NATO-Mitgliedschaft: Sorge Über Haltung des Westens', *Frankfurter Allgemeine Zeitung*, 24 August 1995.

4. See Krister Wahlbäck, 'Der unwägbare Osten: Eine schwedische Sicht neuer Sicherheitsprobleme', *Europa Archiv*, vol. 48, no. 3, 10 February 1993, p. 61.

5. Carl Bildt, 'The Baltic States Belong Inside the Line Between NATO and Russia', *International Herald Tribune*, 5–7 May 1995.

6. See Christoph Bertram, 'Mehr Sicherheit durch Osmose', *Die Zeit*, no. 10, 4 March 1994.

7. See *Security in A Changing World: Guidelines for Finland's Security Policy*, a Report by the Council of State to the Finnish Parliament, 6 June 1995.

8. Former US Secretary of State James Baker's memoirs contain several examples of when Baltic–Russian tensions threatened to torpedo US–Soviet relations because of the repercussions such events had in US domestic politics and on the President. See James A. Baker III, *The Politics of Diplomacy: Revolution, War and Peace 1989–1992* (New York: G. P. Putnam's Sons, 1995).

9. See Nyrup's remarks, made during a tour of the three Baltic states, 26–31 March 1995, in *Berlingske Tidende*, 31 March 1995.

10. Following the December 1995 EU summit in Madrid, the *Financial Times* reported that German Chancellor Helmut Kohl had argued that the Baltic states should not be considered in the first wave of EU enlargement because to do so would encourage their desire for a defence guarantee. See 'Kohl Snubs the Baltics', *Financial Times*, 15 December 1995.

11. For example, Defence Minister Grachev has warned that Russia would hammer together a competing military-political bloc of the CIS countries if the Baltic states were to join NATO. See the report in Jamestown Foundation, *Monitor*, 26 September 1995.

12. See, for example, Chauncy D. Harris, 'The New Russian Minorities. A Statistical Overview', *Post-Soviet Geography*, vol. 34, no. 1, 1995; and Martin Klaft, 'Russians in the "Near Abroad"', *Radio Free Europe/Radio Liberty Research Report*, 19 August 1994.

13. For background on the Russophone minorities, see Lieven, *The Baltic Revolution*, especially chapter 7; Paul Kostvo, 'The New Russian Diaspora', *Journal of Peace Research*, vol. 30, 2 May 1993; Klaft, 'Russians in the "Near Abroad"'; Philip Hansen, 'Estonia's Narva problem, Narva's Estonian Problem', *Radio Free Europe/Radio Liberty Research Report*, 30 April 1993; and Richard Rose and William Daley, 'Conflict or Compromise in the Baltic States', *Radio Free Europe/Radio Liberty Research Report*, 15 July 1994.

14. For example, Latvia's 1994 Citizenship Law was liberalised slightly, to grant automatic citizenship to graduates of Latvian language secondary schools, and the legal status of most non-citizens has now been defined.

15. In Estonia, for example, the language requirements for naturalisation were, if anything, toughened in 1995. Implementation problems range from inadequate resources available for language training to charges that the language exams are sometimes administered in an arbitrary fashion. For recent assessments, see the series of US State Department reports, 'Estonia Human Rights Practices, 1995', 'Latvia Human Rights Practices, 1995', and 'Lithuania Human Rights Practices, 1995' (Washington DC: US Department of State, March 1996). Also see the UN International Convention on Civil and Political Rights (CCPR) Human Rights Committee, 'Consideration of Reports Submitted by State Parties Under Article 40 of the Covenant', CCPR/C/79/Add. 59, 3 November 1995, and Hearings Before the Committee on Security and Cooperation in Europe, 'Implementation of the Helsinki Accords: Ethnic Russians in the Baltic States', 10 August 1992.

16. For further details on Baltic defence cooperation see Juris Dalbins, 'Baltic Cooperation – the Key to Wider Security', *NATO Review*, no. 1, January 1996, pp. 7–10; Vidmantas Purlys and Gintautas Vilkelis, 'Cooperation Between the Baltic States: A Lithuanian View', *NATO Review*, no. 5, September 1995, pp. 27–31; and the 'Joint Statement of the Ministers of Defence of the Republic of Estonia, the Republic of Latvia and the Republic of Lithuania', Tallinn, 23 January 1996.

17. This option, however, would quickly disappear if the Russian military presence in the Pskov region – and perhaps even Novgorod – were to be allowed to grow to such a level that the military situation in the Baltic states would appear hopeless.

18. A useful overview of Nordic efforts, especially those of Denmark, can be found in *Defence Cooperation Around the Baltic Sea in 1996: Documentation from the Danish Ministry of Defence* (Copenhagen: Danish Ministry of Defence, December 1995). See also Hans Haekkerup, 'Cooperation Around the Baltic Sea: Danish Perspectives and Initiatives', *NATO Review*, no. 3, May 1995, pp. 14–18.

19. See the abstract of a study by the Institute of Defence Studies, Moscow, which suggested that the treatment of the Russophone minority coupled with attempts by the Baltic states to join NATO would justify Russian military action against the Baltic states, *Segodnya*, 20 October 1995. Although Russian Foreign Ministry officials disclaimed these views, the document was the object of considerable attention – and some alarm – in the Baltic states. See, for example, the *Baltic Observer*, (Riga), 26 October–1 November 1995. See also the interview with Anton Surikov, one of the authors of the study, entitled 'Who is Dying to Get Under the Wing?', *Sovetskaya Rossiya*, 2 November 1995.

20. The circumstances surrounding this case are especially peculiar: in mid-1995, the nationalist Russian press carried an anonymous article entitled 'Will Russian Troops Invade the Baltics?', summarising an ostensible study by a previously unknown research institute called 'Feliks', presumed to be linked to Russian intelligence. For further details see Bernd Nielsen-Stokkebye, 'Was Feliks zu sagen hat', *Frankfurter Allgemeine Zeitung*, 22 June 1995.

21. See the interview with Yuri Deryabin entitled 'Deryabin: Sweden Talks More Clearly About Neutrality Than Finland, Russian Envoy Urges Baltics To Remain Non-Allied', *Helsingin Sanomat*, 11 December 1995.

Chapter 9
The Costs of NATO Enlargement

Ronald D. Asmus, Richard L. Kugler and F. Stephen Larrabee

What will it cost to enlarge NATO? The question of costs is moving to the forefront in the enlargement debate as the Alliance prepares to decide on a first tranche of new members. Opponents of enlargement insist that the costs will be so high that enlargement should not take place. Proponents claim that the costs are affordable. Across the Alliance, elected officials – those who control the purse-strings – are starting to inquire what enlargement will mean for the tax-payer – American, British, Polish or other.

Establishing what NATO enlargement will cost is not just a financial calculation, but also a political and strategic one. The costs of enlargement will depend on who joins the Alliance, how new Article 5 commitments are implemented in terms of military strategy, how defence postures in both new and old members are adjusted, and how the financial burdens are distributed among NATO members. Addressing the cost issue requires the Alliance to grapple with many problems that have previously been held in abeyance. The Alliance cannot move forward on enlargement and expect the support of NATO parliaments and publics unless it clarifies the implications and consequences of enlargement, including its costs.

This chapter provides a framework and methodology for assessing what NATO enlargement will cost, as well as estimates for a range of alternative defence postures that an enlarged NATO might embrace. Providing such estimates requires making some assumptions on issues that the Alliance has not yet officially decided. For illustrative purposes, the analysis presented here assumes that the first tranche of enlargement will concentrate on the Visegrad countries – Poland, the Czech Republic, Hungary and Slovakia – even though the latter's prospects have clearly diminished. The framework and methodology used, however, could easily be applied to a broader as well as a narrower list of candidate countries.

The methodology employed here calculates what it would cost to fund measures associated with enlargement. This does not mean, however, that NATO budgets must rise by an equivalent amount. Savings might be made elsewhere in order to permit enlargement with little or no increase in overall spending. Moreover, it is important to point out the risks and costs of not enlarging, especially if this leads to new instability in East-Central Europe. If East-Central Europe had to be defended without NATO, the costs to the countries in the region and to the Alliance could be much higher. Whereas critics of enlargement in the US insist that it will drain US military resources away from higher-priority global missions, such a view is short sighted. By stabilising East-Central Europe, enlargement not only reduces the potential for instability in this historically troubled region; it also allows the US and its European NATO allies to focus on other potential crisis areas beyond Europe's borders.

Figure 1: Establishing the Framework

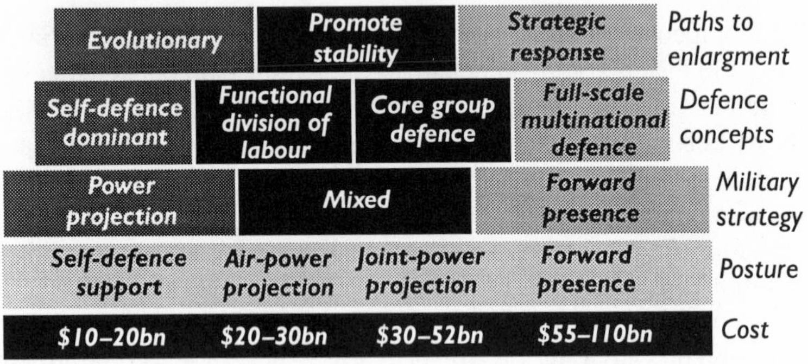

Evolutionary	Promote stability	Strategic response		Paths to enlargment
Self-defence dominant	Functional division of labour	Core group defence	Full-scale multinational defence	Defence concepts
Power projection	Mixed		Forward presence	Military strategy
Self-defence support	Air-power projection	Joint-power projection	Forward presence	Posture
$10–20bn	$20–30bn	$30–52bn	$55–110bn	Cost

This chapter provides general cost estimates in order to assist Alliance leaders in making basic political and strategic judgements. Its specific objectives are threefold. First, building on the analytical framework of chapter 5, we define a spectrum of possible defence postures and calculate their associated budgetary costs.[1] Over a 10–15 year period, the budget cost for the entire Alliance could be as low as $10 billion or as high as $110bn, depending on the posture chosen. This spectrum covers a wide range of alternatives from the least to the most ambitious (see Figure 1).

Second, we establish a political and military framework for assessing which posture NATO should choose. Our analysis is based both on the analytical framework established in chapter 5, as well as the initial criteria laid down in the 1995 'Study on NATO Enlargement'. The answer to the question 'how much is enough?' requires NATO to examine its assumptions regarding the political rationale for enlargement and the specific military requirements to be fulfilled.

Third, and equally important, we examine the set of political and military trade-offs inherent in deciding how to build the posture and how to distribute the burdens among both current and new members.

The costs of NATO enlargement are likely to be modest for several reasons. NATO enlargement is currently not threat-driven; rather, it is part of an overall strategy of projecting stability to the region and unifying Europe. The strategic requirements that NATO will have to fulfill under enlargement are moderate and will remain so, barring a future deterioration in Europe's strategic environment.

Enlargement will raise important military issues and requires changes in the postures of both current and new members. But it will not require a major military build-up of new forces. An enlarged NATO can meet its requirements by upgrading East-Central European defences and by preparing current NATO forces for projecting power to the region in case of crisis. There is no requirement today for deploying large numbers of NATO combat forces in these countries, which will help to contain costs.

If NATO opts to rely on a joint-power-projection strategy using both ground and air capabilities to reinforce new NATO members in Eastern Europe during a crisis, then the total costs are likely to amount to somewhere between $30 and $52bn over the 10–15 year period, depending upon the level of capabilities deemed necessary.

The US Congressional Budget Office (CBO) issued a study in March 1996 claiming that the costs of enlargement could be higher than this chapter's estimate.[2] The CBO's estimates are mostly driven by a postulated NATO strategy of preparing for war against Russia. In contrast, our approach is not threat- but rather goal- and capability-based. It aims to provide political reassurance to the region and develop flexible military assets for NATO to deal with a wide spectrum of contingencies. It is anchored in the premise of avoiding confrontation with Russia, not preparing for a new Russian threat. These two studies reflect very different assumptions and frameworks for assessing NATO defence requirements and the budget costs associated with them. Hence, the programme proposed here is more austere and our costs lower than the CBO's.

Later in this chapter we will examine an illustrative $42bn package. This translates into some $3–4bn per year over the next decade for the Alliance as a whole, divided between current and new members. The budgetary impact of this package would be less than 1–2% of NATO's current defence spending. To put this cost into perspective, it is roughly equal to that of a single US major weapons system (such as buying a new fighter aircraft, for example) and represents about two-thirds of the life-cycle cost of acquiring a single US Army division or a Navy carrier battle group.

Such costs can, if current priorities change, be absorbed through readjusting current defence budgets or, alternatively, making very small defence increases. The budgetary impact on new members is likely to be greater – but so too will the strategic benefits that accrue to them. Their ability to pay these costs will depend on the health of their economies and the size of their defence budgets. They will need help from NATO in areas such as common infrastructure and security assistance.

Steady multiyear planning and programming makes sense and will help spread the costs over time, thus making the annual burden easier to manage. If NATO and current members use the time before enlargement to start preparing for it, they can spread the costs out over a longer period and avoid the need to increase defence preparations once new members have joined. Perhaps the best approach would be for NATO to develop a steady multiyear plan similar to the Alliance Defence Initiative launched in 1970 (AD-70), the 1978 Long Term Defense Program (LTDP) or the Conventional Defense Initiative (CDI) launched in the mid-1980s.

Putting Costs in Perspective

Before turning to details and numbers, it is important to step back and put the costs of enlargement into perspective. First, alliances save money. Collective defence is cheaper than national defence. If the new democracies in Eastern Europe face the prospect of providing for their security and defence on their own, using national means, this would require them to assume an enormous defence burden, something their small and still-fragile economies can ill afford. Alternatively, they could simply live with insecurity. History has taught, however, that this is a recipe for nationalism and the kind of geopolitical jockeying that has made this region one of Europe's most unstable and crisis-prone in the past.

Or these states could join the Alliance and contribute their share to a collective defence effort that will enhance deterrence and stability in their region. One of the great attractions of NATO membership to these countries is that it will allow them to keep their defence expenditures modest and to focus their resources on economic reconstruction. This does not mean that NATO membership will be a free ride. On the contrary, NATO membership will require these countries to spend their resources differently than they otherwise might if they had to provide for their own defence using national means, and to increase spending in some areas while decreasing it in others. But it would allow them to purchase a greater degree of security at a much lower cost than would otherwise be the case.

Second, while money is obviously tight, the Alliance is neither poor nor inflexible. Both current Alliance members and candidate members are already planning to spend significant amounts on defence in the years ahead. NATO is, after all, an alliance of some of the world's wealthiest countries. NATO's current European members together spend nearly $160bn annually on defence, a figure that does not include the portion of the US defence budget devoted to European defence.

If these current rates of defence spending for the Alliance as a whole are projected over the next 15 years, NATO will spend nearly $3 trillion dollars on European defence.[3] Moreover, while considerably poorer than the West Europeans, the East-Central Europeans will also spend a significant amount on defence. For example, the Visegrad countries, which currently spend under 3% of their gross domestic product (GDP) per annum on defence, are likely to spend somewhere between $90 and $125bn on defence over the same period.

While stringency will be required, a moderate defence preparedness programme over a multiyear period is affordable. Viewed in relation to what NATO will be spending for its entire European defence posture, the costs of enlargement will be small. The costs to current NATO members can, assuming the political will exists, be accommodated through reprogramming or modest spending increases. The burdens on the new democracies in East-Central Europe, however, are likely to be heavier. At present, for example, the Visegrad countries spend only about $5bn altogether on defence per year. But over a period of years, their economies will grow as reforms take effect and they should be able to afford larger military budgets. Thus, over time, they will acquire growing flexibility to fund the necessary defence programmes that will accompany their admission to NATO.

NATO currently has a surplus of assets in several key areas that could be used to compensate for East-Central European weaknesses. The Alliance's comparative advantage in these areas should allow a sensible division of labour regarding roles and missions which would enable new members to concentrate their future defence investments in other key areas. For example, NATO countries have the world's most modern and powerful air forces. In an enlarged NATO, the Alliance might opt to have current members assume responsibility for many air missions, thus saving the East European countries the expense of a costly air-modernisation effort.

In short, the issue is whether and how NATO and new members can best use available resources to get the job done. This will require careful coalition planning and long-term programmes that build new capabilities over time. Such challenges are nothing new to NATO. The scope of this challenge is no more demanding than previous tests that the Alliance has successfully passed. During the Cold War, building NATO's defence in Central Europe started almost from scratch in 1950. It took three decades for the Alliance to meet many of its military objectives, but it managed to do so in a gradual fashion. A similar result is achievable in Eastern Europe over the long run. The issue is less one of overall economic means than of the political will to pursue the necessary defence changes.

Third, the costs of enlargement must also be seen against a broader strategic canvas. The Alliance has already made implicit security commitments to the region. If Poland were threatened, would NATO not act to defend it? In our view, the answer is clearly that the Alliance should – and would – even today. If that is the case, then codifying that commitment through NATO will enhance stability and deterrence, thus decreasing the likelihood that Poland will ever be threatened in the first place.

Equally important, enlargement will require the kinds of changes in the strategy and force postures of NATO countries, especially in Europe, that dovetail with the Alliance's overall reform agenda, and in particular the strategic interests of the United States. Surveying the array of possible new Article 5 missions in Eastern Europe – as well as non-Article 5 missions, such as crisis management beyond Europe's borders – it is clear that NATO's most important weakness is its limited capacity to project forces over distance. This is a particular problem for those European countries whose forces were designed only to defend their own territory.[4] NATO has begun to revise its strategic concept to place greater emphasis on power projection, and the allies have already taken several steps towards creating lighter, more mobile forces. Enlargement can give added impetus to this trend if the Alliance adopts a military strategy of relying on power-projection to reinforce the region in a crisis.

Thus, enlargement is a 'two-for-one' deal. The projection capabilities that NATO should acquire in order to carry out enlargement are precisely the capabilities that will also be required for non-Article 5 missions elsewhere. Once NATO forces are able to deploy to Eastern Europe quickly in a crisis, they will also be capable of deploying elsewhere. Improving the capability of NATO's European members to operate in both sets of missions will greatly benefit the United States by allowing a more equitable burden-sharing arrangement for handling future crises in and around Europe. From a US military perspective, this is one of the greatest benefits that could emerge from the enlargement process.

Defining the Key Tasks for Enlargement
Four tasks will determine what measures are needed to prepare NATO's defences for new Article 5 missions in East-Central Europe. These tasks can be performed in many ways, thereby giving rise to a wide spectrum of alternative defence postures. How these tasks are performed will also determine how NATO spends its money. These four tasks include:

• *Preparing East-Central European Forces for NATO Membership.* The Visegrad countries currently plan to field about 20 mobilisable divisions and 1,000 combat aircraft, of which Poland will contribute the largest share. Provided that NATO is willing to commit combat forces as reinforcements to help address an array of contingencies, these forces are likely to be enough to meet East-Central European force needs. Indeed, once NATO enlarges, these countries may opt for smaller and more modern and ready forces. But their forces will require improvements in a host of areas – readiness, modernisation and sustainability – in order to render them capable of operating effectively with those of other NATO allies.

The task of preparing East-Central European forces for NATO membership has two components. The first is making improvements that are a normal part of defence planning and are not a result of joining NATO. These measures include, for example, buying new weapons to replace obsolescent models and adjusting force structures to reflect new doctrine. Such measures will be the responsibility of the new members, who will be funding them from their own budgets. The estimated cost would be $30–40bn if expensive, high-technology systems are bought, but far less if new members select rebuilt models from Western inventories (for example, used but refurbished F-16s). Because NATO allies will help carry out important missions, these countries will not need a gleaming collection of new weapons, and would be better advised to focus their spending in other higher-priority areas. Even so, NATO security assistance (loans and grants of excess equipment) may be needed to help new members afford these improvements, while still leaving enough funds to pursue the second component: measures that are unique to joining NATO. These include those necessary to foster compatibility, interoperability, integration and operational effectiveness within NATO. Our analysis focuses on costs for these measures.

• *Upgrading Infrastructure for East-Central European and NATO Forces.* Enlargement will require upgrading infrastructure for both East-Central European and NATO forces. These countries have inherited a large military infrastructure from the Cold War, but major parts of it are either in need of modernisation, not tailored to NATO's requirements or simply located in the wrong place. The purpose of such upgrading would be to enable joint and combined operations between the forces of current and new NATO members.

• *Basing NATO Forces in East-Central Europe.* The 'Study on NATO Enlargement' concluded that there is no *a priori* need for permanently forward deploying allied forces on the territory of new members, but that the Alliance reserves the right to do so if future conditions so dictate. If any deployments are made, they will probably be limited to command staffs, support troops and perhaps small combat forces for training. Any future requirements are unclear, but there is already a consensus that such deployment should be limited for economic, political and strategic reasons in order to contain costs and to underscore that enlargement is not aimed against Moscow.

• *Preparing NATO Forces for Projection and Regional Reinforcement.* Preparing Alliance forces for projection will be the greatest challenge facing current members. In all likelihood, projection and reinforcement will be the primary vehicle through which current Alliance members project stability to East-Central Europe. NATO's current problem is hardly a lack of forces. In NATO's major subordinate commands, Armed Forces Central Europe (AFCENT) and Armed Forces Northwest Europe (AFNW), the Alliance (including French forces), even after the post-Cold

Figure 2: Four Alternatives Define the Spectrum

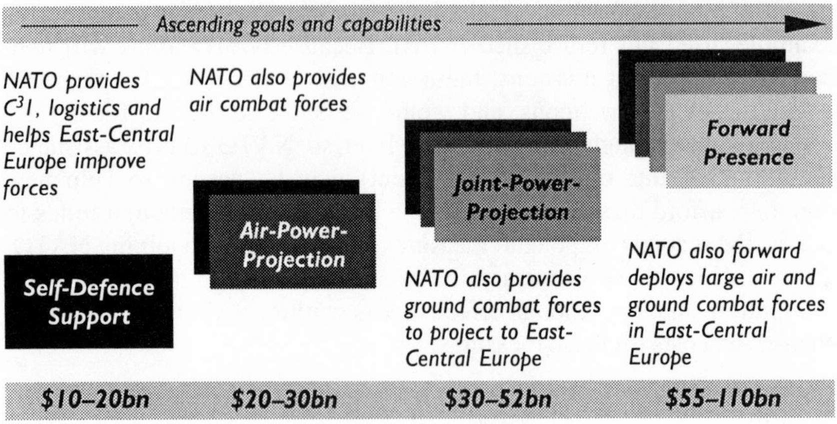

————— Ascending goals and capabilities —————▶

NATO provides C^3I, logistics and helps East-Central Europe improve forces

Self-Defence Support

$10–20bn

NATO also provides air combat forces

Air-Power-Projection

$20–30bn

Joint-Power-Projection

NATO also provides ground combat forces to project to East-Central Europe

$30–52bn

Forward Presence

NATO also forward deploys large air and ground combat forces in East-Central Europe

$55–110bn

War drawdown, will have some 25 mobilisable divisions and over 1,800 combat aircraft. This posture will be more than sufficient to meet any future needs that might arise in the region. NATO's problem, however, is that few of these forces are configured for reinforcement missions eastwards. A sufficient number of forces will have to be configured for such missions, a step that will cost money.

Defining the Spectrum of Options
Based on these tasks, Figure 2 lays out four broad defence postures – alternatives along a spectrum – available to the Alliance for implementing new Article 5 commitments. Their associated costs are also shown. Budget

costs include acquisitions (normally 80% of the total), as well as operations for a multiyear period, around 10–15 years. These calculations are based on US Department of Defense and NATO planning factors, along with RAND's own estimates.[5]

The four broad options examined are Self-Defence Support, Air-Power-Projection, Joint-Power-Projection and Forward Presence. These are labelled according to the missions that current NATO members would be asked to perform, and they should be viewed as building blocks, each one providing the foundation upon which the next could build.

As we pointed out in our earlier chapter, there is no hard-and-fast rule for how the Alliance should implement Article 5 commitments. During the Cold War, Article 5 commitments were implemented in very different ways, even among so-called front-line states such as Norway, West Germany and Turkey. Moreover, NATO's own military strategy and defence postures have evolved considerably over time and under changing political, economic and strategic circumstances. Thus, new members joining NATO in the 1990s have to decide for themselves and in conjunction with current Alliance members which posture makes most sense under current strategic circumstances. The options presented here are designed to illuminate the possible choices and the trade-offs involved.

Self-Defence Support

The Self-Defence Support option assumes that new members will be able to provide their own adequate combat forces to meet their security needs and that the role of other Alliance members will be limited to providing help in areas such as command, control, communications and intelligence (C^3I) and logistics. This option's main goals are: to maximise the effectiveness of East-Central European forces by making them compatible with NATO's integrated structure; improve them so that they meet NATO standards; and configure them for defence strategies aimed at defending their own borders.

For illustrative purposes, we have developed a $20bn package concentrating on six programme areas where East-Central European forces would need to be strengthened. Some of these measures would be funded by the East-Central Europeans themselves, but others would be funded under the NATO common infrastructure programme. The precise allocations and their distribution would have to be negotiated and are discussed in greater detail below.

This package would focus on building a NATO theatre command structure, principal subordinate command centres and communication links to East-Central European militaries. It would provide funds for building a medium-high-altitude surface-to-air missile system and would allow East-Central European aircraft to be rewired so they could communicate with

NATO's system and employ NATO's air-to-air missiles. It could also fund improvements aimed at promoting technical compatibility (the ability to use common NATO equipment, such as fuels, fuelling nozzles, radio frequencies and so on).

This option would also upgrade East-Central European infrastructure to permit operations in expected areas. A key improvement would be the petroleum, oil and lubricants (POL) pipeline distribution system, which is presently inadequate to provide the fuels needed for sizeable NATO operations. Similarly, this option allows for selective upgrades of the road and rail system in the region to enable reinforcement missions. It would also provide for improved readiness and training as well as measures to draw East-Central European forces closer to NATO doctrine. And it would fund the purchase and store of 20 days' worth of stocks of war reserve munitions (WRM). The $20bn price-tag on this package could be lowered if East-Central European countries were content with lower performance and cheaper systems. For example, the $20bn package assumes the purchase of the *Patriot* air-defence system. If the East-Central Europeans chose the Russian SA-10 system, the price could fall to $14bn.

The important impact that even this initial package would have on the defence establishments of these countries should not be underestimated. The structures, doctrines and practices of East-Central European forces remain radically different from those of NATO, reflecting the Warsaw Pact legacy. Despite initial reforms, the work required to achieve full interoperability and integration is vast – and will take years, if not decades, to accomplish. The Self-Defence Support option aims to initiate this process by pursuing high-leverage measures that enable these countries to defend themselves better, albeit within a NATO context.

This option does not provide for is NATO combat forces to carry out new Article 5 commitments. Nor does it supply a framework for NATO and East-Central European forces to work closely together in developing common doctrine and practices for combined operations. The key question is whether such a posture is sufficient to meet the security needs of these countries.

Air-Power-Projection
This option builds on the above Self-Defence Support option. Air-power would be added to NATO C³I and logistics support. The Alliance would provide air-power for contingency operations in East-Central Europe from bases in Western Europe. NATO would not station large air forces on East-Central European territory in peacetime for combat missions, but it would deploy them forward when required as reinforcements in a crisis. If necessary, NATO would provide a full spectrum of air assets for air superiority, deep strike interdiction, close air-support and reconnaissance.

The precise costs of this option would depend on the package of air assets. We examined two suboptions. The first package consists of five fighter wings equipped for deployment to East-Central Europe in a crisis; the second suboption increases the package to ten fighter wings. These two suboptions are consistent with the level of air forces envisioned by NATO's rapid-reaction forces, but constitute only 13–30% of AFCENT and AFNW's total force posture. The ten-wing package, in total, would cost about $30bn: $20bn for the Self-Defence Support foundation, and $10bn for NATO's air forces. On average, each fighter wing costs about $1bn for a full set of rapid-deployment assets and reception facilities.

The $10bn additional cost derives from programme improvements in five areas. These include, first, wing upgrades. Although United States Air Force (USAF) wings are equipped with mobile logistics and command structures, some West European wings would require upgrading. Second, NATO fighter wings would require Co-located Operating Bases (COBs) and Minimum Essential Facilities – East-Central European bases capable of receiving NATO air units with facilities to support them. Third, each COB would also require adequate munitions and POL for military operations. Fourth, host-nation support would also be needed. Finally, funding would have to be set aside for NATO air wings to conduct rotational exercises with East-Central European forces.

If a power-projection strategy is employed, air-power is a relatively inexpensive way for NATO to augment East-Central European forces with its own combat forces. NATO air-power is highly effective and could greatly enhance the effectiveness of East-Central European forces. This option would take advantage of NATO's comparative advantage and allow a degree of role specialisation. But it would assume that the East-Central Europeans are capable of handling their own military requirements for ground forces.

Joint-Power-Projection

This option would build on the two previous options through a power-projection strategy employing *both* air and ground combat forces. As in the Air-Power-Projection option, these forces would remain stationed in Western Europe and would deploy forward in a crisis. NATO's current members would commit armoured and mechanised forces to perform a broad spectrum of missions in Eastern Europe, ranging from border defence to peacekeeping and crisis management. NATO ground forces would also make specialised contributions in key areas such as artillery, aviation and deep-strike.

The precise cost of this option would depend on the package of air and ground combat forces and associated improvement measures. We examined several suboptions consisting of different packages of air and ground forces. The most potent and expensive option consists of ten NATO divisions and ten fighter wings. This package totals $52bn: $20bn for the Self-Defence Support basics; an additional $10bn for ten NATO air wings; and a further $22bn for reconfiguring ten NATO ground divisions for projecting onto the territory of new members in a crisis. In contrast, a smaller package of five NATO divisions and five air wings would cost $38bn. A middle option of ten fighter wings and five divisions, similar to the US 'building bloc' posture for Asia and the Persian Gulf, would cost $42bn. This last package is examined in more detail below.

Funding for ground forces would include division upgrades. Again, US army units are already equipped with the mobile logistics required for such missions, but many West European forces are not. Improvements would be needed in combat-support and combat-service-support functions, especially at the corps and higher echelons. On average, the costs for configuring a division along these lines would be $1.2–1.4bn. Second, reception facilities would have to be provided in East-Central Europe in the form of appropriate railroad off-loading sites, assembly and training areas in order to ensure that this reinforcement function can be carried out. Third, ground forces would require pre-deployed WRM and POL to permit operations until a supply line could be established. Fourth, they would also require host-nation support. Fifth, while there would be no need to preposition equipment for nearby West European forces, it might be sensible to establish prepositioning of material configured in unit sets (POMCUS) for a single US brigade. Finally, funding would have to be included to deploy NATO-designated units periodically to East-Central Europe, where they would exercise with local forces.

A rough rule of thumb is that, whereas it will take about $1bn to equip a NATO fighter wing with a full set of rapid-deployment assets and reception facilities, the cost of re-equipping a ground division for carrying out this new mission is about $2bn. Reconfiguring NATO ground forces for deployment and reinforcement in East-Central Europe is more costly,

Figure 3: More Posture Equals More Cost

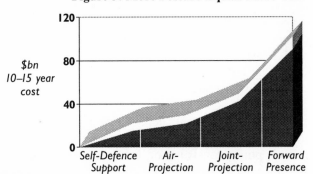

but these forces provide important capabilities that air-power cannot provide alone. The life-cycle cost of buying a heavy armoured division is about $60bn; the added cost of configuring it to deploy eastwards is only $2bn – a 3–4% increase that greatly enhances its effectiveness for power projection.

Forward Presence
This option is discussed here purely to illustrate a worst-case scenario where new members faced the threat of a large, short-warning military attack, and where NATO might opt to respond to such a threat with a strategy similar to that used to defend West Germany during much of the Cold War. Such a strategy would stress the forward deployment of

Figure 4: Alternative Postures Require Different Mix of Investments

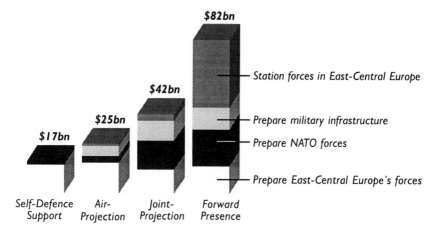

substantial numbers of allied forces on East-Central European territory in order to conduct major military operations on short warning.

This option is substantially more expensive than the three preceding options. Again, the exact cost would depend on the specific package NATO chooses. For illustrative purposes, we examined one suboption where NATO provides ten divisions and ten air wings for defending East-Central Europe – and decides to deploy all these units forward. This package would cost an estimated $110bn. We also calculated another suboption where the same force is earmarked for defending the region, but with only three divisions and five wings deployed forward, at a cost of $70bn.

The costs of a forward-presence strategy are substantially higher because of extra investment in four areas: creating bases and training areas for these units; establishing command staffs and facilities for major operations; providing a much larger logistics network and facilities for large-scale operations on short notice; and building facilities for allied forces' families and dependants.

Such a posture is clearly not needed today. Politically, it would be perceived as very threatening by Moscow; economically it is very expensive; and strategically, it is unnecessary. It would only make sense in a situation where the Alliance faced a large short-warning threat, such as the one that existed during the Cold War.

Figure 3 shows the costs of alternative force postures. As NATO adopts increasingly ambitious postures, the costs increase. The curve's slope is initially steep as NATO invests in the key elements of Self-Defence Support; it then flattens out as increments of air-power are introduced into the calculus. The further addition of ground forces leads to a rise in the slope, owing to the higher marginal costs associated with reconfiguring ground forces for projection and reinforcement. The cost curve rises dramatically under the Forward Presence option because of the high costs associated with permanently forward-deployed combat units.

If these costs are broken down according to the four tasks discussed earlier, the mix of NATO investments changes significantly from option to option. Under Self-Defence Support, the bulk of funds would be invested in upgrading the forces of new members in East-Central Europe. As forces shift towards more ambitious postures, the relative percentages shift. NATO would invest a greater portion of resources in infrastructure, as well as preparing the forces of current members to project both air and ground forces.

For the Joint-Power-Projection posture, nearly 40% of the costs are invested in measures that will make the forces of current members more flexible and deployable for a broad range of missions, not just in East-Central Europe. Once they have been reconfigured to deploy to eastern Poland, they are also deployable elsewhere. Under the Forward-Presence option, the sharp increase in costs is caused by the decision to station large numbers of combat forces in the region. For this option, nearly half the costs result from forward stationing (see Figure 4).

Another factor affecting costs is the number and size of the countries being admitted to the Alliance. The largest share of these costs will go to extending an Article 5 commitment to Poland because of its size and location. Once the Alliance has assumed that commitment, the additional marginal costs of extending the same guarantee to the Czech Republic, for example, would not be large, because of its smaller size and because NATO can use many of the same forces and even some of the same infrastructure. Issues such as whether Slovakia should or should not be included in an initial tranche of NATO enlargement are mainly political and strategic, not economic. The marginal cost of including Slovakia in NATO would be small given its size and the investment that NATO would already have made in building the capability to defend the region. As more small members are admitted, the costs of enlargement rise, but it is the initial cost of defending a large country like Poland that constitutes the major outlay.

Choosing the Right Posture

How should NATO choose among the options here? NATO will be pursuing the goals of ensuring credible commitments, building adequate military capabilities for potential contingencies, and promoting the integration of new members. At the same time, it will not want to embrace an agenda that is too disruptive politically, too expensive economically, and too provocative to Russia strategically. How much is enough? Answering this questions requires revisiting the issue of why NATO is being enlarged in the first place and what we expect the armed forces of new and old members to accomplish.

The political considerations in the calculus were outlined earlier in chapter 5, which identified three alternative paths for enlargement, each with its own rationale. The 'Evolutionary' path posits that NATO faces no immediate security dangers in East-Central Europe, and therefore should enlarge slowly, in parallel with the European Union. The 'Promote Stability' sees enlargement as vital to supporting democracy and filling the security vacuum to the east. The 'Strategic Response' path asserts that NATO should enlarge only if a new Russian threat emerges. The Clinton administration and NATO's enlargement study have embraced the 'Promote Stability' rationale. Yet it is no secret that some in NATO prefer a different route. These differences are likely to re-emerge as NATO moves from rhetorical declarations to concrete decisions about what new Article 5 commitments will mean in practice.

Obviously, these three paths imply very different stances for NATO defence preparedness. Proponents of the 'Evolutionary' path are likely to conclude that the Self-Defence Support option will suffice. They see no threat or prospect of instability, and are not worried about a security vacuum. To them, any additional forces would be superfluous, if not counter-productive. Because proponents of the 'Promote Stability' path are more worried about military imbalances and strategic vacuums, they are likely to conclude that a more robust posture is needed to attain NATO's objectives. They are thus likely to endorse a power-projection posture, including either air forces or air and ground forces, as necessary. Because believers in the 'Strategic Response' path foresee a military threat from Russia, they will probably deem a power-projection posture inadequate, and will want a forward presence instead.

These curves are illustrative. In reality, each individual will have his or her own personal curve, depending on his or her underlying strategic assumptions about enlargement. The point is that NATO – both current members and candidate members – must define where they stand in order to fashion a consensus on what should be done. Assumptions on how much is enough may differ among governments in Warsaw, Madrid, Bonn and Washington. Only when the Alliance has debated these issues and translated its political decisions into guidance on defence-posture choices will it be able to answer the question of which option is appropriate in overall political and strategic terms – and what spending will be needed.

Figure 5: Military Appraisal Determines Requirements

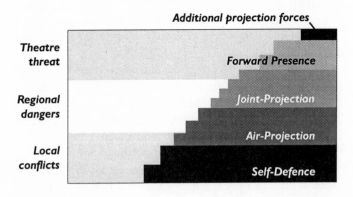

In contrast, a defence planner would approach the issue from a very different angle, by asking: what does NATO want these forces to be able to do in operational terms? Figure 5 reflects this military calculus. It shows NATO's ascending capabilities in ways reflecting the spectrum of defence options, and it matches these capabilities against an ascending spectrum of planning requirements, displayed on the y-axis. 'Local conflicts' refers to a requirement for defending new members in low-intensity operations and for deterring against a single medium-size power. 'Regional dangers' refers to the requirement for deterring against a coalition of medium-size neighbours and culminates with the task of deterring a single-axis regional Russian threat. 'Theatre threat' refers to a requirement to deter a hostile Russian-led Commonwealth of Independent States (CIS) military bloc that posed an offensive military threat to an enlarged Alliance.

Using this chart, a military planner can determine how the defence postures correspond to varying security horizons. If the Alliance adopts the view that its forces in East-Central Europe only have to be prepared to handle local risks, then Self-Defence Support, perhaps coupled with modest Air-Power-Projection assets, may suffice. If the objective is to balance and deter regional dangers, Air-Power-Projection will only suffice to a certain degree. A Joint-Power-Projection strategy might be needed to cover the broader spectrum of regional dangers, as well as a limited Russian threat. The Forward-Presence strategy would be required only if the Alliance were to face a theatre-wide short-warning threat.

Figure 6 combines these political and military perspectives. Its key point is that underlying assumptions about the political rationale for enlargement and NATO's military requirements must be consistent. It suggests that the Self-Defence Support posture is the proper response if the 'Evolutionary' path is chosen and the only military concern is local conflicts. Similarly, the combination of a 'Promote Stability' path along with defence plans focused on regional dangers add up to a coherent set of arguments for a Joint-Power-Projection posture. 'Strategic Response' and a theatre threat equal Forward Presence. To be sure, there will be 'Evolutionary' hawks as well as 'Promote Stability' doves, and other gradations of opinion. What NATO needs is a shared strategic and military approach that translates into agreement on a corresponding defence posture.

Figure 6: Choosing Among Alternative Packages

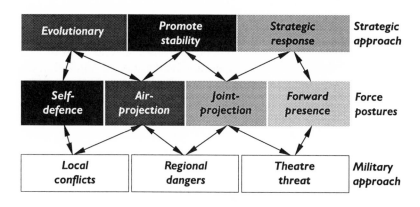

The NATO enlargement study implies support for a Joint-Power-Projection posture, while leaving open the issue of exact force levels. Such a posture would guarantee that NATO could deter regional instability and cover a wide spectrum of regional contingencies, short of a new Cold War with a Russian-led CIS. It would: more effectively promote both burden-sharing and military integration in the Alliance; give NATO the capability of not only handling a single contingency, but also two smaller concurrent events; and it could lead to a substantial upgrading of the Alliance's projection capabilities to help compensate for NATO's currently limited crisis-management capabilities. NATO's current military strategy emphasises the need to deter regional dangers and risks. It sets as a benchmark the capability to defend the borders of each individual subregion of the Alliance. Thus, this posture is fully consistent with NATO's existing planning guidance and strategy, not a new departure. As a practical matter, there are many potential contingencies that can be handled only by a joint posture that includes the projection of ground troops as well as air-power. The Bosnian conflict has shown the difficulties of relying solely on air-power. It is hardly a model for implementing new security guarantees in East-Central Europe. Each of these packages make sense under differing assumptions and strategic circumstances. The key point is that NATO's political assumptions and military objectives must be in harmony and must make political and strategic sense in today's Europe.

Building the Posture

The Alliance faces the task of not only choosing a defence posture, but also deciding how to build it, and how to share the burdens among current and new members. The pace at which the posture is created will determine when the costs must be paid. Burden-sharing will affect how the costs of enlargement are distributed among the participants. These decisions, too, will require NATO to face difficult trade-offs and to strike a balance among different objectives.

While NATO has proceeded cautiously in deepening military cooperation with candidate members, there are several reasons why it should start intensifying this cooperation as the time of admission draws closer. First, Article 5 commitments apply the day new members join, not 10–15 years later, after a defence programme has been completed. The Alliance needs to begin preparing current and new members so that new commitments, when extended, do not lack credibility. Second, concrete steps taken now can demonstrate the Alliance's intent, help create momentum and build consensus, and thus promote stability in the region – the underlying purpose of enlargement. Third, starting early allows the Alliance to spread the costs over a longer period, thus easing the defence burden for any given year.

Fourth, there are also costs to not acting early. The East-Central Europeans today face many crucial defence restructuring decisions. As matters now stand, they are unable to make many of these decisions because they do not know how their forces and programmes should fit into NATO's strategy of carrying out new Article 5 commitments. These countries need guidance now from NATO to avoid misallocating their modest defence resources. If the Alliance gives them clear guidelines on the defence strategy that NATO will employ in their region, this would help provide them with a blueprint for assessing how to restructure their own forces, for deciding where they can afford to cut, and in what areas they should concentrate their

Figure 7: Percentage of Force Posture in Place

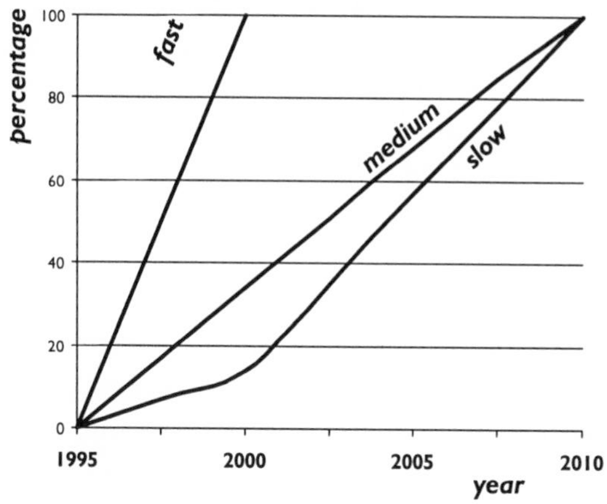

investments. The longer the Alliance waits, the greater the risk becomes that these countries will waste both time and money.

The mechanisms for providing such guidance already exist. NATO's Planning and Review Process (PARP) is one instrument for introducing candidate members to collective defence planning and combined operational planning. As accession draws near, the NATO biennial Force Goals review – which coordinates Alliance requirements with member-nations' contributions – can be expanded to include candidate members by providing them with resource guidance and defence priorities, and by monitoring their progress through the performance-measurement system. What is lacking are Alliance decisions and a consensus on what should be done.

How much of the NATO defence package should be in place on the day of accession and how much can the Alliance afford to build once these countries have already joined? This is a highly political issue and one which has previously been largely ignored. Because Article 5 will take effect the day these countries accede to the Alliance, NATO would ideally want to have the *entire* defence posture in place *before* assuming any new commitments. In reality, NATO will not build up its full defence posture or even a sizeable portion of it before enlarging. The real question is: what is the minimal amount of that posture that must be in place in order to secure enough support within Alliance countries to ensure that enlargement will be ratified – and that also ensures that the Alliance can provide deterrence if something unexpected happens? How high – or low – should Western leaders set the bar for admission day? This decision will determine the pace for defence preparations both before and after enlargement. If 100% is too much to expect, should the goal be set at 30% or 10%? And what political and military criteria is such a decision based on?

Figure 7 addresses this issue and its implications. It assumes that the first tranche of new members will enter NATO around the year 2000. The three tracks reflect alternative approaches. The 'Fast Track' would have the entire programme completed by the date of accession. The steepness of the curve indicates the kind of urgent programme that would have to be pursued to accomplish this goal. The 'Slow Track' estimates what would be accomplished if efforts under way continue at their current pace – 10% of the desired posture – and are accelerated once the candidate countries join. The illustrative 'Medium Track' represents a significant acceleration of efforts – perhaps a doubling or tripling of current activities – in order to build a posture's critical components and create momentum.

The issue is not only the numerical percentage of the overall force posture that should be in place on the date of accession; the content of the 10% or 30% that the Alliance wants to achieve is equally important. Which 10% or 30% will the Alliance consider 'critical' capacities? Alliance officials will need to ascertain which capabilities are 'critical' and to be accomplished before accession. This short list might include acquiring basic C^3I interoperability necessary to ensure that effective command authority can be exercised over NATO and new members' forces if they have to perform missions together. Similarly, such a list should include key infrastructure elements such as a POL system, power grids or main lines of control (LOCs), as well as 'bare-bones' bases, reception facilities and training areas. Technical compatibility of weapons is also a critical goal.

While full interoperability may take years, if not decades, to achieve, new countries should establish key cornerstone units capable of 'side-by-side' operations with NATO forces. Cornerstone units will be the first to be integrated into NATO command structures and multinational force postures. For example, Poland might select a division and a fighter wing as cornerstone units; smaller countries might select a brigade and an air squadron each. These units would be the focal point for restructuring, receiving interoperable equipment, and training and exercising with NATO forces.

NATO will also have to decide the sequencing of this process. Should the Alliance insist that the East-Central European countries change their national defence postures first, or should NATO countries take the lead in adapting their forces, thereby giving the East-Central Europeans more time and breathing space to find resources and make the necessary adaptations? Or should both improvement efforts take place in parallel? Which of these three alternatives would be more effective in terms of achieving NATO's twin objectives of promoting stability in the region while not antagonising Russia?

The Alliance will also have to decide how the costs of enlargement will be distributed. In large part, this will be a function of the strategy and the posture chosen, as well as NATO's own rules on funding procedures. Existing NATO practices call for each member-state to fund its own forces, and for Alliance members to share the costs for common infrastructure. Thus, if a Self-Defence Support posture is chosen, new members will be responsible for funding the bulk of the defence-preparedness measures, since these measures would involve their national forces. Adopting a power-projection strategy would result in a larger share of the burden falling on existing NATO members.

Figure 8 shows the kind of overall breakdown of costs that could result from the $42bn programme discussed earlier. The East-Central European members would fund the 19% of the package devoted to preparing their own forces. Current NATO members would pay for upgrading their own forces – some 61% of the programme. Twenty per cent of the programme would be funded through infrastructure investments. This would almost double NATO's current infrastructure budget. Responsibility for providing these funds would have to be negotiated.

Figure 8: An Illustrative Breakdown of Costs: Joint-Power-Projection Funding Profile

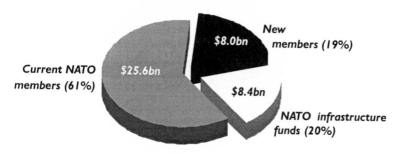

These percentages are not fixed, but could change according to which posture is adopted. Whereas the East-Central Europeans' share of the Joint-Power-Projection posture is only 19%, their share of the Self-Defence Support posture would be 55%, even though the overall amount of money they contributed to each posture would be similar. As NATO moves from Self-Defence Support to a Joint-Power-Projection option, the strategic and economic responsibility assumed by current NATO members will increase.

A final controversial question that must be answered is: whose forces, among current NATO members, will be committed to carrying out these new Article 5 commitments? While all NATO countries sign up in principle for such commitments, not all of them will necessarily carry them out in practice. There is a division of labour, roles and missions in the Alliance. Often only a subset or core group of countries ends up committing their forces to any specific mission. Which countries will assign their forces to defending East-Central Europe? This is not merely a strategic issue because those countries committing their forces will also have to bear the financial burden of re-equipping their forces to do so. The larger members of the Alliance that are committed to enlargement, including the United States, have a clear financial interest in getting more countries involved in undertaking these commitments in order to share the financial burden. Figure 9 shows how the burden on the US can be reduced if the number of participating countries extends beyond the core group of the US, the UK, France and Germany.

Figure 9: Broad Participation by NATO Allies Reduces US/Core Group Burden

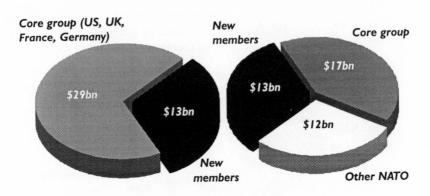

If deemed necessary, NATO could consider a 'no-cost' option of enlargement: enlarging with no net spending increases. The Alliance could pursue this option by economising elsewhere in its defence plans. Current members, for example, could generate sufficient savings by cutting some 5% of their forces in Western Europe – a step that would have little impact on Alliance security since NATO's current forces are larger than any plausible theory of requirements. New Alliance members could, in turn, reduce their still-large combat forces and overheads by 15–25%. Further savings could be gained by pursuing multinational integration in the areas of logistics, procurement and other areas. Smaller forces, less overhead and more integration would free up resources to develop increasingly capable forces and to begin funding NATO enlargement measures. These steps are undoubtedly politically difficult, but they are possible if NATO decides that, for whatever reasons, it does not want to increase defence spending.

Conclusion

What will NATO enlargement cost the tax-payer in the US and Europe? The answer depends on which countries join NATO, and when they accede; what strategy and force posture is chosen to implement new Article 5 commitments; how much of the posture NATO decides must be in place on the date of accession; and how NATO decides that the costs will be shared. None of these questions has yet been answered. The Alliance must start to address them if it wants to ensure a solid basis of political support as it heads down the enlargement path. NATO has coped with similar challenges before. With clear political and strategic guidance, the Alliance can embark on a step-by-step programme that will build real capabilities over time. Waiting will not make the effort any easier and may make it harder.

While the costs of enlargement are not trivial, they are also not overwhelming, when placed in context. The Alliance will be spending considerable sums of money on European defence in the decade ahead. Although the $42bn package discussed here may seem expensive at first glance, it represents a minute portion of planned NATO defence spending over the coming decade. When spread out over a 10–15 year period and distributed among both new and old members, the costs are not enormous. Indeed, the entire programme's costs are only about one-quarter of what NATO's European members currently spend on defence in any given year.

There is no reason for the Alliance to fear the cost issue and the debate that will undoubtedly accompany it. There are straightforward answers to the questions that will undoubtedly be asked. The strategic benefits that will accrue from these strategic investments are considerable. There are also ample reasons to start early in addressing these issues. The longer the Alliance waits, the greater the accumulation of unresolved issues and the danger of political overload and resource mismanagement. If NATO delays too long before giving guidance to new members, it risks these countries investing their resources in a fashion inconsistent with Alliance objectives.

As the key actor in the Alliance, the United States will have to take the lead in forging a consensus on these issues. At the same time, however, support on Capitol Hill for enlargement will be heavily influenced by the willingness of the US' European allies, as well as new allies, to pay their fair share. Major contributions by current members, as well as new members, will be essential. The US also has a strong interest in ensuring that these reforms feed into and dovetail with NATO's overall reform agenda. How large the US share will be ultimately depends on how large a role Washington wants to play politically and militarily in East-Central Europe and in Europe as a whole. The US will have to pay its fair share of common infrastructure funds and cover the costs incurred by US forces when carrying out new Article 5 commitments. Thus, for a $42bn package, the US annual share could range from $420m to $1.4bn, depending on how those decisions are made. This is hardly an onerous price to pay for ensuring the stability of East-Central Europe – a region where instability and geopolitical competition helped fuel two World Wars and the Cold War this century.

Notes

1. See Asmus *et al.*, chapter 5.

2. *The Costs of Expanding the NATO Alliance* (Washington DC: Congressional Budget Office, March 1996).

3. The current European members of NATO spend about $160bn on defence. $160bn x 15 years = $2.4 trillion. Adding in US defence spending on US forces in Europe, currently $5bn per year, and assuming a growth rate of 2–3%, the total approximates to $3tr.

4. Only France and the UK have modest expeditionary capabilities. During the Cold War, the German armed forces were deliberately structured to prevent them from being deployable elsewhere. However, Bonn has now initiated a major restructuring of its armed forces and is creating a new Crisis Reaction Forces designed to allow for one major operation beyond Germany's borders (comprising up to one army division along with corresponding air assets) as well as simultaneous participation in smaller peacekeeping or humanitarian missions. For further details, see Ronald D. Asmus, *Germany's Contribution to Peacekeeping: Issues and Outlook*, MR-602-OSD (Santa Monica, CA: RAND, 1995).

5. As with any analysis of a new defence undertaking, estimating costs is an uncertain endeavour. These estimates should be viewed as illustrative, not definitive. Further and more detailed studies will be required to develop actual programmes. If programme requirements are defined in different ways, costs will rise or fall accordingly.

Part III
New Functions

Chapter 10
Combined Joint Task Forces in Theory and Practice

Charles Barry

In January 1994, NATO leaders approved an initiative to give the Alliance's decades-old integrated military structure strikingly different capabilities for the future. Alliance military authorities were directed to adopt a command-and-control concept known as Combined Joint Task Forces (CJTF), the method used so successfully in the 1991 Gulf War. Of course, much has already been done to streamline NATO's military apparatus. Both the number and size of its military headquarters have shrunk since the end of the Cold War. However, the command and control (C^2) structure that remains is still optimised for NATO's core task of collective territorial defence; it is both too rigid and too cumbersome for NATO's new contingency missions. Flexible C^2 mechanisms to address crisis response, as called for by the 1991 Alliance Strategic Concept, and for peacekeeping, are lacking. As a result, some NATO commands are having to improvise in places such as Bosnia.

The CJTF concept is intended to give NATO's military forces mobility and flexibility and to make them better suited for crisis response across a spectrum of new peacetime operations. Just as important, CJTF capabilities are to be acquired without adding structure: they will be created primarily by 'dual-hatting' selected personnel within existing organisations; by modifying procedures; and by new employment concepts. To be sure, there will be some costs – largely to improve mobility and to modernise automation resources in the areas of command, control, communications and intelligence. Nevertheless, strict guidance to keep investment to a minimum should translate into a modest price for CJTFs.

Although NATO remains, at core, an alliance for collective defence, its immediate tasks have changed. The two-hour reaction criteria for corps-size formations to meet a Soviet attack and the static defence on Western Europe's borders have gone. NATO military structures must now be able to provide a different type of security capability for its members. That security – what members expect from the Alliance – lies in having a military option to respond to any crisis that threatens the collective interests of NATO members. US Senator Richard Lugar referred to this change in focus when he challenged NATO either to develop the capability to operate 'out of area' or to go out of business.[1] NATO's decision to establish CJTF (proposed, incidentally, by the US not long after Lugar's remarks) is an assertion that the Alliance will be 'in business' in the coming era.

What is unique about NATO's CJTF initiative – and unprecedented in military doctrine – is that it will permanently institutionalise the multinational task-force concept, which has always been a temporary command-and-control arrangement employed by *ad hoc* coalitions. In fact, deploying CJTFs will, for the first time, become the primary *modus operandi* of a standing alliance in peacetime.[2] Such action is analogous to organising a professional football team among players accustomed to playing infrequently and with little practice as a team. For more than 40 years, NATO's strength has been its robust, highly integrated but static military structures prepared to execute the broad, enduring mission of territorial defence. In contrast, task forces are formed rapidly, employed for specific short-term contingencies and then disbanded. With the CJTF concept, NATO's military hopes to invent a unique, hybrid capability that combines the best attributes of both coalition and Alliance forces – rapid crisis response by highly trained multinational forces, backed by pre-established political terms of reference, standardised procedures, regular exercises and in-place infrastructure. CJTF will give the allies a stand-by capability for peacekeeping, peace-enforcement and other contingency operations called for under the 1991 Alliance Strategic Concept. Of course, CJTFs must also be available for collective defence, if required. To realise those capabilities, NATO will have to agree to a new C^2 concept, new common procedures and a new regime of exercises. Regular CJTF exercises, like the large annual manoeuvres undertaken during the Cold War, will gradually yield a valuable reservoir of staffs, units and service members experienced in new operations and procedures for NATO; but the future lessons learned will relate to crisis response. In short, NATO will have the same highly capable forces for use in crises *beyond* its borders that it has always maintained for defence *of* its borders.[3]

The task-force concept is not new for the United States. It was a staple of US doctrine even before the Goldwater–Nichols Department of Defense Reorganisation Act of 1986 directed the US Armed Services to place greater emphasis on joint and combined operations. NATO allies, too, have employed the task-force concept in such places as the Falkland Islands (1982), Zaire (1991) and the Persian Gulf (1991). In fact, if a Soviet attack against the West had materialised, NATO would have relied heavily on joint and combined doctrine for its collective territorial defence.

Yet, US officers will find some aspects of NATO CJTFs quite different from the US-dominated task forces to which they have been accustomed. Grafting a rapid-response technique like CJTF onto a consensus-driven alliance will be neither fast nor easy. It is one thing to develop contingency plans, operational concepts and doctrine for one nation; it is quite another to harmonise the rapid deployment of forces by 16 or more nations. Successful implementation will depend upon both innovative thinking and a genuine commitment to adapt much more completely for what lies ahead. Therefore, as the CJTF concept gradually gains form and substance, it is worth examining its implications for NATO doctrine, command structure and operations planning.

NATO Adapts

CJTF was not born in isolation but is the latest in a series of adaptations made by the Alliance in its struggle to keep up with change and remain relevant in a fundamentally different security environment. Broadly speaking, NATO has pursued three primary objectives in its reform efforts. First, the Alliance is adjusting its political and military structures to new missions, the most important of which is crisis management. If NATO cannot cope with regional crises, it cannot meet the needs of its members, and public support for it will certainly erode. Crisis management in the future will call for smaller multinational forces with the flexibility to respond to contingencies over a wide geographical area. Second, the Alliance is attempting to extend security and stability beyond its borders, especially to the new democracies in Eastern Europe and to the troubled areas in the south, both regions where crises are likely to occur. Third, NATO has embraced its European members' resolve to create a collective defence capability of their own, known broadly as the European Security and Defence Identity (ESDI). Consistent with these themes, the United States proposed the CJTF concept at NATO's Defence Planning Committee meeting at Travemünde, Germany, in late 1993, and, at their summit meeting in Brussels in January 1994 (as noted earlier), NATO leaders directed that it be developed.[4] The stated aims were: to adapt NATO's force structure for new missions; to project security and stability towards the East by giving partner-states a way to join NATO in crisis response; and to support ESDI by offering the WEU a 'separable but not separate' military capability that would not be a costly duplication of NATO's structure.

Defining the CJTF Concept
What exactly is a CJTF? US joint-forces doctrine describes a 'task force' as a temporary force for carrying out a specific mission, and as normally

operational (as opposed to strategic or tactical) in nature. Joint task forces (JTFs) involve components from two or more services, while combined task forces (CTFs) include forces from two or more countries.[5] Although US doctrine does not define a 'CJTF' *per se*, its character can be easily derived from these related definitions.

An early goal has been to agree on definitions, as an unambiguous lexicon is critical to arriving at any sound conceptual framework.[6] Promulgating an official NATO definition of CJTF has been delayed by political differences. However, in light of the 1994 summit language and related US doctrine, a CJTF can be described as: a multinational, multiservice, task-tailored force consisting of NATO and possibly non-NATO forces capable of rapid deployment to conduct limited duration peace operations beyond Alliance borders, under the control of either NATO's integrated military structure or the Western European Union (WEU). Presumably, the CJTF headquarters that NATO ultimately adopts will be similarly tailored and sized to the task force itself, with command, staff and liaison representation corresponding to the size of participating national forces.

A CJTF headquarters' size will be determined by the mission, as well as by the size and composition of the force to be controlled. The US experience is to build a task force at an organisational level that is appropriately sized for the mission. For example, an army brigade task force is organised around a brigade commander and his staff for smaller operations (even as a joint-combined force in given scenarios), but larger operations call for task forces organised around a division or corps headquarters. NATO staffs working on CJTF are following a different model. Rather than call upon several echelons to maintain CJTF C^2 contingency plans, NATO leans towards establishing CJTF headquarters only at some of NATO's eight remaining Major Subordinate Commands (MSCs). The designated MSC would augment a CJTF headquarters nucleus staff with additional 'staff modules' (from its own or other headquarters) to meet each C^2 operational requirement. The staff module concept should be carefully scrutinised to determine its strengths and weaknesses.

Consensus Building: Limited Success and Cautious Optimism
The initial focus of CJTF planners has been to agree on a CJTF concept that modifies existing headquarters in ways that allow them to incorporate a CJTF C^2 capability. Work on this plan began in early 1994 on two levels. First, at the Military Committee (MC) level and above, the political aspects of definitions, terms of reference and oversight were addressed. Resolving political issues is a slow process, but the CJTF has proved particularly awkward because it touches on deeply held US and French differences over NATO's future role. Second, at the Major NATO Command (MNC) level, a tri-MNC (later, a bi-MNC) working group, under the executive agency of the Supreme Allied

Commander Europe (SACEUR), completed a draft operational concept for CJTF C^2 in March 1994.[7] Since then, the CJTF C^2 concept has been left unresolved pending consensus at the political level. Meanwhile, Allied Command Europe (ACE) and Allied Command Atlantic (ACLANT) undertook 13 follow-up studies to define many aspects of the headquarters concept in greater detail, including operating procedures, training and equipment requirements. The results of most of these studies were presented to NATO's Military Committee in September 1994. Subsequently, work at the military level has had to wait for political progress to catch up. As 1996 begins, there is hope for speedier progress.

The central political issues frustrating the CJTF initiative concern the role of the MNCs in the planning and conduct of so-called 'non-Article 5' operations. The French view resists extending the MNC's authority to non-Article 5 tasks, at least not without increased oversight in the form of additional staffs at NATO headquarters, either formal or informal.[8] France wants more political input earlier in the planning process to preclude dominance of crisis response by the MNCs, particularly SACEUR, that France believed (as a self-selected outsider to the military command) existed during most of the Cold War. The US-led position is that the North Atlantic Council (NAC), under current arrangements, exercises sufficient political control. In any case, it would be a mistake for political oversight to take place at the operational level of MNCs. Most important, the US wants to ensure that NATO does not end up with two chains of command, one for Article 5 and another for non-Article 5. In light of the Balkan crisis, where only NATO's military structure has the capacity to respond, it seems clear that MNCs must have a role in non-Article 5 operations. While US–French differences about the need for additional staff oversight are real enough, solutions incorporating dual staffs (albeit expensive) have been used in the past to break a political impasse. The preservation of a single chain of command, however, must be absolute: any deployed CJTF, even if WEU-led, is vulnerable to attack, which then becomes an Article 5 situation and is thereby an MNC responsibility.

Other contentious issues include defining the support role of NATO commanders during WEU-led operations, the potential for the WEU to select its own headquarters – including national commands and the new Eurocorps headquarters – to function as European-led CJTFs, and the WEU's access to NATO assets. From an outsider's perspective, it seems the role of supporting Commander-in-Chief should be based on US doctrine, which already incorporates this function in a proven concept. A solution to the use of national commands by the WEU may be possible if the WEU pre-designated headquarters can be drawn close enough to NATO's military organisations. They would have to participate in planning, exercises, common C^2 procedures, robust information connectivity and handover provisions if an Article 5 situation were to arise. The issue of WEU access to NATO will require the categorisation of resources – at least into those to be made routinely available, such as intelligence – and those necessarily provided on a mission-by-mission basis, such as strategic air-lift. Another challenge will be the cost accounting of assets provided from nations and from one organisation to another.

At the start of 1996, there is cautious speculation that most issues are moving painstakingly towards compromise. General agreement on most of the issues that have dogged the CJTF concept's approval seem near at hand, although agreeing the details of implementation may still prove difficult. France's recent decision to end 29 years of non-participation in NATO's military organs falls short of a return to full engagement but is nonetheless encouraging. With Partnership for Peace (PFP) well established, and if NATO can focus on CJTF sufficiently while its troops are operating in Bosnia-Herzegovina, there is reason to believe that real progress towards an agreed concept can be made by the spring 1996 ministerial meetings. In any case, the contentious matter of overhauling NATO's integrated military system, both the realisation of CJTF and the broader task of revamping the expensive and outdated command structure itself, must move forward with greater resolve.

In addition to building consensus on C^2, NATO has worked on the deployability and composition of potential CJTF forces, principally as an unofficial aim of otherwise scheduled NATO exercises by both land and maritime forces. For practical reasons, this process is less pressing, because, if a crisis erupts, forces can be assembled in improvised CJTFs, as illustrated by *Operation Desert Storm*. More pertinently, the NATO Peace Implementation Force (IFOR), *Operation Joint Endeavour* – a hybrid of coalition forces and standing headquarters – is illustrative of the potential for CJTF under NATO. Although short of what CJTF's proponents promise, IFOR works: it includes forces from NATO members and other contributing states, and an effective C^2 arrangement is in place. Ultimately, CJTFs will offer much greater prospects of success than *ad hoc* crisis-response arrangements. CJTFs will give NATO forces and cadres that are more capable because of regularly conducted multinational planning, training and exercises.

CJTF Structural and Operational Issues

The Headquarters

The essential underpinnings of CJTF C^2 are few but important. The scheme adopted must:

- support the three main objectives of the NATO transformation process mentioned earlier (respond to new missions; be adaptable for new members and non-members alike; and provide support for the WEU's operational needs);
- ensure that collective defence requirements can take priority if they arise;

- preserve both the transatlantic nature of the Alliance and a single integrated military structure; and finally,
- be done with minimum added cost.

These criteria dictate that CJTFs be organised within NATO's integrated military structure (or, at the very least, immediately appendable to it), and that they rely primarily upon the resources of selected MSCs. Whatever headquarters organisation is ultimately adopted, it must be capable of timely, effective response to crises beyond NATO borders; able to coordinate between the Alliance and the WEU; and able to accommodate participation in staff planning by non-NATO countries (especially in Central and Eastern Europe) both during pre-deployment activities and during actual task-force operations.

The functional requirements of CJTF headquarters will include assimilating and disseminating intelligence; receiving and committing forces; and maintaining communications among subordinate, higher and 'lateral' elements, such as humanitarian agencies, local civil authorities or even other militaries. The conduct of logistical sustainment and the management and control of airspace are other features that must be designed into the CJTF headquarters.

To limit costs and to avoid creating additional structure, selected ACE and ACLANT MSCs will organise CJTF headquarters 'nucleus' staffs by 'dual-hatting' existing billets for CJTFs. This nucleus will be developed into a complete staff, drawing initially from the personnel and equipment assets of the host MSC. Additional resources will come from subordinate commands and from other MSCs. When not involved in operations or exercises, the only active element will be the CJTF nucleus staff. The CJTF's deputy chief of staff, possibly a general or flag officer from the host MSC, will direct the small nucleus staff in CJTF-related information management, administration, operational planning, training and exercises. The commander, the chief of staff and perhaps other key staff would be designated only when the CJTF is activated for a particular operation.

Which of NATO's eight MSCs will establish nucleus staffs has not yet been decided. As with all important decisions, NATO must consider more than just military factors in command arrangements. For both political and geographic reasons, ACE may need the flexibility to form a CJTF under any of its three MSCs: Allied Forces North-west Europe (AFNORTHWEST), Allied Forces Central Europe (AFCENT) and Allied Forces Southern Europe (AFSOUTH). ACLANT favours employment of a sea-based CJTF headquarters under Striking Fleet Atlantic (STRIKEFLTLANT), but could also establish nucleus staffs at Eastern Atlantic (EASTLANT) or Iberian Atlantic (IBERLANT) commands. Both ACE and ACLANT want the ability to employ both types of CJTF, either land-based or sea-based, in order to have the greatest operational flexibility. Nonetheless, in practical terms, it is not likely that NATO could justify (or would want) CJTFs within more than three or four of its MSCs overall.

No response times have been agreed for deploying lead CJTF C^2 elements or forces, but usually, once an operation is approved politically, an immediate military response is expected. An initial deployment time of less than 30 days should thus be anticipated.[9] When alerted for either an exercise or actual contingency operation, a CJTF headquarters will come up to full strength by drawing on the assets of the host MSC as well as other staffs to augment its nucleus staff. The nucleus staff will have trained as a close working team and remain generally constant from one operation to the next. However, the actual size of the headquarters will be tailored by the addition of staff 'modules' – either functional staffs as a whole or additions to core elements of the nucleus itself. The ultimate headquarters' size will be determined by the size of the operation, the force to be employed and the requirements for special staffs, such as civil–military coordination or chemical operations. A fully augmented CJTF could be quite large and provide C^2 for sizeable multinational forces drawn from all services and many outside agencies. Conversely, a much smaller CJTF might be deployed to provide C^2 for a small contingent of only land and air forces.

It is critical, according to the US and all allies except France, that the task-force lines of command lead clearly back to the MNC responsible for Article 5 defence in the region concerned, since a CJTF operation could escalate unexpectedly into a defence of alliance territory or forces. For WEU-led CJTFs, procedures to recall a force to NATO control, including a national headquarters should that eventuality be agreed, must be developed and exercised. This is because territorial defence is considered, even by the WEU, to be executed under Article 5 of the Washington Treaty (NATO).[10] Once deployed, a CJTF under NATO would report either directly to the regional MNC or through an MSC, depending on factors such as geography and overall mission profile. One variable in determining the role of the MSC is whether the CJTF is land-based or sea-based. The benefits of an intervening headquarters generally increases for land-based operations, while maritime forces tend to operate over greater distances without additional C^2 echelons.

The CJTF will operate under agreed NATO standing operating procedures (SOPs) and standardisation agreements (STANAGS). Non-NATO nations engaging in CJTF operations must be proficient in these procedures in order to participate successfully in contingencies. When a headquarters is activated, national approval to allow all assigned personnel to deploy will be needed to avoid eroding command and staff efficiency on the brink of deployment.[11] In addition to the NATO staff, non-NATO nations contributing forces to a CJTF will augment the headquarters with essential liaisons and staffs. This is an area where NATO's PFP will play a crucial role by developing the capability for non-NATO states to integrate smoothly into CJTFs. The capacity to operate together with NATO, and to respond to crises that are affecting their own regions, will be a tangible extension of security and stability to partner-states.

Since CJTFs can anticipate extended deployments, a personnel rotation plan will be required for continuity in headquarters' staff performance and in the tempo of force operations. UN peacekeeping forces generally follow a six-month rotation plan and, historically, peace operations tend to extend over long periods. It is thus possible that a CJTF will have to operate (perhaps in a hostile environment) for a number of years. Conversely, over time, long-running operations such as peacekeeping must necessarily be converted to more permanent arrangements than a task force comprising resources borrowed from other headquarters and agencies. This is an issue that CJTF planners have yet to address.

Mission Profiles
Another key factor in designing CJTFs is the limited purposes for which they will be employed, that is, to conduct peace operations outside the NATO area as that area is defined in Article 6 of the North Atlantic Treaty. Peace operations (the so-called 'non-Article 5 operations') are described in NATO's Military Committee document 327, 'NATO Military Planning for Peace Support Operations', and encompass conflict prevention, peacekeeping, humanitarian aid and peace-enforcement. The missions for CJTFs will fall into these four categories. At the operational level, Supreme Headquarters Allied Powers Europe (SHAPE) has drafted separate military doctrine for peace operations.[12] WEU military missions can be found in the 1992 Petersberg Declaration and are similar to NATO's MC 327, including humanitarian and rescue operations, peacekeeping and peacemaking.[13]

The geographical areas into which NATO (or the WEU) may agree to deploy a CJTF is, ultimately, a political question, although military capabilities and limitations must also be considered. In contemplating geographic regions where a CJTF might be deployed, it can be assumed that any mission will aim to protect collective Alliance interests – interests that are likely to include preservation of peace in the lands and waters immediately adjacent to NATO territory. Security interests might also extend to distant areas where conflict could threaten European security and stability.

The accumulation of a ready reservoir of military personnel experienced in collective crisis response will be a significant by-product of CJTF planning, procedural agreements, exercises and training. An experienced cadre is a crucial factor in any military undertaking, both inside NATO and, as was demonstrated in the 1991 Gulf War, in *ad hoc* coalitions. Some urgent missions, such as non-combatant evacuation, initial disaster relief and search and rescue, may be executed on the spot if there is no time for the political decisions and assembly required for CJTF. Nonetheless, such immediate situations will benefit from the availability of veterans of CJTF planning and training.

Logistical Support

CJTF logistical support will be a major challenge for an alliance that is used to the luxuries of interior lines of communication, fixed bases and a wealth of host-nation support. NATO's infrastructure, logistics planning and support must meet the challenges of rapid deployment, long and potentially unsecured lines of communication and remote, bare-base operations. While NATO will probably adhere to the principle of national responsibility for supplies and services for CJTF support, there will be unique transport and distribution requirements that will need a multinational capability. Depending on the operational environment and the size of the task force, logistics coordination might be handled by either an integral logistics staff or – in more demanding situations – by an independent combined-joint logistics command.

In addition to support for national forces, support must be planned for headquarters and support elements assigned directly from NATO. Service support for these elements will be another responsibility of the logistics coordination staff. When a CJTF is detached to the WEU, NATO's logistics concepts and infrastructure system will follow and provide the same measure of support as if the CJTF were NATO-led. Host-nation support, another historic staple of NATO logistics, will be unreliable or unavailable in most out-of-area crises, and in humanitarian aid operations it will be self-defeating for the CJTF to rely upon (or compete for) the meagre resources available to the population being assisted. In sum, a comprehensive logistics concept will have to provide for task-force self-sustainment, a factor unknown to NATO planners.

Communications and Information

A crucial task will be to create the necessary communications and information-system architecture to support a radical new operational concept. A deployed CJTF headquarters must be able to communicate not only through traditional rearward, lateral and forward military linkages, but with local governmental, non-governmental and international agencies. The absence of deployable long-range, multiple-user systems has already been identified here as a critical shortcoming.

Lack of interoperable systems is a second critical deficiency. Although the NATO Integrated Communications System (NICS) is sophisticated, it is essentially fixed and non-deployable. Nor is NICS designed for connectivity with non-NATO forces (such as East European partners). Operational level NATO–WEU links are also absent.

In the near- to mid-term at least, CJTFs will be heavily dependent on the United States and one or two other countries for strategic and operational communications and intelligence systems. In this regard, space-based systems will be particularly helpful in extending existing NICS networks to deployed CJTFs, either afloat or ashore. Some Europeans have voiced the goal of acquiring their own command, control, communications and intelligence capabilities, to be resident in the WEU. Current levels of defence spending, however, militate against the quick replacement of national capabilities.

Employment Options

Military planners envisage three CJTF employment scenarios. The basic scenario, the one that satisfies the urgent requirement to modify the existing military structure for new missions, is the deployment of a CJTF consisting of forces solely from NATO member-countries. However, in order to design a CJTF headquarters concept suitable for command and control of non-NATO forces, as well as operating under the control of the WEU, the tri-MNC planners considered three employment scenarios: a 'NATO-only' CJTF; a 'NATO-plus' CJTF (including some non-NATO states); and a WEU-led CJTF. A CJTF headquarters could be deployed under any of these options, depending upon NATO political decisions and the nations actually involved.

• *NATO-Only CJTF.* A NATO-only CJTF might involve forces from up to 15 NATO members (the sixteenth member, Iceland, has no military forces), although, even if NATO agrees to act, some allies may elect not to contribute forces. Since CJTF forces must be ready on short notice, the forces which member-states might offer to a CJTF are likely to be NATO reaction forces, particularly the ACE Rapid Reaction Corps (ARRC), the Multinational Division (Central) or the standing naval forces in the Atlantic (STANAVFORLANT) and Mediterranean (STANAVFORMED).[14]

Forces earmarked for CJTF contingencies will have to concentrate their planning on peace-support operations, and engage in significantly different training and exercise regimens from those they undertook during the Cold War. Some of the greatest challenges for NATO military staffs are likely to be strategic deployment and sustainment requirements. Units previously accustomed to a single mission close to fixed support bases will find themselves in scenarios more closely resembling those of the US Army's 18th Airborne Corps, a unit devoted almost exclusively to contingency operations.

• *NATO-Plus CJTF.* Because CJTFs might be employed in crises affecting PFP partners as well as NATO, the Alliance hopes that partner-states will join a 'NATO-plus' CJTF operation. NATO-plus is a particularly desirable aspect of the CJTF initiative and is accorded high priority by both CJTF and PFP planners. The capability to operate together with NATO militarily is a central objective of PFP activities. As shown by the intense effort being made by partner-state forces participating in IFOR, being part of a CJTF operation is seen as a demonstration of military compatibility with NATO. Thus far 27 states have accepted the invitation to join PFP, and NATO has agreed to 16 Individual Partnership Programmes.[15]

Under PFP's Partnership Work Plans, partner militaries are exposed to NATO procedures and standards and participate in peace-support operations planning and exercises. In a crisis, skills honed under the PFP programme can be used in a CJTF response, effectively extending NATO's stabilising role beyond its members' territory. Even if not actually called on to deploy, the planning and capability developed under PFP and through CJTF exercises are likely to foster a greater sense of security to partner-states, especially as military-to-military contacts deepen and the pool of personnel with NATO-plus CJTF experience grows.

In the near term there will be formidable obstacles to overcome, especially language problems (the official NATO languages are French and English, but the working language in the NATO military structure is English), and, in some cases, cultural differences. There will also be doctrinal discrepancies in all manner of military operations. In the short term, equipment incompatibility will not be an insurmountable obstacle, as NATO has long managed a wide variety of different items in all its major (and not-so-major) equipment categories. To succeed in fast-moving contingency operations, however, NATO must revive efforts at standardisation and interoperability, especially in the area of command and control. Some logistics standards, such as those for fuel and ammunition, must also be given priority. These concerns aside, the capability exists today to operate together in a crisis.

• *WEU-Led CJTF.* On a case-by-case basis, NATO members may, by decision in the North Atlantic Council (NAC), provide a CJTF headquarters and related support assets to the WEU to conduct a WEU-led CJTF operation. The forces themselves would be solicited by the WEU from its members, associates and Associate Partners – 21 countries in all.[16] Under this option, a NATO military command (MNC or MSC) would probably assume a support role. In June 1994, the WEU provided NATO with a concept paper outlining broad operational requirements for a CJTF, but direct staff-to-staff participation was only agreed to in April 1995.[17] Although all the details have yet to be worked out, some observations can be made on how a CJTF might operate under the WEU and what challenges it will face.

Once a decision is taken in the NAC, NATO will direct one of its MSCs to stand up a CJTF and prepare for deployment. During the stand-up process, the CJTF headquarters will be missioned and force-tailored. At an appropriate point, control of the CJTF would be transferred to the WEU. There is a possibility that, as negotiations between the WEU and NATO on the concept for a European-led (WEU) CJTF unfold, the way may open for employment of a national headquarters from a WEU member-state as a CJTF headquarters, in lieu of a NATO-provided headquarters. The prospect of national headquarters has aroused concerns that NATO might be weakend, or that Europe could see a shift back to national (as opposed to multilateral) militaries.

As well as the option of using a national headquarters, another potential candidate for a WEU-led CJTF is the Eurocorps, a five-nation headquarters responsive to NATO, but outside NATO's integrated military structure. So far as the WEU is concerned, either of these options is more desirable than 'borrowing' part of NATO's structure by accepting a NATO CJTF headquarters.

The size of a WEU-controlled operation, and hence composition of the CJTF headquarters and forces deployed, is expected to be smaller than that of NATO-led operations. This is based on an unstated assumption that, if a crisis is large enough to concern all the allies (not just NATO's European members), then NATO would direct the operation. Another factor is that, while WEU missions under the Petersberg Declaration are essentially the same as NATO's, the WEU is only in the initial stages of adapting to its new role and has no formal military C^2 structure similar to NATO. In sum, the WEU will be incapable of unaided large-scale operations for the foreseeable future.

In developing NATO–WEU agreements on CJTF, a central issue is identifying the role of SACEUR or the Supreme Allied Commander Atlantic (SACLANT). One view is that either SACEUR or SACLANT could be designated as the 'supporting commander' to the WEU operational commander. Because these are, conveniently, also US national commanders, they could provide NATO resources as well as agreed US support assets. The supporting-commander concept is borrowed from US C^2 doctrine, and will have to stand the test of Alliance scrutiny, particularly on the political level. Another issue is the adequacy of a WEU political–military structure directing a CJTF operation, especially where operational and strategic factors interface. The WEU has few structures in place to match the robustness of the NATO Military Committee, International Military Staff (IMS) or MNCs. The WEU is studying this problem, but wants to avoid creating redundant structures. Instead, it may strengthen its operations headquarters concept or have the state that provides the operations headquarters act as go-between for the WEU Council and the CJTF or force commander.[18]

Conclusions: Realising an Operational Capability

CJTF is far from an operational reality. Indeed, the concept itself remains on NATO's drawing board because of ineluctable political wrangling in both the NAC and the WEU Council. There are formidable problems to solve before the concept's minimum requirements are met. National doctrines on techniques such as task-force employment, defining the C^2 linkages between commands, airspace control and the use of technologies (especially for information processing and decision support systems) must be harmonised by the Alliance and adapted for multinational uses. One positive note is the existence of numerous STANAGS that have been refined over 40 years for collective defence operations – these will be a valuable foundation for new procedures.

A particularly important issue for NATO to address is the impact of potential national decisions not to permit deployment of personnel assigned to a CJTF headquarters that has been activated for an operation. Answers to this question will require a firm grasp not only of the aims of the CJTF initiative, but also of the multinational political and military context in which a solution must be devised. Other issues will require more time to solve, among them the dearth of English-speaking commanders and staff officers in Eastern European militaries. No doubt language will be a barrier to interoperability for some time. On the institutional side, a long-term commitment will be needed to develop the modalities for close WEU–NATO cooperation in crisis response. These two organisations are just beginning to establish the transparency and reciprocity necessary for effective coordination.

Further questions, such as the divisions of labour among MNC, MSC and a CJTF during operations; the interoperability of national, NATO and WEU communications and intelligence systems; the nature of training and exercises; and the assessment of deployment requirements, are all virgin territory for NATO military planners. In addition, NATO's venture into completely new command-and-control and force-employment concepts coincides with the much-heralded revolution in military affairs (RMA). RMA is a forward-looking phenomenon drawing on the impact of information technologies on warfare (and all military affairs, including peace-support operations), and the subsequent transformation of military operations and organisations with the goal of gaining and maintaining strategic, operational and tactical information dominance. Whether NATO's concept for the future – CJTF – can harness the fruits of this revolution will be a huge factor in its operational success. Yet, practically speaking, if NATO's military structure is to remain relevant it has no choice but to place itself at the leading edge of RMA concepts and technologies – and that will mean reversing years of declining investment in modernisation, especially in communication and information systems. Fortunately, NATO military commanders understand the gravity of these issues and are beginning to tackle them.

Regardless of the intent to minimise costs, some modernisation expense associated with the CJTF initiative will be unavoidable, such as capital investment in CJTF-specific equipment, training and exercises, and operations and maintenance. The call to spend resources on CJTF will have to overcome the recent tide in defence-spending cuts, which has not yet begun to subside.

CJTF project officers within NATO and WEU staffs have made modest headway despite the slow progress on political issues. The allies are aware that, unless NATO can find the military tools for deterring and responding when their collective interests are threatened, the Alliance's utility in terms of security will wither and fall into disuse even as security problems multiply. They also know that Central and East Europe – where the most unstable areas along NATO's borders exist – must be drawn closer to NATO to achieve a permanent peace in Europe. They know, too, that the EU's fledgling ESDI needs help to grow stronger, and perhaps eventually become free-standing in many regional crisis situations. That will lead to a greater balance in the transatlantic partnership which many believe is essential to keep NATO strong. CJTF, more than any other initiative since the Cold War, offers hope that these objectives can be achieved.

Despite the enduring challenges in C^2, logistics and communications, both ACE and ACLANT have the capability to respond to crisis now. This is most evident in the detailed planning for peace operations in former Yugoslavia. The final CJTF concept may, in fact, reflect much of what has been learned daily by AFSOUTH in *Operations Deny Flight* and *Sharp Guard*, and is now being discovered anew on the steep learning curve of *Operation Joint Endeavour*. What this portends for the future of the Alliance is a completely new NATO capability that addresses the security concerns of its members and partners while preserving the nature of the most successful security and defence alliance in history.

That goal is, of course, worth pursuing. But two years have passed since NATO's highest authorities approved the notion of CJTF, with only recent painstaking progress on political differences. Compromises are long overdue. Alliance leaders should seek an expeditious settlement of the remaining issues, based on a spirit of trust and cooperation, and a resolute determination to keep the Alliance strong. They should then direct NATO military commanders to make CJTFs available for employment as quickly as they can. It is time to finish putting into theory what the Alliance, in Bosnia, is now having to do in practice.

The views expressed in this chapter are the author's own and not those of the National Defense University, Washington DC, or the US Department of Defense.

Notes

1. Senator Richard Lugar's remarks to the Overseas Writers Club, 23 June 1993, as reported in 'NATO's Last Chance' by Stephen S. Rosenfeld, *Washington Post*, 2 July 1993, p. A19.

2. Peacetime for NATO is essentially anything short of collective defence under Article 5 of the North Atlantic Treaty. In future, NATO intends to rely primarily on the CJTF concept to provide a military response to crisis in non-Article 5 situations.

3. The point here must not be lost: NATO needs to exercise common procedures in order to be successful in multinational operations. Exercises also expose the militaries to each other's unique methods and make battlefield success more likely with fewer casualties. Most of the forces of NATO allies that joined the 1991 Gulf War coalition had experienced working with the US through NATO (apart from the French, with predictable results). Similarly, CJTF provides a set of techniques as a vehicle – a game

book – for working together in future conflicts. NATO's long investment in teamwork should be seen as wise for the future just as in the past.

4. See NATO Declaration of Heads of State and Government at the North Atlantic Council meeting in Brussels, 10–11 January 1994, para. 9.

5. See Joint Chiefs of Staff, *Dictionary of Military and Associated Terms*, JCS Pub. 1 (Washington DC: Government Printing Office, 1987), pp. 76, 200–2 and 367; and Joint Chiefs of Staff, *Doctrine for Joint Operations*, Joint Pub. 3-0 (Washington DC: Government Printing Office, 1993), p. II-15.

6. Competing definitions plague the broad doctrine of peace-support operations, a NATO term which is identical to the US term 'peace operations'. More confusion surrounds the category of 'peacemaking', which in both UN and NATO parlance is a strictly diplomatic undertaking, while the WEU gives it the meaning that the UN and NATO reserve for 'peace-enforcement', which involves combat operations. The meaning of peace-enforcement can also be misleading. *NATO Doctrine for Peace Support Operations* (draft), dated 28 February 1994, refers to the Korean and Gulf Wars as the best examples of 'peace-enforcement'. One can only wonder, then, what constitutes 'war' in the lexicon of peace operations.

7. Initially Commander-in-Chief Channel (CINCHAN) participated along with Allied Command Europe (ACE) and Allied Command Atlantic (ACLANT) as they completed work in March 1994 on the initial draft CJTF C2 concept. However, Channel Command was de-activated, as previously planned, in July 1994, leaving only two NATO MNCs. These two MNC commanders are SACEUR and SACLANT – both Americans.

8. France left the integrated military structure in 1966 in order to operate independently except in the event of an actual attack on NATO territory. Thereafter, France sought increased political oversight on the activities of the major NATO commanders. Since 1990, France has especially resisted the evolution of military planning for non-Article 5 scenarios. At the December 1995 NATO ministerial meetings, France announced it would join the Military Committee and the activities of the Defence Planning Committee. While this is a positive development, it is unclear what it will mean in terms of progress towards further adapting the Alliance's integrated military command structure.

9. As an indicator of expected response times, NATO's ACE Rapid Reaction Corps (ARRC) alerted to cover the potential withdrawal of UN forces in Bosnia – and a prime force for CJTF operations – planned to deploy its headquarters to the theatre in 7–15 days, according to the ARRC Commander, Lt-Gen. Mike Walker, British Army. See Charles Miller, 'Reaction Corps is Set to Cover UN Pullout', *Defense News*, vol. 10, no. 17, 1–7 May 1995, p. 8.

10. With the signing of the Washington Treaty in 1949, the exercise of military responsibilities for collective defence under the 1948 Brussels Treaty was transferred from the Western Union (forerunner to the WEU) to NATO. See *NATO Handbook* (Brussels: NATO Office of Information and Press, 1995), pp. 196–97. Nonetheless, recent commentators on the WEU's re-activation correctly observe that the Brussels Treaty remains a collective defence treaty, suggesting that some see a future WEU role in collective defence, in addition to crisis response.

11. States with representatives assigned to CJTF headquarters staff positions will be asked to agree to deploying them even if they do not provide forces. However, the nature of a voluntary alliance means that deploying either forces or individual personnel will always be a national prerogative.

12. Excluding peace-enforcement operations, which are essentially conventional combat operations and are addressed adequately in existing NATO military doctrine.

13. See 'On Strengthening WEU's Operational Role', Section II of the Petersberg Declaration, the public announcement following the meeting of WEU Foreign and Defence Ministers to determine guidelines for the future development of the WEU in Bonn, Germany, 19 June 1992. Note that the WEU term 'peacemaking' equates with peace-enforcement in UN terminology. In conjunction with the creation of a military planning staff, the Petersberg Declaration designated the above missions and directed the staff to conduct contingency planning.

14. The Multinational Division (Central) is fully operational and includes Belgium, German, Dutch and British forces.

15. Theoretically, PFP is open to all 53 members of the Organisation for Security and Cooperation in Europe (OSCE). See Williams, chapter 11.

16. The WEU has ten full members, three Associate Members, nine Associate Partners and five observer countries – 27 countries in all that participate in WEU activities. Group breakdowns are as follows: the full members are Belgium, France, Germany, Greece, Italy, Luxembourg, the Netherlands, Portugal, Spain and the UK; Associate Members are Iceland, Norway and Turkey – three NATO members not in the EU; Associate Partners are Bulgaria, the Czech Republic, Estonia, Hungary, Latvia, Lithuania, Poland, Romania, and Slovakia; and, finally, observer countries include Austria, Denmark, Finland, Ireland and Sweden. Full and associate member-countries pledge military forces to the WEU for planning through a process – similar to NATO's Defence Planning Questionnaire – known as 'Forces Answerable to WEU' or FAWEU. Associate Partners may also offer forces for WEU operations. Thus, because Iceland has no military forces, a total of 21 countries can provide forces to the WEU. At present there are no provisions for observer-country forces, but this might change in the future.

17. See WEU note C(94)103, 'Criteria and Modalities for Effective Use by the WEU of CJTF', 28 June 1994 (classified WEU restricted).

18. The WEU C2 concept for operations is principally *ad hoc*; each operation's command arrangement is unique. Political authorities designate an Operation Headquarters, typically an existing national headquarters of a member-state, a Force Headquarters and a force commander. The command-and-control structures are usually chosen based upon national contributions. The WEU internal document that covers these procedures is WEU C(93)38, 'Secretary-General's Note, Organization and Operation of WEU in Times of Crisis', 28 April 1993 (classified WEU restricted).

Chapter 11
Partnership for Peace: Permanent Fixture or Declining Asset?

Nick Williams

Partnership for Peace (PFP), NATO's military cooperation programme with non-NATO states, has now been in operation for two years. Since its launch at the NATO summit in January 1994, it has attracted 27 countries and generated an increasing level of military cooperation, transparency and interoperability between NATO and Partner forces. The aims of the initiative were ambitious and far-reaching. In the words of the NATO Summit Declaration, PFP would 'forge new security relationships between the North Atlantic Alliance and its Partners for Peace'.[1] Within a relatively short time, PFP has in fact done just that – to the extent that it is now difficult to imagine a NATO without Partners or indeed a real Partnership without the detailed mechanisms of cooperation that PFP introduced. In the words of Richard Holbrooke, US Assistant Secretary of State for Europe, 'PFP has become an integral part of the European security scene'.[2]

Yet, right from the outset, doubts were expressed about PFP's real long-term value. Some saw it as a 'quick fix', enabling NATO to postpone the hard question of NATO enlargement. Others saw it as a very small evolution in NATO's policy of cooperation which had been in place and moving forward since 1991 under the North Atlantic Cooperation Council (NACC).[3] What the criticisms had in common was the idea that PFP in itself had little intrinsic value: its importance could only be judged in relation to enlargement and the extent to which it hastened or delayed the admission of new members to NATO. Such assessments were not entirely surprising given that, at the January 1994 summit, allied leaders made a commitment to the eventual enlargement of NATO and simultaneously to a Partnership that would extend cooperation throughout Europe. As PFP would play a significant part in the process of enlargement, it was difficult to judge whether NATO's priority was to extend cooperation or to move towards enlargement.

Initial evaluations of PFP thus tended to concentrate on the initiative's extrinsic value – the fact that 'active participation in PFP would play an important role in the evolutionary process of the expansion of NATO'.[4] And the consensus among outside observers seemed to be that PFP effectively stalled the process. The fact that Russia endorsed PFP during US President Bill Clinton's visit to Moscow immediately following the NATO summit confirmed the suspicions of those who felt that the Alliance had effectively taken a step back from, rather than towards, its enlargement. The Joint US–Russia Declaration described PFP as an 'important element of an emerging new European Security architecture' – implying that PFP was intended more as a permanent structure than as a preparatory process for NATO membership.[5] At a related news conference, in August 1994, Russian President Boris Yeltsin expressed his satisfaction that NATO had not been expanded.[6] A few months later, US Senator Richard Lugar famously described PFP as a 'policy for postponement'.[7]

Partnership for Peace: A Multi-Purpose Framework
The problem with analysing PFP solely as a function of enlargement is not that such an interpretation would be misguided. Without the enlargement debate heating up over the course of 1993, PFP might not have materialised in the form it did. Instead, the problem is that such assessments are one-dimensional: they assume that if PFP is inefficient as a mechanism for advancing NATO enlargement, then it is evidently efficient as a means of avoiding it. These assessments overlook the innovative features of PFP, which make it a genuine contribution to military and defence-related cooperation in Europe, irrespective of NATO enlargement.

A close examination of PFP's various features would reveal that it is not a single coherent, monolithic scheme, with only one purpose and one means for achieving it. Rather, it is a framework that accommodates several different purposes and is flexible enough to further those purposes simultaneously. Such ambiguity may make PFP difficult to analyse, but it is a major factor of the Partnership's success in attracting and maintaining such a large number of countries, from a wide geographical area and with very different security traditions and expectations. As Table 1 indicates, PFP has a wide range of participants:

Table 1: Current Standing of Non-NATO States in NATO Programmes

Country	Date of Signature	IPP	In PARP[a]	In IFOR[b]
Central Europe				
Poland	2 February 1994	✓	✓	✓
Hungary	8 February 1994	✓	✓	✓
Slovakia	9 February 1994	✓	✓	✓
Czech Republic	10 March 1994	✓	✓	✓
South-east Europe				
Romania	26 January 1994	✓	✓	✓
Bulgaria	14 February 1994	✓	✓	✓
Albania	23 February 1994	✓	✓	–
Slovenia	30 March 1994	✓	✓	–
Malta	26 April 1995	–	–	–
FYROM	15 November 1995	–	–	–
Baltic States				
Lithuania	27 January 1994	✓	✓	✓
Estonia	3 February 1994	✓	✓	✓
Latvia	14 February 1994	✓	✓	✓
Eastern Europe				
Ukraine	8 February 1994	✓	✓	✓
Moldova	16 March 1994	✓	–	–
Russian Fed.[c]	22 June 1994	✓	–	✓
Belarus	11 January 1995	✓	–	–
Non-NATO EU				
Sweden	9 May 1994	✓	✓	✓
Finland	9 May 1994	✓	✓	✓
Austria	10 February 1995	–	–	✓
Caucasus				
Georgia	23 March 1994	–	–	–
Azerbaijan	4 May 1994	–	–	–
Armenia	5 October 1994	–	–	–
Central Asia				
Turkmenistan	10 May 1994	–	–	–
Kazakhstan	27 May 1994	–	–	–
Kyrgyzstan	1 June 1994	–	–	–
Uzbekistan	13 July 1994	–	–	–

Sources: The Peace Implementation Force (IFOR) and Allied Forces Southern Europe (AFSOUTH) *Fact Sheet*, 4 January 1996; *NATO Review*, Brussels, various years.

Notes: [a] PARP stands for Planning and Review Process.
[b] These Partner countries had expressed an interest in participating and were subsequently invited to contribute to IFOR by NATO's then Acting Secretary-General, Sergio Balanzino. Egypt, Pakistan and Malaysia have also been invited to participate. Offers from other countries continue to be assessed.
[c] Russia and Ukraine have enhanced relationships with NATO in addition to PFP.

- those whose chief objective is to join NATO quickly (Central Europeans), and those whose chief objective is to prevent it (Russia);
- those who wish to associate closely with the Alliance, and those who traditionally have tried to keep their distance from military blocs (the former 'neutrals');
- those who wish to act within NATO, and those who merely want to learn from it (the Central Asian republics). Such a programme, by definition, requires a range of purposes that reflect the diversity of interests of its participants.

Within PFP it is possible to distinguish three separable 'purposes', each with its own logic and each with sufficient value to attract participation in its own right. This does not mean that within PFP there is a series of separate compartments in which Partners pursue different programmes of cooperation. Rather, PFP contains several possibilities and potentialities. Partners differ somewhat in what they wish to get out of PFP. Equally, NATO can have different approaches to, and expectations of, its various Partners.

Partnership for Peace as an Intensification of NATO's Outreach

The Framework Document that Partners sign on joining the initiative confirms that PFP was established 'within the framework of the North Atlantic Cooperation Council'.[8] And the most evident and visible effect of PFP has been to intensify the cooperation that NATO undertook in launching the NACC. The NACC was formed in December 1991 in order to overcome the residual security effects of the Cold War by promoting 'dialogue, cooperation and partnership' between former adversaries. The intention was partly to prevent the re-emergence of new divisions in Europe and partly to help and influence the emerging democracies in the East as they developed independent security policies, many of them for the first time. As NATO's new Strategic Concept of 1991 made clear, 'cooperation' was not, as many commentators have assumed, a peripheral part of NATO's work, but a central element of a new strategy in which NATO aimed to become a major stabilising influence for the whole of a fully democratising Europe.

For many former Warsaw Pact countries that joined the NACC in 1991 and 1992, the association with NATO represented a highly symbolic break with the past. Membership of NACC was an assertion of their independence and signalled their ambition to integrate into Western security and economic institutions. They expected to learn and benefit from NATO's expertise in the short term; for the longer term they expected to be allowed to join the Alliance.

The NACC, however, made no concession to those countries that wished to become members of the Alliance. It made, and still makes, no distinction between the 22 countries which join the allies within it.[9] Its annual work plan, which provides for consultation and information exchange in a range of political and security-related matters, is open to all Partners.[10] Inevitably, the concept of equality within the NACC reflects the optimism of the period in which it was founded: that all former communist countries were equally committed and in principle capable of democratisation and integrating into a common, cooperative security system. In the conception of then NATO Secretary-General Manfred Wörner, NATO was a pole of attraction to which Eastern Europe would be naturally drawn for its security.[11] Through the NACC, NATO could induce and accelerate a process of European security integration to which all countries naturally aspired.

PFP was intended to take this process a major step further. At its launch, it was presented as a practical programme that would transform the relationship between NATO and participating states: 'This new programme goes beyond dialogue and cooperation to forge a *real* partnership'.[12] The partnership would have five objectives, none of them entirely new, and all of them traceable in some form or other to what the NACC had already achieved or aimed to achieve:

- to facilitate transparency in national defence planning and budgeting processes;
- to ensure democratic control of defence forces;
- to maintain the capability and readiness to contribute, subject to constitutional considerations, to operations under the authority of the UN and/or responsibility of the Conference [now Organisation] on Security and Cooperation in Europe (OSCE);
- to develop cooperative military relations with NATO, for the purpose of joint planning, training and exercises in order to strengthen their ability to undertake missions in the fields of peacekeeping, search and rescue, humanitarian operations and others as may subsequently be agreed; and
- to develop, over the longer term, forces that are better able to operate with those of the members of the North Atlantic Alliance.

PFP broadened and deepened the integrative process represented by the NACC in two main ways. First, the Partnership was explicitly offered to all OSCE (formerly CSCE) countries able and willing to contribute to the programme: this meant that countries that were not part of the Cold War Alliance system could join, and Austria, Finland, the Former Yugoslav Republic of Macedonia, Malta, Slovenia and Sweden have done so. Second, PFP emphasised practical programmes of cooperation, rather than generalised consultation and information exchange.

One of the innovative features of PFP, which makes possible deeper forms of cooperation than within the NACC, is the concept of Individual Partnership Programmes (IPP). IPPs allow each country to agree on a programme of activities with NATO and develop its Partnership at its own pace and within its preferred scope. Yet, despite this new possibility for countries to differentiate themselves within PFP, all countries choose their activities from the same basic menu. There is no scope, therefore, for NATO to develop a form of relationship with one country which it could deny to another. NATO, after consulting Partners, sets the menu, and Partners pick what they want and what they can afford to do: its emphasis is on self-differentiation.[13] As in the NACC, PFP seeks to influence each country equally towards a close relationship with NATO based on shared values and the common objective to build a more stable Europe.

In joining PFP, countries formally reaffirmed their shared values – such as a commitment to freedom and democracy – and recalled their international obligations – such as respecting existing borders and settling disputes peacefully. Much emphasis is placed on the democratic and civilian control of military forces, and transparency in defence planning is promoted. This is well within the concept of the NACC, which aims to build stability in Europe through spreading shared democratic values and reducing suspicions between neighbouring countries. Although in retrospect this idea may appear optimistic, or even romantic, it is evident that the desire to join or associate with NATO (and hence the United States) remains a powerful incentive in the continuing adaptation to a new European security environment.

Partnership for Peace as a Framework for Joint Action
In many respects, therefore, PFP remains firmly within the NACC framework while representing a more sophisticated approach to developing relationships with individual Partners. The Partnership introduces no new mutual security obligation or commitment. In return for active participation within PFP, the Alliance undertakes to consult with any Partner that considers its political independence or territorial integrity to be under threat. In other words, there is a hint of solidarity in the event of a threat, but no commitment to the defence of a Partner. PFP thus maintains the distinction between allies and Partners that characterises the NACC, and preserves collective defence as the prerogative of NATO itself.

Yet PFP does make a very significant operational advance over the NACC. It was conceived not just as a means of further intensifying the dialogue and cooperation that already existed, but also as a new framework for joint action in the sphere of peacekeeping. The framework document states that the Partnership 'is established as an expression of a joint conviction that stability and security in the Euro-Atlantic area can be achieved only through cooperation *and common action*'.[14] The protection and promotion of shared democratic values is considered fundamental to the Partnership. It is true that the NACC had also aimed to facilitate cooperation in the field of peacekeeping, and had made progress.[15] Yet much of the emphasis was on doctrinal rather than operational issues – developing a common approach to peacekeeping rather than establishing a real operational capability.

That PFP reflected an increased emphasis and urgency in the area of operational capability can be discerned more clearly in the mechanisms of PFP than in its objectives. These objectives, as noted earlier, do not go much further than what NATO had already been trying to achieve through the NACC process. Indeed, the most striking aspect of PFP is that it has introduced a structural and procedural depth previously absent in NATO's cooperation activities. The key features in this respect are:

- *Authority of the Council.* PFP operates under the authority of the North Atlantic Council (NAC): its direction and motivation come from the 16 allies and not the NACC. This gives PFP a dynamism that is inevitably missing in NACC, which lacks the resources but also the military structure to exploit the possibilities of joint action.

- *Partner Representation at NATO.* The permanent representation of Partners at NATO headquarters in Brussels and in a specifically formed Partnership Coordination Cell at Mons, Belgium, alongside Supreme Headquarters Allied Powers Europe (SHAPE), is a major structural innovation. The advantage of having Partners in place is that it facilitates the active contribution of Partners to the planning and development of the Partnership. It also considerably improves the understanding of NATO and communications between NATO and Partners. This is a particularly important asset when NATO is planning an operation, such as the Peace Implementation Force (IFOR) in Bosnia, which involves Partners.

- *Promotion of Interoperability.* Promoting interoperability between NATO and Partner forces has been the primary military objective under PFP. Field Marshal Sir Richard Vincent, Chairman of NATO's Military Committee, underlined the importance of interoperability in October 1995, and gave the example of non-NATO countries' inclusion in NATO contingency planning for Bosnia.[16]

Vincent also mentioned that NATO had already made available over 800 NATO standardisation documents, which are being progressively incorporated into Partners' military doctrine, concepts of operations and standard operating procedures. Over time, this standardisation will start to affect future equipment requirements, with a high priority on command, control and communications (C^3) systems.

- *The Planning and Review Process.* The fact that PFP is an evolving programme with a marked accent on joint action was underlined by the introduction of a biennial Planning and Review Process in January 1995. Under this process, which mirrors NATO's long-standing defence planning system, forces and resources that Partners have made available to PFP become the focus of a planning and review cycle. The first cycle focused on setting objectives for force interoperability.[17] As with NATO's own defence planning, the performance of Partners in meeting the objectives set will be assessed and evaluated in the next cycle, scheduled for 1997. Over time this process is designed to have a significant influence in moving interested Partners towards greater interoperability with NATO forces. The extent to which Partners and allies develop the capacity for joint action is also tested in a programme of PFP exercises which are growing in number and in sophistication – 80 are to be held in 1996.[18]

Taken together, the mechanisms of PFP amount to a formidable array of levers for cultivating a multinational peacekeeping capability, in which the constituent elements are interoperable and trained to the necessary minimum standards. These mechanisms are modelled on, and replicate within PFP, those of NATO. Taken individually, of course, there has been a tendency to underestimate or even ridicule the various aspects of PFP. George Brock of *The Times* referred to the first military exercise under PFP as 'a hastily convened military Kabuki play', and pointed to the fact that instruction was being given by US officers, 'who will almost certainly never take part in peacekeeping operations on European soil'.[19] The IFOR experience, however, should reduce the temptation to micro-criticise PFP.

Partnership for Peace as a Means of NATO Membership
PFP's third purpose, as previously noted, has received the greatest interest – preparing Partners for eventual NATO membership. Unlike mechanisms for general cooperation and joint action within PFP, the way in which PFP actually advances the process of enlargement is not readily discernable. By participating actively in a broad range of Partnership activities and processes, countries must inevitably familiarise themselves better with NATO procedures. It also helps Partners to organise themselves for working closely with NATO at political and military levels. Yet, to date, there is no scope within PFP for developing a pre-enlargement relationship with NATO that would definitively identify a country as heading for NATO membership. As in the dentist's waiting room, the length of the wait is not affected by the quality of the magazines the patient chooses to read.

Achieving interoperability with NATO forces for the purpose of peacekeeping is open to all Partners, as is the general exchange of defence planning and budget information provided for under the Planning and Review Process. The one way that is open to Partners who wish to demonstrate their credentials for membership is to participate in as many exercises as possible, to negotiate an extensive Individual Partnership Programme and to be seen as among the most active and capable of Partners.[20] All this serves to confirm the obvious: certain countries, notably the Central Europeans, want to join NATO and are ready to do what is needed to achieve this goal.

The progress that has been made towards NATO enlargement has not been the direct result of PFP. In January 1994, NATO leaders launched PFP and made a simultaneous commitment to enlarge NATO. Although they indicated that they would 'expect and would welcome NATO expansion', there was no indication of when that expectation might be fulfilled. It would be an evolutionary process, taking into account political and security developments throughout Europe.[21] The lack of precision regarding the mechanics of enlargement raised the question of whether enlargement would come at the end of the PFP process or could be earned through active PFP involvement. This uncertainty ironically benefited the new initiative. It led most countries to join PFP within the first few months in a competitive rush towards what German Defence Minister Volke Rühe referred to as the 'door opener'.[22] The decision to initiate a specific study on enlargement by NATO foreign ministers in December 1994 underlined the point that enlargement was in fact a separate process from PFP.

The 'Study on NATO Enlargement', completed in September 1995, affirms that enlargement 'will occur through a gradual, deliberate and transparent process'.[23] It envisages a strong role for PFP in preparing countries for membership, and emphasises the concept of Partners' self-differentiation. NATO would not, as yet, pick candidates for membership, but candidates would, through a Planning and Review process, for example, help to identify themselves by adopting 'certain minimum standards'.[24] Simultaneously, the study indicates that PFP will continue to be important *after* NATO enlargement in strengthening European security in general. At first glance these two parallel objectives might seem incompatible, as enlargement will remove some of the most active countries from the 'receiving' end of the Partnership (thus weakening PFP) while simultaneously risking alienating politically significant Partners such as Russia (thus widening the gap PFP is intended to reduce). It would nonetheless be premature to write the obituaries for PFP. With enlargement making measurable progress, PFP is now entering a new phase in its development, and there is an increased incentive for NATO to use PFP as a means of supporting the objective of an undivided Europe.[25]

The Next Steps

The enlargement study has given PFP a new impetus and clearer focus for the future, first as a preparation mechanism for membership of the Alliance, and second as a means of cooperation with countries that do not join NATO at first or at all. It is clear that, for the first function, PFP will have to develop further practical measures to assist specific countries in understanding NATO and adapting to its procedures. Equally, for PFP to fulfil its parallel function and make a valuable contribution to European security beyond enlargement, there will have to be a 'deepening' of cooperation within PFP to enhance its value as an instrument of security for allies and Partners alike. For countries that do not become members, PFP is intended to 'constitute a continuing vehicle for active cooperation with NATO' and to provide 'concrete evidence of NATO's continuing support and concern for their security'.[26]

Russia In or Out?

So far in the implementation of PFP there has been a positive equilibrium between its various parts, and sufficient ambiguity in its purpose to attract and maintain the participation of a diversity of countries, including, most notably, Russia. After considerable discussion between NATO and Russian officials, Russia was persuaded to join PFP in June 1994. This was taken as the start of a much closer relationship. NATO and Russia agreed to develop an extensive Individual Partnership Programme corresponding to Russia's size, importance and capabilities.[27] They also agreed to develop a political relationship *outside* PFP.

In practice, Russia's relationship with NATO has been marked more by the development of political consultations outside PFP than by military cooperation within it – understandably so, given the central importance of Bosnia to both during this period. Moreover, former Russian Foreign Minister Andrei Kozyrev tended to make cooperation in PFP conditional on the pace of the enlargement process. For instance, he refused to move forward with the next stage of PFP in December 1994 because he considered that NATO, in initiating its enlargement study, was substituting a policy of rapid enlargement for Partnership.[28] As he emphasised in December 1995, Moscow's position is quite straightforward: 'Yes to cooperation; no to enlargement'.[29] Without Russia in a close relationship with NATO, *after enlargement*, it would be difficult for the Alliance to sustain its claim that it wants to prevent new divisions of Europe, and that enlargement supports the objective of an undivided Europe.

1996 will see the next phase of the enlargement process, in which interested Partners will have the opportunity to learn more about the specific details of Alliance membership through an intensified bilateral dialogue.[30] This will be outside PFP. Within PFP, NATO plans a further enhancement of practical work to facilitate eventual membership for some and, for others, to strengthen their long-term Partnership.

This twin-track approach maintains the parallel incentives of potential membership and real Partnership that have characterised PFP from the outset. Yet, as each phase of the enlargement process unfolds, the risk of Russia withdrawing from the Partnership, and of interest waning among those who see their chances of joining NATO remaining remote, appears to grow.

The withdrawal of Russia from PFP would strike a blow, which, although not fatal, would deprive PFP of a considerable amount of its potential, both as an instrument of joint action and as a means of cooperation with countries that do not join the Alliance in the first wave. It is more likely, however, that, having participated in IFOR and established a working relationship with NATO in such a key operation, Russia will exploit rather than reject the opportunities open to it. Russia's concentration on establishing a prestigious relationship with the Alliance outside PFP has borne fruit in the offer by NATO to develop 'permanent mechanisms of consultation' with Russia.[31] This should go some way towards reassuring the Russians that the Alliance is committed to a constructive relationship with it. More usefully, it should ensure that consultation could, in future, proceed more fluently than appeared to be the case in relation to the key stages in the Bosnian crisis, when Russia sought consultations before key decisions, not notification after them.

There is growing evidence that Russia sees engagement with NATO as in its strategic interest, both despite enlargement and because of it. As Russia's Ambassador to NATO, Vitaly Churkin, stated in an interview in *Izvestiya*, 'cooperation with NATO is necessary'. In relation to enlargement he suggested that 'if NATO's expansion has become such a long drawn-out affair, it is because of pressure from Moscow'. He pointed to Russia's clear interest in becoming part of the 'NATO scenery' and using the time available before enlargement for active diplomacy.[32] The 'permanent structure of consultation' on offer would give Russia considerable scope for doing so.

The case for a stronger Russian military engagement with NATO is equally forceful, particularly since, by concentrating on the political side of the equation, Russia, before IFOR participation, had neglected the military side. Russia joined PFP after the Central European countries, and it delayed the development of its IPP. The participation of a Russian brigade in IFOR redresses the balance and sets a very positive precedent. It was facilitated by the presence of Russian General Leonti Shevstov at SHAPE for several weeks in October 1995, where he and his team familiarised themselves with NATO's military organisation and thinking. As reported in the Russian newspaper, *Krasnaya zvezda*, his assessment was reasonably positive.[33] Although as a military officer he could not rule out NATO as a potential threat, he endorsed the value of cooperating with it. In Bosnia, 'common unified tasks have to be performed. Thus it is a question of organising good working cooperation'. Of NATO he was complimentary: 'NATO is not a country but 16 states. And over many years people there have worked out a good structure and format for cooperation'. It seems that, for Russia, the balance of initiatives both political and military remains weighed in favour of greater cooperation and engagement in PFP.

Conclusion

As NATO enlargement proceeds, there is a risk that PFP's delicate equilibrium will be disturbed; its value both as a means of promoting cooperation and as a means for preparing a large number of countries for common action could be overtaken by an emphasis on enlargement. At some stage in the process –

however gradual and steady it might be – there will have to be a shift from self-differentiation by Partners to identification of candidates by the Alliance. At that point it may well be necessary to clarify some of the ambiguities in PFP that have helped it appeal to such a broad constituency of countries.

The possibility of PFP becoming a declining asset rather than the permanent fixture it was designed to be does exist – but it is small. The Partnership's value has always been misunderstood and misrepresented and only now, after two years of experience, is its strategic importance in creating common approaches to peacekeeping coming to be appreciated. IFOR will provide many political and military lessons – the most obvious of which will be the need to maintain and strengthen a system that has made such a broad coalition possible. With PFP structures effectively shadowing NATO's military structure, PFP is capable of generating important add-ons to any peacekeeping deployment, add-ons which are trained and ready to participate in an international force with NATO as a strong inner core. PFP's operational value is likely to ensure not just its survival, but also its vigour.

The views expressed in this chapter are the author's own and not those of NATO or Alliance member-countries.

Notes

1. NATO Summit Declaration, Press Communiqué M-1(94)3, 11 January 1994, Brussels, para. 14. NATO documents referred to in this chapter are available on the internet, at gopher NATO.int or http://www.nato.int.

2. Richard C. Holbrooke, 'America, A European Power', *Foreign Affairs*, vol. 74, no. 2, March–April 1995, p. 44.

3. The North Atlantic Cooperation Council was formed in December 1991 to promote dialogue, cooperation and partnership between NATO and former members of the Warsaw Pact. It now has 38 members.

4. NATO Summit Declaration, Press Communiqué M-1(94)3, 11 January 1994, Brussels, para. 13.

5. The text of the US–Russian declaration issued by the US Information Agency, 14 January 1994, and ITAR-TASS, 14 January 1994.

6. See Michael Mihalka, 'European–Russian Security and NATO's Partnership for Peace', *Radio Free Europe/Radio Liberty Research Report*, vol. 3, no. 33, 26 August 1994, p. 38.

7. 'NATO Enlargement and US Public Opinion', speech by Richard G. Lugar, Center for Strategic and International Studies Conference on 'NATO's Role in European Stability', Washington DC, 3 March 1995.

8. See NATO Press Communiqué M-1(94)2, 'Partnership for Peace: Invitation', issued by the Heads of State and Government, NAC, Brussels, 10 January 1994. For a full description of the PFP process, see Gebhardt von Moltke, 'Building a Partnership for Peace', *NATO Review*, vol. 42, no. 3, June 1994, pp. 3–7.

9. The members of NACC are: Albania, Armenia, Azerbaijan, Belarus, Bulgaria, Czech Republic, Estonia, Georgia, Hungary, Kazakhstan, Kyrgyzstan, Latvia, Lithuania,

Moldova, Poland, Romania, Russia, Slovakia, Tajikistan, Turkmenistan, Ukraine and Uzbekistan. As participants in PFP, Austria, Finland, Malta, Slovenia and Sweden have observer status in the NACC.

10. See 1996–97 NACC Work Plan, *NATO Review*, vol. 44, no. 1, January 1996, pp. 28–30. This also sets out the PFP topics on which PFP activities are based.

11. Interview in *Weser Kurier*, 17 January 1992.

12. NATO Press Communiqué, M-1(94)2, Brussels, 10 January 1994, italics added.

13. See von Moltke, 'Building a Partnership for Peace', pp. 3–7.

14. *Ibid.*, italics added.

15. The NACC *Ad Hoc* Group on Cooperation in Peacekeeping issued a report in June 1993 which identified a range of areas where further work could be done. See Press Release M-NACC-1(93)40, 'Report to the NACC *Ad Hoc* Group on Cooperation in Peacekeeping', Athens, 11 June 1993.

16. Sir Richard Vincent, speech to the Atlantic Treaty Association, Toronto, 7 October 1995.

17. See NATO Basic Fact Sheet No. 9, 'Partnership for Peace', Brussels, November 1995; also NATO Defence Planning Committee Communiqué, M-DPC/NPG-2(94)126, Brussels, 15 December 1994.

18. See 'NATO–PFP Training Paves Way for Coalition Missions', United States Information Service Report (Eur 205), 30 August 1995, in which US Joint Chiefs of Staff Chairman John Shalikashvili describes PFP exercises as an opportunity to introduce NATO standing agreements and operating procedures to Partner nations.

19. 'A Military Kabuki Play', George Brock, *The Spectator*, 1 October 1994, p. 18.

20. Polish Foreign Minister Andrzej Olechowski originally interpreted PFP as a means by which Partners could self-select the members for NATO membership. He was reported as saying that 'Poland must take the best of what is offered … it is up to a particular country how quickly it enters the Alliance'. Bulgaria, by contrast, was more welcoming because PFP offered equal chances to all. See Associated Press Reports, 14 January 1994.

21. NATO Press Communiqué M-1(94)3, para. 12.

22. See Reuter Press Report from the Press Conference, Travemünde, Germany, 22 October 1993, when the idea of PFP was first discussed by NATO Defence Ministers.

23. 'Study on NATO Enlargement', Brussels, 1 September 1995, para. 7.

24. *Ibid.*, para. 40.

25. See *ibid.*, paras 16 and 34–37, for example.

26. *Ibid.*, para. 36.

27. Summary of Conclusion of discussions between the North Atlantic Council and Foreign Minister of Russia, Brussels, 22 June 1994, published in *NATO Review*, no. 4, August 1994, p. 5.

28. See Andrei Kozyrev, 'Partnership or Cold Peace?', *Foreign Policy*, no. 99, Summer 1995, pp. 3–14.

29. *Agence France Presse*, Report of 6 December 1995, Brussels. See also Timothy Heritage, Reuter, 'Bosnia Deal Busts East–West Ties', Moscow, 29 November 1995.

30. See NATO Final Communiqué M-NAC-2 (95) 118, Brussels, 5 December 1995.

31. *Ibid.*, para. 4.

32. Leonid Mlechin, 'Sulking at the World is No Way to Behave', *Izvestiya*, 24 November 1995.

33. Mikhail Pogorely, 'General Leonti Shevstov, the First "One of Ours" at NATO', *Krasnaya zvezda*, 14 November 1995, p. 3.

Chapter 12
NATO's Role in Counter-Proliferation

Robert Joseph

The North Atlantic Alliance is often criticised for having made little progress in forging policies and implementing programmes responsive to the security conditions of the post-Cold War environment. NATO's response to the proliferation of nuclear, biological and chemical (NBC) weapons may well become an important exception to this record. Proliferation is increasingly perceived within the Alliance as both a political and a military threat that could undermine NATO's ability to conduct essential defence missions, both in regional conflicts beyond its borders and in protecting Alliance territory and populations, especially as proliferant states acquire longer-range and more sophisticated delivery means. Although allies continue to differ on the immediacy of the problem and the most effective means of response, there is an emerging consensus that NATO should act to protect against this growing threat.

With the fundamental change in the Soviet threat, regional conflicts now represent one of the major challenges to Alliance interests and a likely setting for military involvement. As NATO restructures its forces to deal with these conflicts, acquiring the capabilities to deter and defend against the regional NBC and missile threat becomes essential, perhaps the most important stimulus for force planning and defence analysis in the decades ahead. As a result, the Alliance's ability to respond effectively to the proliferation threat may well be the key indicator of NATO's ability to adapt to the new security environment.

Alliance progress in addressing the proliferation threat has been impressive. Allies have agreed on an assessment of the risks, as well as on the security implications of, and military requirements to meet, the proliferation challenge. The success of the ongoing NATO initiative in this area, however, will only be assured when the allies make national and collective commitments to field the military capabilities necessary to counter the proliferation threat and to incorporate the threat in the Alliance defence planning process, including in joint military doctrine, operational plans and training.

This chapter discusses the reasons underlying NATO's intensifying concern about NBC and missile proliferation and describes Alliance efforts to meet the challenge.

The Setting

One early casualty of the end of the Cold War was NATO's long-standing strategic outlook. Although NATO's Cold War doctrine had undergone periodic shifts to accommodate changes in Warsaw Pact forces and advances in technology, such as from rapid and massive nuclear retaliation (Military (MC) Committee document 14/2) to flexible response (MC 14/3) Alliance leaders had been guided by a consistent strategic principle – deterring and defending against the Soviet threat. Although the Alliance did periodically consult on 'out-of-area' operations, such operations had little influence on major force goals or defence planning.

One of the most central events that has helped to shape the Alliance's post-Cold War strategic concept was the Iraqi invasion of Kuwait in August 1990. Less than ten months after the Berlin Wall was dismantled, Iraq's aggression and the coalition's response demonstrated the profound changes that had taken place in the international security environment. Not only did regional threats now seem pre-eminent, but the very nature of deterrence and defence appeared to be radically altered. Cold War concepts such as graduated escalation and mutual assured destruction had little relevance in confronting an expansionist Iraq, whose leader did not share Western values or observe the 'accepted' rules of conflict.

In fact, the *Operation Desert Storm* experience raised questions about warfare itself. On the one hand, the coalition's overwhelming qualitative superiority in conventional forces quickly defeated Iraq in a spectacular, high-intensity war. On the other hand, the Iraqi use of ballistic missiles against coalition forces as well as against Israeli and Saudi cities, and the threat of Iraqi use of chemical and biological weapons, compelled the United States and its major allies to think about the potential implications stemming from the proliferation of NBC weapons in the hands of hostile states seeking political and territorial changes in regions of vital interest to the West.

In light of the *Operation Desert Storm* scare, and recalling the extensive use of chemicals and ballistic missiles in the earlier Iran–Iraq War, leaders in key allied capitals confronted the grim reality that the probability of NBC use could be much higher in a future conflict. The timing of the 1991 Gulf War was fortuitous in that Iraq attacked Kuwait before acquiring nuclear weapons; it is now known that Iraq was further along in the process than was thought at the time. Moreover, the coalition was successful in deterring the use of chemical and biological weapons, largely because of Iraqi 'mirror-imaging' about whether the coalition (and Israel) would respond to such use with nuclear weapons.[1] Alliance leaders understood they could not rely on luck in the future.

As a result of the Gulf experience, NATO leaders at the November 1991 summit in Rome acknowledged the 'problem' of nuclear, biological and chemical weapons proliferation, as well as increasingly capable missiles as a means of delivery. In the new 'Strategic Concept' articulated at the Rome meeting, proliferation was elevated to a subject requiring 'special consideration'.[2] Soon thereafter, the Alliance initiated several significant efforts, including the relevant intelligence groups giving greater attention to the threat of proliferation and the initiation of conceptual work on extended air-defence and theatre-missile-defence (TMD) requirements.

Nevertheless, despite the concerns evident at the Rome summit, it took more than two years – and a strong push from the United States – before the Alliance began a sustained effort at the policy level to develop the political–military framework necessary for understanding and responding to the overall threat to the Alliance posed by NBC and missile proliferation. It was not until the 1994 Brussels summit that NATO leaders declared proliferation to constitute 'a threat to international security' and established as a goal the development of 'an overall policy framework to consider how to reinforce ongoing prevention efforts and how to reduce the proliferation threat and protect against it'.[3] Underlying this sense of urgency were several factors which, when taken together, made the need for Alliance action apparent.

Growing Awareness of the Proliferation Threat

During the Cold War, proliferation was associated almost exclusively with nuclear weapons – the Alliance viewed it as an important political problem, but not one central to NATO security. Most allies accepted the conventional position that proliferation could best be prevented through political means, including diplomacy, arms control and restrictions on exports of sensitive technologies and materials. In those cases where traditional non-proliferation tools had failed – such as with Israel, India and Pakistan – no direct security threat was apparent. In fact, possession of a nuclear-weapon capability by these 'unacknowledged nuclear powers' was considered by some to be a stabilising element which, although troubling in several respects, could serve to enhance deterrence, and thereby prevent conflict in volatile areas. Overall, stopping and 'rolling back' proliferation were not an Alliance priority.

By January 1994, this almost benign view of proliferation had begun to erode. Mounting evidence had demonstrated that potential adversaries in regions of vital interest to the Alliance were determined to acquire NBC weapons and missiles as political and military tools to advance very aggressive, and in most cases anti-Western, agendas. In the eyes of proliferant states, possessing NBC weapons would not only add to their regional stature, but would also offer an asymmetrical counter to the West's massive superiority in conventional forces.[4] Longer-range delivery systems, especially ballistic missiles, would optimise the political effect of brandishing NBC weapons and thereby add to the utility of these weapons in deterring Western intervention in regional disputes.

Although all NATO members agreed that prevention was essential and that traditional measures required strengthening, many now began to accept that additional measures, and specifically military measures, were necessary to protect against the growing threat. Between the Rome and Brussels summit meetings, several events served to bring about this dramatic shift. These events, acting as a series of shocks, altered the Alliance's perception of the contemporary security environment and the need for NATO to respond to ensure its ability to function effectively in this new and potentially more dangerous environment.

Proliferation Shocks

The first shock came in the aftermath of Iraq's defeat in *Operation Desert Storm*. By the end of the first year of inspections by the UN Special Commission on Iraq (UNSCOM) and the International Atomic Energy Agency's (IAEA) Action Team on Iraq, it had become clear that the Iraqi NBC and missile programmes were far more advanced than had been assessed by Western intelligence agencies. An account of the early findings by one of the chief inspectors emphasises the scope of the discoveries: 'during the inspections in Iraq after the Gulf War, an immense military production establishment was found that was producing or striving to produce a broad range of chemical, biological, and nuclear weapons and missiles capable of delivering them'.[5] The meaning of these discoveries, coming not long after the IAEA had failed to detect Iraq's covert nuclear programme, seemed inescapable: 'the failed efforts of both the International Atomic Energy Agency safeguards inspectors and national intelligence authorities to detect prior to the Persian Gulf War a nuclear weapons programme of the magnitude and advanced character of Iraq's should stand as a monument to the fallibility of on-site inspections and national intelligence when faced by a determined opponent'.[6]

In short, traditional non-proliferation methods had failed to stop the Iraqi NBC and missile programmes. Iraq had been able to violate arms-control commitments without detection and, in some cases with the help of Western businesses, to manipulate export controls using front companies and other types of deception to acquire the technology and expertise to produce these weapons. Together with Iraq's impressive indigenous efforts, the UNSCOM and IAEA evidence led to the conclusion that barriers to possession of NBC and missile capabilities were collapsing. Iraqi use of chemical weapons in its war with Iran and against its own population had already demonstrated that the barriers to use of such weapons had also been breached. Baghdad's later revelations of Iraqi activities prior to *Operation Desert Storm*, including filling bomb and *Scud* warheads with chemical and biological agents for use against coalition forces, as well as against Saudi and Israeli cities, would only confirm this conclusion.[7]

The hope that Iraq might be a unique problem was soon diminished. By early 1992, on the basis of evidence derived from the initial on-site inspections of North Korean facilities at Yongbyon, the IAEA began to suspect that Pyongyang had earlier reprocessed plutonium from fuel rods for a nuclear-weapon programme.[8] The United States, reacting to this finding, began an intensive diplomatic initiative, both in the region and within the United Nations, to bring North Korea back into compliance with the Nuclear Non-Proliferation Treaty (NPT). In March 1993, in violation of its commitments to permit special inspections of suspect sites, Pyongyang announced its intention to withdraw from the NPT – making headlines in the world press as speculation grew about the likelihood of armed conflict on the peninsula.

In June 1993, North Korea again modified its position, postponing its withdrawal from the NPT but continuing to refuse IAEA requests for full regular and special inspections of its nuclear facilities. After six more months of stalemate, IAEA Director General Hans Blix announced at the December 1993 IAEA Board of Governors meeting that the safeguards system in North Korea 'cannot be said to provide any meaningful assurance of peaceful use'.[9] By spring 1994, US officials were stating publicly that Pyongyang may have acquired sufficient plutonium to build at least one nuclear bomb.

Once again, the traditional methods of prevention had failed. When confronted about its programme, North Korea was not repentant but bellicose and threatening. The North Korean ballistic-missile programme, combined with chemical and possible biological weapon capabilities, took on a new significance. For the United States, this crisis would be the top security priority throughout autumn 1994, suspended at least for an interval with the US–North Korean framework agreement of 21 October 1994.

Whereas the military threat from North Korea might be discounted by European allies as remote, growing evidence of NBC and missile proliferation in several Mediterranean and Gulf states appeared to present prospects of direct risks to NATO security interests. North Korea's flight test of the 1000km-range *No-dong* missile in 1993, as well as intelligence findings that Pyongyang was developing two new missiles, the *Taepo-dong* 1 and 2, both with ranges of several thousand kilometres, aroused concern.[10] If North Korea were to export the *No-dong* and *Taepo-dong* missiles for hard currency to the same countries to which it had exported *Scud* missiles, much of Central Europe would then be within their range. Because the southern flank of the Alliance – from Turkey to France – would be most vulnerable to attack by medium-range missiles from states such as Iran and Libya, NBC programmes in these states were particularly worrying.

Even after signing the Chemical Weapons Convention in 1992, Iran continued the expansion of its chemical weapons (CW) capabilities to permit the production of hundreds of tons of chemical agents each year. Iran's biological weapons programme, which dated back to the early 1980s, was assessed in 1992 as capable of producing biological agents. At the same time, Tehran's ambitions to restart its nuclear programme – stalled as a result of Iraqi attacks – became increasingly clear from covert acquisition efforts (as well as open purchases of 'dual-use' technologies) and from statements by Iranian leaders. By 1994, the US estimated that, with significant foreign help – such as that offered by Russia in its proposal to rebuild the Iranian nuclear infrastructure – Iran could possess a nuclear weapon by the end of the decade. In the ballistic-missile area, by the early 1990s Iran had, with North Korean assistance, expanded its inventory of *Scud* missiles to include the 500km-range *Scud*-C.[11] Some analysts also considered that Iran could be one of the first purchasers of the North Korean *No-dong* missile.

Regarding Libya, experience had repeatedly demonstrated to NATO members the need for protective measures to deter the erratic behaviour of its leader, Colonel Moamar Gadaffi. The use of CW by Libyan forces in Chad had provided a clear message that Gadaffi would use whatever weapons he possessed. The 1986 Libyan launch of ballistic missiles against the US facility on Italy's Lampedusa Island, east of Tunisia, also sent a clear message – especially to the Italians. In the early 1990s, Tripoli's investment in both chemical-weapons production and ballistic missiles increased. The Libyans constructed a new CW plant at Tarhunah and reportedly signed an agreement to purchase *Scud*-Cs and perhaps *No-dong* missiles from North Korea. Reports also surfaced of Libya's interest in biological and nuclear weapons.[12]

In addition to the concerns generated by Iraqi, North Korean, Iranian and Libyan programmes, in the early 1990s, NATO members became increasingly aware of additional proliferation risks stemming from the dissolution of the former Soviet Union. The greatest attention focused on the 'leakage' of sensitive materials, technologies and expertise which could dramatically accelerate the NBC and missile programmes of proliferant states. Beginning with the Nunn–Lugar programme of US assistance to Russia and similar French, UK and German efforts, the West gave high priority to improving security at nuclear facilities and helping to stem the loss of weapons experts who might be tempted to sell their knowledge to the highest bidder. Increasingly frequent press headlines of attempted nuclear smuggling from the former Soviet Union gave urgency to such assistance. However, continuing questions about Russian compliance with its legal obligations relating to both biological and chemical weapons impeded progress and added to the existing concerns about proliferation.[13]

By the time of the Brussels summit, the optimism within the Alliance following the fall of the Berlin Wall and the coalition's victory in *Operation Desert Storm* had dissipated. Fears of a reversal of political and economic reforms in Russia, reflected in the resurgence of ultra-nationalism, and NATO's inability to act effectively to resolve the tragedy of Bosnia, contributed to this change. Perhaps equally important were concerns about the growing proliferation threat to NATO's security interests. On this latter point, substantial common ground existed in key NATO capitals.

National Perspectives

Of the NATO allies, the United States assigned the highest priority to addressing the security dimensions of proliferation, including the need for defence programmes to protect against the threat. In December 1993, then US Secretary of Defense Les Aspin had formally announced the Defense Counter-proliferation Initiative. The Initiative set as one objective strengthening efforts to prevent proliferation through enhancing traditional non-proliferation tools, such as diplomacy and export controls. But the Initiative's major emphasis was on the military dimension of the threat, specifically on the need to protect US troops from the effects of NBC weapons. To achieve this capability, the United States would need to equip and train its forces to deter and defend against the regional NBC and missile threat.[14]

Two major catalysts had provided the rationale for the Counter-proliferation Initiative. First, combat experience in the 1991 Gulf War had demonstrated a number of critical limitations on the US ability to fight a regional adversary armed with NBC weapons and missiles. For example, the United States had been notably unsuccessful in destroying mobile missiles. *Operation Desert Storm* also had made evident the need to improve the US ability to attack such targets as biological-weapons facilities while limiting collateral effects. Second, the 1993 US national security assessment of post-Cold War defence requirements, the *Bottom-Up Review*, identified the need to reorient US armed forces to fight and win two major regional conflicts simultaneously. The probability of NBC use or threat of use in connection with such conflicts was perceived to be high. Thus, military measures would have to be undertaken to ensure the operational effectiveness of US forces for both deterrence and war fighting purposes.[15]

The French view of the proliferation threat at the time of the Brussels summit was perhaps best revealed in an official *White Paper* published in spring 1994.[16] The *White Paper* identified NBC and missile proliferation as a serious danger to the nation's vital interests. The threat was described as twofold:

first, NBC weapons threaten French national territory, currently from the former Soviet Union, and in future from the Mediterranean basin, especially Algeria; and, second, NBC raises the stakes for future intervention by French forces in 'strategic zones' outside Europe. In this connection, France indicated acute concern that its ability to project power could be radically circumscribed by the spread of CW and biological weapons (BW) and ballistic-missile capabilities, particularly in Africa and the Middle East.

The *White Paper* described proliferation as a key dynamic in reshaping the environment within which France, Europe and the NATO Alliance would need to defend their interests in the years ahead. French willingness to expand its participation in the 'new' Alliance, which later would include rejoining the NATO Military Committee, was motivated by a range of factors, from military necessity (planning for combined operations) to a desire not to be excluded from important deliberations. Paris also wished to benefit from possible technological cooperation with the United States and other NATO allies (perhaps in the field of missile defences), to maintain US engagement in NATO and ensure that Germany continued to forswear nuclear weapons.

Like France, in early 1994, the United Kingdom viewed NBC and missile proliferation as a serious security concern which, in the first instance, could present a direct threat to British deployed expeditionary forces.[17] To London the problem was global, encompassing two separate dimensions: the former Soviet Union, especially as a potential source of material and expertise for proliferant nations; and the Third World, where proliferation would present even more difficult deterrence and defence challenges for the future.

To counter the regional proliferation threat, the UK advocated a comprehensive political and military approach that would both respond to underlying regional and global causation and also provide the operational military means to deter and defend against the NBC threat. Deterrence of NBC use, primarily through maintaining a credible nuclear retaliatory capability and a firm declaratory policy, was viewed as possibly the military component's most essential element in the response to proliferation. London supported the need for a NATO initiative as a means of ensuring a credible Alliance response to future regional contingencies even more strongly than Paris, as well as for the defence of NATO territory beyond the current decade.

Prior to the Brussels summit, Germany appeared the most reluctant of the major allies to accept the need for an Alliance defence initiative to counter the proliferation threat. Yet even Bonn recognised the requirement to move beyond sole reliance on preventive measures. A 1994 German *White Paper* described NBC proliferation as a risk to regional and global stability and called for 'an all-embracing approach, encompassing the numerous and diverse elements, from classic non-proliferation and disarmament through development aid to politico-military measures'.[18] Although the emphasis in shaping this policy had focused primarily, if not exclusively, on the political aspects of the challenge and response, Bonn was gradually coming to accept that military force may be necessary to deal with states that possess NBC capabilities. Moreover, following the July 1994 Constitutional Court decision permitting German military participation in peacekeeping operations outside the NATO area, it became clear that Germany would no longer be able to avoid participation in military coalitions facing such adversaries. For these reasons, the German Ministry of Defence acknowledged NBC and missile proliferation to be a future military threat both to out-of-area peacekeeping and to NATO territory.

Other European allies, such as Italy and the Netherlands, shared the view that proliferation represented a growing security threat to their national interests, as well as a potential challenge to the health of the transatlantic partnership and to NATO's ability to function in the post-Cold War environment. Although differences existed among NATO members as to the urgency and precise nature of the proliferation threat, as well as the best means of responding to it, a consensus had begun to emerge that prevention measures alone were no longer sufficient – protective measures would also be vital to meet the threat. In this context, similarities in allied views provided the foundation on which an Alliance effort could build.

Alliance Objectives and Progress to Date
NATO Objectives
Following the 1991 Rome summit, NATO undertook a number of activities relating to the growing risks of proliferation. These activities, however, focused almost exclusively on prevention. In particular, the allies devoted themselves to more frequent consultations on potential proliferant countries, as well as on related measures, such as export controls and coordination of national efforts to stem the leakage of sensitive materials and technologies from the former Soviet Union.

While technical committees had continued work in the well-established field of passive defence, especially in the protection of individual soldiers from chemical attack, the Alliance had initiated relatively little new work on the broader issues associated with deterring and defending against the threat if prevention failed. The principal exception was the development of a 'conceptual framework' for air defence that incorporated the theatre-ballistic and *Cruise*-missile threat, including considerations of the potential for industrial cooperative efforts.

Although important, by late 1993 these Alliance efforts were considered insufficient to meet the challenge of proliferation, especially in the area of defence measures. As a first step to remedy the perceived inadequacies, NATO leaders at the Brussels summit directed the preparation of an 'overall policy framework'. Only with such a framework could the Alliance assess the security implications of proliferation and respond effectively and efficiently to the growing threat. A comprehensive approach across the spectrum of political and military measures was considered essential.[19]

Prevention of proliferation – or reversing proliferation through diplomatic efforts if prevention failed – would remain the primary goal. In fact, prevention was perceived as even more vital in the current environment. For that reason, reinforcing traditional non-proliferation tools was seen as a top Alliance priority. Yet, given the experience with states such as Iraq and North Korea, NATO leaders now concluded that a determined proliferant would probably succeed. As a result, it became incumbent on NATO as a defensive alliance to consider the requirements for protecting its members and forces if prevention and reversal failed.

To undertake the mandate directed at the Brussels summit, NATO established two expert working groups. The first, the Senior Political–Military Group on Proliferation (SGP), was assigned the task of developing the broad policy framework for the Alliance approach to proliferation and, on a continuing basis, of determining how NATO can best complement ongoing prevention efforts in other forums. The second, the Senior Defence Group on Proliferation (DGP), was charged with identifying the security implications of proliferation for Alliance defence planning, assessing allied military capabilities to protect against the threat and recommending additional capabilities that may be required. In addition, the DGP was asked to consider how NATO's defence posture might strengthen the Alliance's prevention efforts.

The composition of the two working groups reflected their taskings. The SGP would be chaired by NATO's Assistant Secretary-General for Political Affairs and would comprise primarily political officers from the national missions. The DGP would consist principally of defence experts from capitals and would be co-chaired by a US Assistant Secretary of Defense and by a European allied representative of comparable rank. This high level of representation was considered necessary to give the defence dimension greater visibility and weight in national capitals.

Responding to the summit mandate and working with the DGP, the SGP took the lead in rapidly producing a document entitled 'Alliance Policy Framework'. Issued as an agreed statement of NATO policy at the June 1994 Foreign Ministers meeting in Istanbul, the document provides a very broad description of NATO's objectives and its role in preventing and protecting against the proliferation threat. The treatment of measures to prevent proliferation consists primarily of a list of non-proliferation arms-control agreements and export-control regimes supported by NATO members. In the section 'The Political Dimension', the Alliance's 'role' is described in conventional terms. Reaffirming that the principal goal is to 'prevent proliferation from occurring or, should it occur, to reverse it through diplomatic means', the statement notes the allies' intention to consult frequently and to examine how NATO might assist in implementing and strengthening existing non-proliferation arrangements.[20]

Most significantly, in the section entitled 'The Defence Dimension', the 'Alliance Policy Framework' concludes with the observation that proliferation of 'weapons of mass destruction' (WMD) occurs 'despite international non-proliferation norms and agreements'.[21] It then acknowledges that 'NATO must address the military capabilities needed to discourage WMD proliferation and use, and if necessary, to protect NATO territory, populations and forces'. As a means to accomplish this goal, the statement ends by describing additional work to be conducted, including the intention to assess the threat to NATO, both current and potential, posed by proliferation and the implications of the threat for NATO defence efforts. Although unstated in the public release, this assessment comprises two central elements of the DGP work programme.

Whereas the SGP's work, especially its treatment of the 'political dimension' of NATO's response to proliferation, was essentially descriptive, the work of the DGP would clearly be groundbreaking for the Alliance. For the first time, NATO would undertake a comprehensive assessment of a non-Soviet or Warsaw Pact threat and determine the military measures that must be taken to deter and defend against that threat, ensuring that NATO forces could operate and prevail in an NBC context. Much more than symbolism, the fact that the French would serve as the first European co-chair of the Senior Defence Group revealed the significance of this effort and yet another fundamental change for the Alliance in the new security environment. Although French participation would impose limits on what the DGP could examine in certain areas, such as in nuclear doctrine, where long-standing differences continued to persist, this unprecedented French involvement in a NATO defence initiative added much more than it detracted.

In May 1994, the DGP met for the first time. At this meeting, the group agreed on an ambitious work programme to fulfil the Brussels summit's mandate by spring 1996. The first phase of the effort would examine the risks to NATO posed by the NBC and missile programmes in potential threat countries, both on the periphery of the Alliance and further afield. The second phase would focus on the consequences of the proliferation threat for defence planning and on the range of capabilities required to respond. The third phase of the work programme would assess Alliance and national capabilities in light of the identified requirements. On the basis of this assessment, the group would examine measures to overcome deficiencies, including the potential for cooperative acquisition initiatives.

Progress to Date: Defining the Threat
The DGP completed the first phase of its work programme – the risk assessment – in December 1994. The assessment examined potential threats to NATO

to the year 2010 stemming from NBC and missile proliferation in the Mediterranean and the Middle East, as well as from illicit transfers of material and expertise from Eastern Europe, the former Soviet Union and from suppliers outside the NATO region, such as North Korea and China.[22]

The risk assessment resulted in the identification of even greater common ground among NATO members and made evident the need to differentiate among NBC weapons, recognising that they possess different attributes and uses.[23] Such differences include the following:

- *Nuclear weapons* appear to be the most prized by proliferant states. While the utility and legitimacy of nuclear weapons have been increasingly questioned in the West, proliferators appear to value possessing even a few crude weapons highly. Presumably, such a capability could be used to coerce neighbouring states and deter non-regional states from responding to aggression, in particular by giving an aggressor the ability to hold populations in the region hostage or those in the intervening state's homeland. The trend towards acquiring longer-range ballistic missiles, capable of striking NATO territory in the future, may best be understood in the context of seeking this coercive leverage. At a minimum, a regional opponent's possession of nuclear weapons would complicate coalition-building both within and outside the region of conflict.

- *Biological weapons*, although still often considered less threatening than nuclear weapons, have emerged as a key threat. Technical advances, including micro-encapsulation to produce more stable agents for use over longer periods, have undermined many of the previous assumptions about the military utility of BW agents. Given the spread of the dual-use technologies involved, the pursuit of BW is now seen as a relatively inexpensive path to acquire a weapon capable of mass destruction – the so-called 'poor man's atomic bomb'. Moreover, small quantities of these highly lethal agents permit multiple-delivery modes and attack options to advance tactical goals. It is clear, for example, that BW can now be used in a more discriminate fashion, such as against naval task forces or on the battlefield against such critical targets as ports and airfields.

- *Chemical weapons* are clearly seen by proliferant states as an effective military tool, as well as an instrument of terror. NATO members long understood from first-hand experience the effectiveness of chemicals on the battlefield, and invested significant resources in chemical defences and, in some cases, in offensive programmes for retaliation. Even with effective defences, however, the use of CW would have a dramatic effect on troop performance and, perhaps, profound political consequences on the will to fight. Although use of CW to cause massive civilian casualties would be less effective than biological agents, chemicals could be employed against populations for psychological and political impact – as in the sarin gas attack on the Tokyo subway in March 1995.

In addition, the DGP risk assessment resulted in a set of common allied views on the nature of an NBC-armed adversary which differed fundamentally from the way NATO had perceived the Soviet Union. The 'strategic personalities' of the regional proliferators are very different, and more dangerous, than those of the former Warsaw Pact states. In particular, such states would be less likely to act according to the 'rules' of deterrence and would be more prone to take risks in order to advance the leadership's interests. Proliferant states would also be less likely to have effective command and control, raising the risks of accidental or unauthorised use.

Potential adversaries' employment concepts might well be different from those assumed in the East–West context. In this case, NBC weapons – especially chemical and biological weapons – may best be understood as weapons that weaker enemies could use selectively and in relatively small numbers to achieve special effects precisely because they offer significant psychological, political and military advantages in a regional conflict. Rather than being weapons of last resort, NBC weapons could be weapons of choice, employed early in a conflict in a manner that creates significant, possibly crippling, political and military problems.

Implications for NATO Defence

The DGP began the second phase of its work programme – identifying the political–military consequences of the threat and the capabilities necessary to respond – by exploring the implications of NBC and missile proliferation in three sets of illustrative scenarios: threats against Alliance territory where NATO populations would be at risk; threats to the ability of Alliance members to intervene in regions of vital interest where an NBC-armed adversary could threaten NATO's ability to deploy forces and conduct combat operations; and threats to missions, such as peacekeeping and humanitarian operations, in which NATO forces would be involved.

The DGP examined the implications of NBC proliferation – and particularly chemical and biological weapons – for NATO defence planning and requirements in these scenarios. A number of observations emerged:[24]

- The greatest threat presented by NBC and missile proliferation, at least in the foreseeable future, is to deployed forces. NATO's approach, therefore, should be to give first priority to protecting its forces operating in regional contingencies. As the threat evolves, capabilities will also need to develop. As adversaries acquire longer-range systems, the focus of the Alliance effort may shift to the protection of NATO populations.

- Proliferant states do not have the ability to defeat NATO members in classic military terms. However, an adversary may view its possession of NBC – or even chemical or biological weapons alone – as an effective means to overcome NATO's conventional superiority. Particularly when combined with missile capabilities, these weapons may give the possessor the ability to hold key targets at risk, from troop concentrations to port facilities to population centres, providing possible leverage to coerce NATO decision- making and operations.

- NBC weapons could have a direct impact on the outcome of an operation by disrupting coalition cohesion or by inhibiting the ability of NATO to deploy forces. In particular, loss of staging areas in the theatre, because of threats to or actual use against regional host countries, could compromise the Alliance's ability to carry out the campaign.

- NATO forces will be most vulnerable to NBC attack while entering the region of conflict, when large numbers of forces are concentrated at a relatively small number of airfields and ports. NBC weapons used to disrupt operations at these facilities could have a profound influence on the ability of Alliance forces to carry out their missions.

- NBC weapons could alter the military balance in the region if their use severely degrades the capability of NATO operational forces essential to the conflict. Such degradation could be direct (killing or incapacitating troops) or more indirect. For example, if NBC use occurs or is considered likely, forces will need to operate for extended periods in protective posture, with a major decrement to combat capabilities.

- Uneven capabilities among coalition partners with regard to equipment and training for NBC operations and for defending against the missile threat could offer the enemy opportunities for exploitation.

- Reactions by the civilian population within the theatre of operations could also have a fundamental effect on NATO's ability to conduct operations. Loss of key civilian labour, such as on docks, could seriously impede reinforcement and resupply. The need to divert military resources, for example, missile defences, to protect civilian populations would also detract significantly from the effectiveness of Alliance forces. In addition, large-scale movements of civilians caused by the fear of NBC use could severely impede military movements.

Force Capability Findings

On the basis of these implications, the DGP identified the range of capabilities needed to support NATO's overall political–military objectives for dealing with proliferation: discouraging the acquisition of NBC weapons and related delivery systems; deterring the threat or use of such weapons; and, if necessary, protecting NATO forces and territory from NBC attack. Capabilities were considered in a number of key areas: active defence, passive defence, counter-force (referred to as 'response capabilities'), intelligence and command and control.

In the area of active defences, the DGP reaffirmed the Alliance's position in support of a 'balanced' capability to protect against aircraft and tactical missiles, both *Cruise* and ballistic. For the near term, emphasis is given to acquiring a robust capability for point defence (for protecting limited geographical areas, such as airfields), regional contingencies and, specifically, to the planned improvements to the Integrated Air Defence Programme and to upgrades to anti-tactical ballistic-missile systems such as *Patriot*. In the longer term, the DGP work also recognises the advantages of a multi-tiered capability to intercept longer-range missiles further out.

In the passive defence area – considered central to NATO's defence response to proliferation – the DGP's emphasis is on the need to provide Alliance forces with protection and timely warning capabilities, allowing them to operate effectively in an NBC environment. These include the ability to detect and identify NBC agents at remote distances, individual and unit protective equipment, and decontamination.

In the response or counter-force category, the DGP assessment emphasises the need to possess a range of military capabilities to deny an enemy the ability to strike NATO with NBC weapons. The identified capabilities, essential if NATO is to project a credible deterrent posture, include the ability to conduct strikes against hardened and underground NBC targets which in turn requires enhanced penetration capabilities and the ability to contain collateral effects. Also critical is the ability to conduct operations against mobile targets.

In the category of intelligence capabilities, the DGP's work reinforces the central need for reliable and timely strategic and operational intelligence to ensure the effectiveness of NATO's defences. Improved strategic intelligence – focusing on the 'strategic personalities' of the proliferators and on the adversary's indigenous NBC capabilities and external supply relationships, as well as its employment doctrine and command and control vulnerabilities – can provide an effective tool in both preventing and protecting against NBC proliferation. Accurate and timely operational intelligence, especially wide-area surveillance, is vital to locating targets and providing sufficient warning of attack.

In the area of battle management, the DGP work reinforces the standing requirement for a systems architecture, ensuring effective command and control from timely political consultations to combat on the ground. At the operational level, there is a need to develop and deploy an advanced and survivable Alliance capability to coordinate and integrate NATO military operations, from active and passive defences to the execution of response options to counter the proliferation threat.

The DGP completed its assessment of the operational implications of NBC and missile proliferation in early autumn 1995. Its findings on required military capabilities were summarised in a NATO press statement released after the meeting of Alliance Defence and Foreign Ministers in late November.[25] These findings emphasised the need for the Alliance to possess a 'core' set of capabilities, including:

- strategic and operational intelligence, including early-warning data;
- automated and deployable command, control and communications;
- continuous wide-area ground surveillance to locate and track mobile targets;
- remote and point CW and BW detection, identification and warning;
- extended air defences, including against tactical ballistic and *Cruise* missiles for deployed forces; and
- NBC individual protective equipment for deployed forces.

The report also stressed the need to integrate these core capabilities, and to reflect the proliferation threat in such critical areas as Alliance and national doctrine, training and planning. This is essential to provide the basis for continuing improvements in NATO capabilities as the threat evolves.

In several of these core areas, the Alliance already has or is developing the required capabilities. In these cases, the DGP's findings give further weight to existing programmes as well as demonstrating how supplementing these capabilities with other initiatives – such as layered TMD and special munitions for NBC agent defeat – could assist the Alliance in meeting its objectives of discouraging, deterring and defending against proliferation. In other core areas new initiatives will be necessary.

The DGP is currently working on the third phase of its programme, assessing Alliance and national capabilities with the objective of recommending specific measures to meet existing deficiencies. The Alliance's ability to take such measures will determine NATO's ultimate success in meeting the goals established at the Brussels summit.

The Road Ahead

Alliance defence and foreign ministers accepted the DGP's findings in November 1995, including the need for the core capabilities identified as essential to respond to the proliferation threat. In doing so, ministers also reaffirmed several key principles that had guided the DGP work. In particular, they agreed that NATO's defence posture must provide for alliance cohesion, project reassurance in crisis and protect NATO's freedom of action in the face of the growing proliferation threat. This shared position and consensus on both the proliferation risk assessment and required military capabilities represent real progress in addressing the NBC and missile threat in the context of the objectives established at the Brussels summit.

To succeed in fielding the military capabilities needed to protect against the growing proliferation threat, however, NATO will need to overcome a number of obstacles. These range from the conceptual (such as how the Alliance thinks about the security implications of proliferation and deterrence) to the operational (for instance, the actual commitment of resources to military programmes and making proliferation an integral element of NATO's defence-planning process).

One critical factor is how Alliance political leaders perceive the threat and, specifically, whether they see NBC and missile proliferation as representing a fundamental change in the security environment. Largely as a result of the DGP's work, the political–military community within NATO has clearly begun to accept the view that proliferation can profoundly affect the Alliance's security and its ability to act in regions beyond its borders. Yet the views of the national leadership in several key allied governments are poorly defined. Although progress in the DGP clearly suggests a growing recognition of proliferation as a serious security threat, the argument that traditional non-proliferation prevention policies and programmes are sufficient to meet the challenge may prevail in some capitals, especially when decision-makers are confronted with hard policy and fiscal choices. If this occurs, NATO will almost certainly fail to take the steps necessary to meet the threat.

In some cases, concern over new defence initiatives stems from the view that such measures could be counter-productive if they are interpreted as an intention to provoke conflict through the pre-emptive use of force. The DGP's work, conducted at senior level by representatives from capitals, should help alleviate any such concern of NATO leaders. The group's findings make clear that the choice is not between prevention or protection – the Alliance must do both. Preventive efforts are essential and must be strengthened, but are not in themselves sufficient.

Taking into account a realistic assessment of the threat, the identified military capabilities are equally essential if the Alliance is to succeed in adapting to the new security environment. Indeed, if these capabilities are acquired, they would clearly advance non-proliferation goals by devaluing NBC weapons by denying their use or by mitigating their effects. As NATO ministers have noted, far from being provocative, these prudent defence measures could help discourage NBC and missile acquisition in the first place.[26]

The attainment of the identified military capabilities would also reinforce NATO's nuclear deterrent. In this context, Alliance leaders must re-evaluate long-standing and fundamental assumptions of deterrence. The principal concept of the past – deterrence based on the threat of retaliation and punishment – is likely to be less relevant in a regional conflict involving NBC weapons where the interests are not symmetrical and the conditions for stable deterrence are problematic at best.[27] The threat of a nuclear response to deter NBC use against NATO forces will simply not be credible in all cases. NATO did not rely exclusively on nuclear deterrence in the Cold War, nor can it in the present environment.

While the Alliance must retain the option for an effective nuclear response, it is essential to complement NATO's nuclear forces with a mixture of conventional counter-force enhancements and active and passive defences. Possessing these capabilities will strengthen deterrence and also help to undermine the value of NBC use in the eyes of potential proliferators. Deterrence through denial is a stronger foundation for NATO policy than the concept of massive retaliation which, under a wide range of circumstances, would be perceived as disproportionate or otherwise inappropriate by the Alliance in time of conflict. Moreover, these enhanced conventional capabilities will provide the best hedge against deterrence failure, allowing NATO forces to operate effectively in an NBC environment.

To protect against the proliferation threat, the Alliance will also need to rethink its long-standing position on wide-area missile defences. Given the proliferation of increasingly capable *Cruise* and ballistic missiles, the threat to NATO territory is rapidly approaching. In fact, North Korean ballistic missiles currently under development could provide regional adversaries with the ability to strike substantial sections of NATO Europe with NBC weapons in the next few years.[28] Holding Alliance populations 'hostage' would add a profoundly disturbing dimension to NATO's ability to intervene beyond its borders and would clearly undercut the prospects for deterrence.

The Alliance is committed to deploying effective point defences to protect NATO troops against theatre missiles. This capability will make a major contribution to the Alliance's deterrence and defence posture in countering NBC and missile proliferation. However, protection against the longer-range missile threat, which will possess sufficient range to target NATO territory and populations, is also essential. Concerns about the effectiveness of UK and French nuclear forces (measured in the context of deterring the former Soviet Union) and about the political consequences of amending or abrogating the Anti-Ballistic Missile (ABM) Treaty have for decades dominated the debate and ensured opposition to developing and deploying effective area defences. With the end of the Soviet Union and the expansion of the regional NBC and missile proliferation threat, the rationale behind these concerns requires re-evaluation. Defences capable of meeting and defeating the changed threat are clearly required.

In addition to changing how it thinks about such a threat and about deterrence and defences, the Alliance will need to commit scarce defence resources in a period of declining military budgets to meet the proliferation challenges. The core capabilities identified in the DGP work provide a set of funding priorities. Commitment to acquiring these identified capabilities will only be demonstrated when NATO members fund specific programmes, such as the Joint Surveillance and Target Attack Radar System (JSTARS) and a theatre high-altitude defence area (THAAD)-type TMD system.

Beyond the funding of key defence programmes, the Alliance will be successful in responding to NBC and missile proliferation only when it embeds the threat in overall Alliance defence planning. This will be achieved when NATO takes the threat into account in its force planning process, in its cooperative industrial defence programmes and in its doctrine, operational planning, exercising and training.

In short, NATO's preparedness to deal with proliferation threats is an essential aspect of the Alliance's adaptation to the new security environment. The Alliance work to date provides the necessary framework for success and a firm basis on which to proceed.

The views expressed in this chapter are the author's own and not those of the National Defense University, the US Department of Defense or any other US government agency.

Notes

1. 'UN Says Iraqis Prepared Germ Weapons in Gulf War; Baghdad Balked, Fearing US Nuclear Retaliation', *Washington Post*, 26 August 1995, p. 1. See also 'Crash Nuclear Programme by Iraq Is Disclosed', *New York Times*, 26 August 1995, p. 3; and James A. Baker III with Thomas DeFrank, *The Politics of Diplomacy* (New York: G. P. Putnam's Sons, 1995), p. 359.

2. 'The Alliance's New Strategic Concept', Communiqué of the NATO Heads of State and Government, Rome summit meeting, 7 November 1991.

3. NATO Summit Declaration, Press Communiqué M-1(94)3, NATO Heads of State and Government, Brussels, 11 January 1994.

4. For a discussion of proliferation incentives from a regional perspective, see William Martel and William Pendley, *Nuclear Coexistence: Rethinking US Policy to Promote Stability in an Era of Proliferation* (Washington DC: US Government Printing Office, 1994), pp. 21–26.

5. David Kay, 'Denial and Deception Practices of WMD Proliferators: Iraq and Beyond', *Washington Quarterly*, vol. 18, no. 1, Winter 1995, p. 85.

6. *Ibid.*

7. 'UN Extends Its Sanctions Against Iraqis', *New York Times*, 9 September 1995, p. 3. See also 'Saddam Spills Secrets', *Time*, 4 September 1995, p. 41.

8. William Berry Jr, *North Korea's Nuclear Programme: The Clinton Administration's Response*, Institute for National Strategic Studies (INSS) Occasional Paper 3 (Colorado

Springs, CO: USAF INSS, March 1995), p. 7. In an address to the Asia Society on 3 May 1994, Washington DC, US Secretary of Defense William Perry stated: 'the Director of Central Intelligence, James Woolsey, has estimated that the plutonium from this last unloading already may have been used to build at least one nuclear device'. *US Department of State Dispatch*, vol. 15, no. 19, 9 May 1994, p. 276.

9. US Arms Control and Disarmament Agency, 'Report to Congress on Adherence to and Compliance with Arms Control Agreements', 23 June 1994, p. 14.

10. 'The Weapons Proliferation Threat', The Non-proliferation Center, drawn from Intelligence Community-coordinated unclassified material from the 1994 Annual Nonproliferation Report to the US Congress and from recent testimonies before Congress by senior Intelligence Community officials, Washington DC, March 1995, p. 8.

11. *Ibid.*, p. 11.

12. *Ibid.*, pp. 9–10.

13. US Arms Control and Disarmament Agency, 'Report to Congress on Adherence to and Compliance with Arms Control Agreements', 14 January 1993, p. 14.

14. 'Pentagon Begins Effort to Confront More Lethal Arms in Third World', *New York Times*, 8 December 1993, p. 15. See also, 'Aspin Vows Military Efforts to Counter Arms Proliferation', *Washington Post*, 8 December 1993, p. 7.

15. Mitchel B. Wallerstein, 'Concepts to Capabilities: The First Year of Counter-proliferation', in William Lewis and Stuart Johnson (eds), *Weapons of Mass Destruction: New Perspectives on Counter-proliferation* (Washington DC: National Defense University Press, 1995), pp. 18–19.

16. Ministry of Defense, *Livre Blanc sur la Défense, 1994* (Paris: Service d'Information et de Relations Publiques des Armées, Ministère de la Défense, 1994).

17. Jackie Davis, 'The United Kingdom and Proliferation', unpublished manuscript written for the Center for Counter-proliferation Research, National Defense University, Washington DC, June 1994.

18. Federal Ministry of Defence, *White Paper 1994* (Bonn: Federal Ministry of Defence, 1994), English edition, pp. 80–81. See also Klaus Kinkel, 'Policy Statement on German 10-Point Initiative on Non-Proliferation Policy', *Statements and Speeches*, vol. 17, no. 1 (New York: German Information Center, 15 December 1993).

19. The January 1994 Declaration of NATO Heads of State and Government, Brussels, declared: 'Proliferation of weapons of mass destruction and their delivery means constitutes a threat to international security and is a matter of concern to NATO. We have decided to intensify and expand NATO's political and defence efforts against proliferation, taking into account the work already under way in other international fora and institutions ... we direct that work begin immediately in appropriate fora of the Alliance to develop an overall policy framework to consider how to reinforce ongoing prevention efforts and how to reduce the proliferation threat and protect against it', NATO Press Communiqué M-1(94)3, Brussels, 11 January 1994.

20. 'Alliance Policy Framework on Proliferation of Weapons of Mass Destruction', Press Release M-NAC-1(94)45 issued at the Ministerial Meeting of the North Atlantic Council, Istanbul, 9 June 1994.

21. *Ibid.*

22. These observations are taken from a series of in-depth interviews with US and allied participants in the DGP process.

23. See Robert Joseph and John Reichart, *Deterrence and Defense in a Nuclear,*

Biological, and Chemical Environment (Washington DC: Center for Counter-proliferation Research, National Defense University, December 1995), pp. 4–6, and forthcoming in *Comparative Strategy*, vol. 15, January–March 1996. See also 'Proliferation of Weapons of Mass Destruction: Assessing the Risks', Office of Technology Assessment (Washington DC: US Government Printing Office, December 1993).

24. Based on interviews with US and allied DGP participants. A complementary set of observations focused on the operational implications of NBC for US forces are contained in Joseph and Reichart, *Deterrence and Defense*, pp. 13–18.

25. 'NATO's Response to Proliferation of Weapons of Mass Destruction', NATO Press Release (95) 124, Brussels, 29 November 1995, pp. 3–4.

26. The proposition that NATO conventional military capabilities devalue NBC weapons – 'by reducing the incentives and raising the costs of acquiring or using them' – is stated explicitly in the November NATO press release. Similarly, the press release emphasises how these capabilities complement and strengthen NATO's nuclear deterrent. See 'NATO's Response', p. 3.

27. The need to think differently about deterrence in a regional NBC context is clearly accepted as part of the US Counter-proliferation Initiative. The 1994 US Secretary of Defense Annual Report states: 'new proliferators might not be susceptible to basic deterrence as practised during the Cold War. New approaches are needed as well as new strategies should deterrence fail'. Les Aspin, *Annual Report to the President and the Congress* (Washington DC: US Government Printing Office, January 1994), p. 35.

28. A report in the South Korean press, citing a South Korean intelligence official, credits the *Taepo-dong* 2 missile with a maximum range of 10,000km – see *Seoul Sinmun*, 11 September 1995, report carried in FBIS-EAS-95-175, 11 September 1995, p. 49. See also, 'N. Korean Missile Could Reach US, Intelligence Warns', *Washington Times*, 29 September 1995.

Chapter 13
The Western European Union and NATO's 'Europeanisation'

Philip H. Gordon

Of all the organisations currently existing in the world, the Western European Union (WEU) is among those whose length of existence is the most *inversely* proportional to the actual functions that it has fulfilled. Launched as the 'Western Union' in 1948 by the UK, France and the Benelux states as a response to a growing Soviet threat, the WEU saw its responsibilities subsumed by NATO early the following year, and it never developed the sort of organisation, forces, reputation or credibility required of a defence institution. Despite many revivals, most notably in 1984, when it was officially 'reactivated'; in 1987, when it published a 'platform on European security interests'; and in 1991, when it formally became the European Union's defence arm, the WEU has remained in NATO's shadow, fulfilling a symbolic and potential role – but no real function.[1]

Arguably, the WEU is now emerging from that shadow, and today has both greater responsibilities and military and organisational capacities than at any time in its 48-year existence. In 1988, the WEU undertook its first military operation ever, dispatching mine-sweepers to the Persian Gulf during the Iran–Iraq War. Since then it has participated in a naval blockade of Iraq during the 1991 Gulf War, and from 1992 helped enforce sanctions on Yugoslavia both along the Danube River and in the Adriatic Sea. In 1991–92, the WEU agreed to undertake military missions on behalf of the European Union, and it has begun to build up its capabilities – in the form of a defence planning cell, satellite-interpretation centre and situation centre

258 ■ Philip H. Gordon

– to out carry these missions. At NATO's 3 June 1996 Berlin ministerial meeting, the WEU was given permission to conduct its own military missions using NATO assets, an innovation that would give the organisation much more military capability than it currently has. Many have thus come to believe that the WEU – long seen as moribund – is not dying after all, but is on the verge of unprecedented relevance.

This chapter argues that the WEU is indeed becoming a more capable organisational instrument, but that it is nonetheless unlikely to emerge from NATO's shadow anytime soon. There is a case for a distinct European security organisation, but that case does not seem sufficiently compelling – nor likely to become so – to provoke Europeans into endowing the WEU with the means to conduct anything but minor military operations on their own. If a military crisis in or around Europe is large (such as conflict in North Africa or a renewed Russian threat), it would almost certainly involve the United States and would require US military assets. If it is small (such as a humanitarian crisis in Africa or a hostage-rescue mission in the Mediterranean), it would more probably be dealt with by individual European nation-states or regional groups than by the WEU as a whole. In other words, there seems little reason to believe that the presumed subset of NATO that might want to undertake a military mission in the absence of the United States would be the ten full members of the WEU.

This is not to say that the steps currently being taken to strengthen the WEU do not make sense for Europeans. If the WEU did not currently exist, Europeans would probably want to invent a security organisation of their own, and since all Europeans would not agree on a defence role for the European Union, they would probably end up with an organisation similar to the WEU. But it is also important to understand that the WEU has a long way to go if its role is to be more than symbolic, and that there are few signs of a European willingness to do what would be necessary – in terms of acquiring military hardware, adopting more binding decision-making rules and mustering the political will – for this to happen. Thus the most likely future scenario is that the WEU will remain on its current course – pronouncing itself relevant, making symbolic deployments to prove it, undertaking a few missions here and there, and very slowly building up its actual capabilities, all while leaving – both by choice and necessity – the most important tasks of European security in the hands of NATO and the United States.

The WEU's (Limited) Functions

The WEU has four main functions or potential functions. Together, they are enough to justify the organisation's existence and to make strengthening it a good idea in principle. At the same time, the WEU's functions are limited and likely to remain so.

• *Identity and Visibility.* Perhaps the main function actually performed by the WEU is giving an 'identity' to European security and defence efforts. Most of the actual military operations the organisation has performed were primarily for this purpose: sweeping mines in the Persian Gulf, enforcing sanctions on Yugoslavia and policing the Bosnian city of Mostar were all important tasks, but they were done by the WEU more to give it a role than because it was the most appropriate or only organisation available to undertake them. In some cases, such as enforcing the Yugoslav arms embargo in the Adriatic during 1992–93, the WEU's efforts to stake out a role for itself actually diminished the efficiency of the operation – they caused confusion between the WEU and NATO as to who was doing what until the enforcement operations were combined in November 1993.[2]

Pursuing a European 'identity' is not a bad thing. As Europeans strive to maintain and strengthen their unity post-Cold War and before the EU's planned enlargement, it is important that they continue to stress the concept of solidarity, and there is no area in which European solidarity is more important than in the fields of security and defence. It is thus not surprising – and altogether legitimate – that proponents of European integration stress the need for a more 'visible' European role within the Atlantic Alliance, and that they welcome the apparent US willingness to support this cause. NATO's January 1994 declaration that it supported the development of a European Security and Defence Identity (ESDI), and its June 1996 agreement to create the possibility of WEU-led Combined Joint Task Forces (CJTF) were both important steps in the direction of European visibility in international security.[3]

• *Performing Military Missions.* Identity is important, but it should not be confused with action. Although the WEU has, as noted above, already performed a number of military missions, most of these could have been performed just as well by *ad hoc* coalitions or by NATO; the WEU label was primarily symbolic. In the future, the organisation may acquire a more practical military role. Looking chronologically at the list of WEU military actions undertaken – from the 1988 Gulf mine-sweeping through the 1991 Gulf War and Adriatic sanctions to the 1994–96 Mostar operation – the logic of using the WEU for those actions seems to be becoming less symbolic and more 'real' as time goes on.

At their 19 June 1992 meeting in the Petersberg castle outside Bonn, WEU leaders agreed to strengthen the WEU's operational role, in accordance with the decisions taken at Maastricht the year before to develop the WEU into the defence component of the EU. The Petersberg Declaration listed possible tasks (now commonly referred to as 'Petersberg tasks') that would include: humanitarian and rescue missions; peacekeeping; and combat tasks in crisis-management, including peace enforcement.[4] Participation in such missions would still be voluntary, but now there was an explicit agreement that the

WEU would plan for, and possibly undertake, missions that went well beyond its original common defence commitment.

Since Petersberg, the WEU has taken a number of steps to enhance its operational capability. It has moved its headquarters to an impressive new site in Brussels; established a defence Planning Cell of more than 40 officers; developed a catalogue of military units answerable to the WEU; set up a satellite-interpretation centre in Torrejon, Spain (where it is already training staff and receiving data from the *Hélios* I satellite); arranged for the regular meeting of armed forces chiefs of staff and other military officers; initiated a comprehensive military exercise policy; set up its own Institute for Security Studies in Paris; and begun to create a 24-hour-capable situation centre to monitor and deal with crisis situations more effectively.[5] Without question, the WEU now has more actual military and organisational capability than ever before.

These capabilities are still modest and they are unlikely to expand within the next few years. Even so, there are four types of missions – hypothetically, at least – that the WEU might be called upon to undertake.

First, it is possible to imagine small peacekeeping or military observer missions in Central Europe for which the WEU might be an appropriate force. If US forces were not needed, and if the risks of conflict escalation were low, it might be more sensible for the WEU to undertake the mission as a sign of Europe's willingness and ability to police its own continent than to rely on NATO and/or the United States. To fulfil this function, the WEU would not be the *only* option, but it would be an acceptable one. So long as risks were limited, Washington would probably have no objection to a purely WEU-led mission, and might even welcome one.

Second, there might be similar missions somewhere along Russia's borders – say, in Moldova or the Baltic states – where the WEU would not only be an *acceptable* option, but where it would be more desirable than NATO because of the latter's negative image in Moscow. It is worth noting that although Russia has been hostile to NATO enlargement and has repeatedly warned against it, Moscow seems to have little or no objection to the WEU. (Indeed, say Russian officials familiar with the Western security debate, most Russians don't even know what the WEU *is*.) The WEU might, then, be useful as a more palatable Western force somewhere in Russia's vicinity.

Third, the WEU might be the best force to undertake certain humanitarian, peacekeeping or hostage-rescue missions in Africa. Just as Russians might find it more acceptable than NATO, Africans might be less resistant to a WEU military mission than to one led by former colonial powers like Britain, Belgium or France.

Finally, the WEU might eventually be necessary to undertake military operations not only without US participation, but in the face of US opposition to a mission. Worries in Europe during the early 1990s about the

United States turning inwards or away from Europe – stimulated by the 1992 election of a President with domestic priorities and the 1994 election of a Congressional majority hostile to foreign interdependence – have largely faded, and Europeans, including the French, recognise that building up an independent European Security and Defence Identity is neither immediately possible nor immediately necessary. Although most Europeans would prefer the active involvement of the United States in European security, no one can exclude an eventual scenario in which Washington refuses not only to participate but also to lend its own or NATO's support to a European military action, which would leave Europeans with the options of doing nothing or doing something alone. If ever the latter option seemed the better of bad alternatives, the WEU would be necessary for the job. The very existence of a capable WEU, moreover, might be enough to force the Americans to think twice about their non-support.

• *Outreach to the East.* A third potential function of the WEU is outreach to the East. In addition to its ten full members, the WEU has three Associate Members, nine Associate Partners, and five Observers – EU members that choose not to be full WEU members (see Table below).

Table 1:   Current Members of the Western European Union

Full Members†*	Associate Members†	Associate Partners	Observers*
Belgium	Iceland	Bulgaria	Austria
France	Norway	Czech Republic	Denmark†
Germany	Turkey	Estonia	Finland
Greece		Hungary	Ireland
Italy		Latvia	Sweden
Luxembourg		Lithuania	
Netherlands		Poland	
Portugal		Romania	
Spain		Slovakia	
UK			

Notes: † NATO member, * EU member

Ambassadors to the WEU from all 27 countries meet twice per month, and even though the Central and East Europeans are not full members and cannot vote, they participate fully in most WEU meetings. Associate Partners thus have the opportunity to play a key part in aspects of European security policy-making and to participate in WEU planning and execution of military operations.

This makes the WEU Europe's only security organisation to involve nearly all the Europeans but exclude the US and Russia, and as such the only forum in which Europeans with common security concerns can discuss those concerns in the absence of the two great external actors in European affairs. Since most of the East Europeans are unlikely to join the EU soon, WEU outreach is a useful way of involving non-EU members in important and practical aspects of European affairs immediately. Bulgaria, Hungary and Romania, for example, are full participants in the WEU's ongoing Danube operation, a concrete and no doubt satisfying example of their integration into 'Europe'.

• *Providing for Europe's Defence.* It is not by accident that 'providing for Europe's defence' – what might be considered the WEU's primary function – is listed last here. Technically, of course, this is what the WEU is all about: Article 5 of the WEU treaty requires all signatories to give 'all the military and other aid and assistance in their power' to any of its allies that are the object of an armed attack in Europe. But not only is a direct military threat to a WEU member (with the potential exception of Greece) hard to imagine in the near future, but as long as NATO exists and US troops remain present in Europe, the WEU's original defence role will remain redundant. If the WEU does start giving military guarantees to countries in Eastern Europe with direct security threats (the Baltic states, for example), it would not be in a position to uphold those guarantees without NATO, which is why NATO membership seems a sensible prerequisite for WEU membership. NATO remains Europe's defence guarantee, and if the WEU has military roles to play, they are probably beyond the borders of its current members.[6]

In NATO's Shadow

At its 3 June 1996 ministerial meeting in Berlin, NATO agreed – after more than two years of debate – on the basic principles of Combined Joint Task Forces (CJTFs), a more flexible orientation of NATO command structures that would allow 'coalitions of the willing' to undertake military actions with the support of – but not necessarily the participation of – the rest of the Alliance.[7] At the same time, NATO explicitly accepted the possibility of creating WEU-led CJTFs, in which the WEU would organise and command a military mission but would be able to draw on NATO and even US assets, without necessarily involving US troops. The Berlin decision was hailed by Europeans and Americans alike (and described by the media) as one that would allow Europe to take on more responsibility for its own security, and one that promised a much more important future for the WEU.[8]

If so, and if the WEU does have the potential functions outlined above and is building the means to fulfil them, why conclude that the WEU's role is likely to remain limited? Why assert that the organisation will remain under NATO's shadow, when NATO just agreed to give a greater role to the WEU? The WEU-led CJTF innovation is useful, as are the changes taking place within the WEU, but it is easy to exaggerate the practical importance of both.[9] Indeed, the illusion of NATO's Europeanisation results from the fact that all the main players in the Berlin agreement have an interest in claiming that it is happening: France needs to claim a greater role for Europe as political cover to come back into the Alliance; Germany needs to show progress towards European political unification to reassure its political élite and convince its public to accept monetary union; the UK wants to show that the WEU is strong to forestall calls to give the EU a defence role; and the US administration needs to be able to claim to Congress and public opinion that the Europeans are now prepared to shoulder more of the burden of transatlantic defence.[10] In fact, however, there are numerous reasons to believe that the enhanced role for the WEU pronounced after the Berlin meeting will be hypothetical rather than real.

First, despite the recent efforts to strengthen the WEU's operational role, Europeans are still militarily dependent on NATO and the US for all but small and local military operations. European countries have large and capable armed forces (1.85 million men and women in the WEU members' militaries) and without doubt the economic potential to develop robust capabilities for intelligence, force projection and high-technology combat.[11] At present, however, most of this force remains devoted to and organised for territorial defence, with the UK and France the only two WEU members possessing the capability for even medium-scale (10,000 soldiers) or sustained deployments abroad (the most likely type of mission for the WEU). As the experiences of the Gulf War, former Yugoslavia and even interventions such as in Rwanda made clear, only the United States has the types of military forces necessary to conduct operations that involve getting large numbers of combat-ready troops to a distant location quickly.

There is no sign, either, that Europeans are prepared to alleviate their military deficiencies. European military budgets have been falling rapidly for more than six years and are likely to be cut even further in an effort to meet the deficit criteria for European monetary union in 1999. Whereas the United States, whose military budgets are also falling, still spends 3.8% of its gross domestic product (GDP) on defence, the European members of NATO only spend 2.3% of theirs.[12] It is true that some countries, most crucially France, are reorganising their armed forces to enable them better to project forces and participate in peacekeeping and peace-enforcement missions abroad. The professionalisation of the French forces, and plans to build up an intervention force of up to 60,000 troops, are important and relevant contributions to Europe's military capabilities.[13] But even while it talks of building up European military capabilities, France is cutting defence spending by FF100 billion ($20bn) over the next six years, withdrawing from joint European projects critical to the WEU's autonomy like the Future Large Aircraft transport plane, and sharply cutting its orders of transport and attack helicopters meant to be built together with Germany. German defence budgets are also under great pressure, and even if Bonn agrees to –

and helps pay for – French plans to build new series of optical and radar satellites, the scope for significant development in this area, as in others, is very limited.[14] Estimates of how much it would cost for Europe to create the military capability to conduct medium-scale 'out-of-area' military operations without the United States vary, but the costs involved (including intelligence satellites, floating communications headquarters, mobile logistics and transport craft) would be at least $30bn, an amount unlikely to be added to European defence budgets anytime soon.[15]

The new NATO deal is meant to help Europeans around this capabilities constraint by making NATO and US assets available to the WEU. Thus, the WEU should not need its own independent assets, but it can borrow NATO's whenever needed. NATO, however, has very few assets of its own to lend the WEU. Most of the forces that make up the Alliance are nationally owned and nationally controlled – simply 'earmarked' for NATO use if the national government approves. The only assets actually owned by NATO are an air-defence system; some command, control and communications assets (which are mostly fixed, and therefore of little use for outside interventions); oil pipelines; a system of bunkers and shelters; and 18 airborne warning and control systems (AWACS). What the Europeans would need to conduct anything but small scale and nearby interventions are not NATO assets but national US ones – long-range heavy transport aircraft, air-refuelling capabilities and satellite intelligence systems. The very capabilities the Europeans need but do not have, NATO does not 'have' either.

Even the borrowing of strictly NATO assets, though, depends on the agreement of all 16 members of the Alliance, including (most crucially for the case of WEU-led CJTFs) the agreement of the United States. As pointed out above, one can imagine certain situations in which the US might be glad to lend its support – when missions are small, with goals supported by Washington and little risk of escalation. In many cases, however – even when the US does not want to supply troops but supports an operation – Washington may be reluctant to authorise a WEU-led CJTF and thereby move political control from the North Atlantic Council to the WEU. If US assets are involved (as they probably would be), or if there is any risk of the WEU (with or without NATO assets) getting bogged-down in an operation and requiring the US to help get them out (as was nearly the case in Bosnia), it is difficult to imagine Washington giving the authority for a WEU-led CJTF. It is true that the Clinton administration is generally more sympathetic to the goal of European integration and ESDI than some of its predecessors, but this sympathy should not be exaggerated. It does not include blanket support for lending US or NATO assets to missions that would be led by the WEU. What counts most to American leaders, whether Democratic or Republican, is whether European policies and goals are in harmony with those of the United States, not whether Europeans are united in some 'identity' or not. No one should expect the

US to prefer lending assets to a WEU-mission to conducting such a mission under NATO's own, or bilateral, auspices.

Finally, even when US support for WEU missions exists, the accompanying prerequisite for such missions to take place is that Europeans agree to do them, which is also far from guaranteed. Having focused their security policies on territorial defence for over 40 years, most Europeans have developed a culture of security dependence, and seem reluctant to use force or undertake collective missions without US participation and leadership. An exclusively European extension of NATO's Peace Implementation Force (IFOR) in Bosnia after December 1996, for example, was consistently and vigorously ruled out by European leaders as too ambitious, and too difficult without the United States.[16] European concerns about US 'interference' in a WEU mission even if the US was not participating are legitimate, but that is a reflection of a political-military imbalance within the Alliance that the Europeans seem resigned to living with. If US participation in European security proves to be erratic and undependable, and if Washington consistently refuses to support WEU missions, perhaps the Europeans will respond by developing both the political will and the means to carry out such missions on their own. But such a development seems unlikely, and it is worth noting that even after the great tensions over former Yugoslavia from 1991–95, the European response has been more to ensure that European security remains in the hands of the Atlantic Alliance as a whole than to pursue their strategic independence from the United States.[17]

After the disaster of the 1956 Suez crisis, when the United States undermined a joint British–French invasion of Egypt, the British concluded 'never again be on the wrong side from the Americans' whereas the French concluded 'never again depend on them'. This time, although the French still harbour ambitions for European strategic independence, both countries seem to have reached the earlier British conclusion. Even Paris now recognises that being a global power, for the foreseeable future at least, is beyond Europe's capability or will.

The WEU–EU Relationship

Within Europe, although there is widespread support for the continuing existence and limited strengthening of the WEU, there are two distinct visions about its ultimate role, and primarily about its relationship with the European Union. The first camp, led by France and Germany (and with the support of the more integrationist EU states), sees the WEU as 'the defence arm of the European Union', in the words of the Maastricht Treaty. The second, led by the UK (with support from Finland and a few others), defends the WEU's independence from the EU, and stresses both its role as 'the European pillar of the Atlantic Alliance' (the other part of the Maastricht compromise) and its practical utility, a utility that this group believes a merger with the

EU would undermine. These competing visions are the basis for negotiations over the EU–WEU role at the current EU inter-governmental conference (IGC), just as they were during the Maastricht process of 1990–92.[18]

The French and Germans support an eventual full merger of the two organisations, primarily because they see the EU as a political organisation that 'would not be complete' (according to the WEU's November 1994 Noordwijk Declaration) without a security and defence dimension.[19] Aware that they will not achieve full EU-merger at this IGC, France and Germany support interim steps along this road, such as changing the treaty to allow the EU to 'instruct' (rather than simply 'request') the WEU to undertake military missions on its behalf. Paris and Bonn recognise the practical limits of such a change (since all full WEU members are also members of the EU, the WEU could never be given an 'instruction' that one of them did not support) but want to make the political point that the Council of the European Union, not that of the WEU, should be the supreme political authority, even for defence questions. They accept that some of the 'neutral' countries in the EU (Ireland, Austria, Sweden and Finland) are currently unwilling to play a European defence role or accept military guarantees, but believe that strengthening the EU–WEU link would inspire a greater sense of European solidarity in the neutrals than at present, including in the areas of defence and security. If the neutrals (and Denmark) continue to refuse a defence role, some French and German leaders believe that the EU and WEU should still be merged, but with a possible proviso stating that they were exempted from the WEU's Article 5 security guarantee, making it clear that the countries that did not want to join the WEU would not have a veto in the European Council when decisions concerning the WEU were taken.[20] This too, like the change from 'request' to 'instruct', would be a largely symbolic step, with little practical impact.

The UK also supports a closer relationship between the EU and the WEU, and has proposed a number of steps towards this goal, such as back-to-back meetings of the two organisations' councils (so that decisions agreed by the EU could be accepted by the WEU on the same day) and the 'double-hatting' of officials who represent their countries in each organisation (already implemented by the UK).[21] But the UK is strongly against a merger of the two organisations for several reasons, and even opposes at the language proposed by Germany and France at the IGC proclaiming merger as an eventual goal.[22] First, the British argue that the memberships of the two organisations are different for a reason: some EU member-states (Denmark, Finland and the UK) do not want the EU to have a defence role, and others (the neutrals) are unwilling to participate in certain types of military mission or to extend defence guarantees. To merge the WEU and EU would thus make the WEU less rather than more likely to act. Second, an EU–WEU merger would make extending EU membership to Eastern Europe more difficult by combining it with a defence guarantee that few in the EU would be willing to accept.

Since EU enlargement is an important goal, and since exempting any new EU members from the WEU guarantee would defeat the purpose of a merger, the two organisations should remain distinct. Third, argue the British, removing defence and security tasks from the WEU would take them away from an organisation with defence expertise and experience and give them to an organisation that has none. Finally, and perhaps most important, merger would run the risk of interference by integrated EU bodies like the Commission, European Parliament and European Court of Justice, all of which the UK believes have no role or legitimate involvement in security and defence matters, which should remain purely inter-governmental. The British thus approach the WEU, like they approach most things, in a pragmatic manner: it should be strengthened so that it is useful if and when its members see fit to use it, but there is no need for joining it with the EU in the name of theology.

Some (mostly in Paris and at the EU in Brussels) suspect London's enthusiasm for strengthening the WEU's capabilities and independence is disingenuous, a guise for ensuring that it is strong enough to be kept out of the EU but not so strong that it threatens the primacy of NATO. But while it is true that the UK probably goes further than is necessary in explaining why merger is inappropriate, its arguments ultimately seem difficult to ignore. If *all* of the EU's members agreed on giving defence guarantees to each other (not impossible, given the changing strategic cultures in the neutral countries, the support of the Danish élite for doing so, and the possibility for 'fudging' the issue of Ireland's role), there might be a case for making the WEU an actual part of the EU. This could probably be done in a way that both preserved the WEU's military expertise and made it clear that defence policy should remain inter-governmental, like the WEU. But this is not currently the case, and, even if it were, it would not alter the fact that the EU is planning to take on new members whose entry might be complicated if it entailed giving a WEU Article 5 defence guarantee. Is an EU–WEU merger more important than the eventual entry of the Baltic states into the EU?

European political and security arrangements are messy, and the desire to avoid differing memberships for functional issues (defence, security, monetary policy, open borders and so on) is understandable, but ultimately futile. Merging the WEU with the EU would have its merits, but those merits would be outweighed by the drawbacks and would make the WEU – already unlikely to be employed often or in important cases – even less likely to be used. It seems more sensible to preserve the institution's flexibility and independence, while making its relationship with the European Union as close as possible.

Conclusion
With the United States' renewed commitment to European security as part of IFOR, France's recent *rapprochement* with NATO, and NATO's ongoing

renovation, it would not be unreasonable to conclude that the WEU no longer has a role. Since there is agreement that NATO is the primary European security organisation, since NATO's assets are far more capable than those of the WEU, and since Washington remains engaged in Europe, there is (according to this view) no need for a separate European security organisation that can only be redundant. The WEU, to take the view to its logical conclusion, might as well be disbanded, perhaps in 1998, when its original 50-year mandate comes to an end.[23]

As suggested above, however, disbanding the WEU would not be a good idea. The WEU may not have a leading role to play in Europe, but there are certain limited functions it can fulfill. It is the useful expression of Europe's identity and solidarity in the fields of security and defence. There are certain types of peacekeeping missions, perhaps near Russia's borders or in Africa, that the WEU might be best placed to undertake (especially if the missions require the sustained deployment of troops that the US might be unwilling to commit). And, since US engagement in Europe is likely but can never be guaranteed, the WEU is an ultimate protection against American unreliability as well as leverage in keeping the United States involved. For an organisation that costs only 4% of what NATO costs, that is not such a bad deal.

Yet if the case against the WEU can be exaggerated, it is a different exaggeration that is both more common and more dangerous, and that is the exaggeration of its relevance. The limited steps the organisation has taken to strengthen itself are positive, as is its new relationship with NATO, but neither development should lead Europeans or Americans to believe that there is a new security system in Europe in which Europeans will take primary responsibility for their own regional security, and the United States will only be required in a supporting role. In fact, as suggested above, the theoretical arrangements of WEU-led missions with NATO support are unlikely to be used. There is nothing wrong with Europeans and Americans congratulating themselves on working out mutually acceptable arrangements after so many years of 'burden-sharing' disputes; that both sides now agree that NATO is the first choice and that the WEU is not necessarily in competition with it is a huge achievement. But if Americans now believe that they can count on Europeans to bear most of the burdens and take most of the risks for European security, or if Europeans believe they are less dependent on the United States, then both are mistaken.

Notes

1. The March 1948 'Treaty of Economic, Social and Cultural Collaboration and Collective Self-Defence', or Brussels Treaty, was commonly referred to as the 'Western Union'. It only officially became the Western European Union on 23 October 1954, with the Paris Agreements that modified the Brussels Treaty and brought West Germany

and Italy into the organisation. For a good, brief history of the WEU that covers the 1987 platform, see Sir Russell Johnson, rapporteur, *Western European Union: Information Report* (Brussels: Western European Union, March 1995), pp. 6–16.

2. See Mathias Jopp, *The Strategic Implications of European Integration*, Adelphi Paper 290 (London: Brassey's for the IISS, 1994), pp. 30–31.

3. For the former, see the NATO Summit Declaration of the Heads of State and Government, Press Communiqué M-1(94)3, 11 January 1994, Brussels. For the latter, see the Final Communiqué of the North Atlantic Council Berlin Ministerial Meeting, M-NAC-1(96)63, Berlin, 3 June 1996.

4. See the Petersberg Declaration of the WEU Council of Ministers, Bonn, 19 June 1992; and the discussion in the Assembly of Western European Union, Johnson, *Western European Union*, pp. 33–36.

5. See *ibid.*, pp. 47–55. On the satellite centre, see Assembly of Western European Union, *WEU and Hélios II* (Brussels: Western European Union, 14 May 1996).

6. This is clearly the view of the UK House of Commons Defence Committee, which has concluded that 'the WEU's role in collective defence under the modified Brussels Treaty is of no continuing significance, provided that NATO membership continues to be a prerequisite for membership in the WEU'. See House of Commons Defence Committee, Fourth Report, *Western European Union*, 8 May 1996, p. vi.

7. See the Final Communiqué of the 3 June North Atlantic Council Berlin Ministerial Meeting.

8. See, for example, 'NATO Acquires a European Identity', *The Economist*, 8 June 1996, pp. 43–44; Bruce Clark, 'US Agrees to Give Europe More Say in NATO Operations', *Financial Times*, 4 June 1996; and Rick Atkinson, 'NATO Gives Members Response Flexibility', *Washington Post*, 4 June 1996.

9. See this argument in Philip H. Gordon, '"Europeanization" of NATO: A Convenient Myth', *International Herald Tribune*, 7 June 1996.

10. See 'NATO, CJTFs and IFOR', *Strategic Comments* (London: IISS), vol. 2, no. 5, June 1996.

11. Full WEU member troop strength, not including reserves, is 1.849m. The total for all of NATO's European members is 2.44m. See *The Military Balance 1996–1997* (Oxford: Oxford University Press for the IISS, 1996), pp. 49–76.

12. For figures on defence spending and comparisons with earlier years, see *The Military Balance 1996–1997* (Oxford: Oxford University Press for the IISS, 1996). Also see the discussion in Rick Atkinson and Bradley Graham, 'As Europe Seeks Wider NATO Role, Its Armies Shrink', *Washington Post*, 29 July 1996, pp. A1, A15.

13. French defence reform plans are discussed in Jacques Isnard, 'Le Budget Militaire Sera Réduit de 100 Milliards de Francs en Cinq Ans', *Le Monde*, 24 February 1996, pp. 6–9.

14. In June 1996 it was still uncertain whether Germany would be able to proceed with the Franco-German satellite cooperation project because of cuts in its defence budget. See Giovanni de Briganti, 'Germans May Drop Helios', *Defense News*, vol. 11, no. 5, 24–30 June 1996, pp. 1, 76.

15. According to a recent RAND study, equipping a European intervention force of approximately 50,000 troops would require extra equipment costing $18–49 billion over 25 years (depending on the amount of capability deemed necessary) as well as satellite intelligence systems that would cost between $9bn and $25bn over the same

period. See Morton B. Berman and Gwendolen M. Carter, *The Independent European Force: Costs of Independence* (Santa Monica: RAND, 1993). Other estimates have placed the cost of European military independence at $107bn per year for the rest of the decade. See an estimate by the Royal United Services Institute cited in 'The Defence of Europe: It Can't Be Done Alone', *The Economist*, 25 February 1995.

16. Throughout 1996, UK Foreign Minister Malcolm Rifkind and French Foreign Minister Hervé de Charette repeatedly stressed that, in de Charette's words, 'we arrived with the Americans and we will leave with them'. When European Commissioner Hans van den Broek suggested in early May 1996 that perhaps European troops could stay on in Bosnia without the United States, he was quickly repudiated by de Charette. See *Agence France Presse*, 'EU Commissioner Slammed for Bosnia Comments', 7 May 1996.

17. For a demonstration of how this conclusion was reached by France, where it is most striking, see Grant, chapter 3.

18. For a discussion of the various European positions on this issue at the IGC, see 'European Foreign Policies: Institutional Compromises', *Strategic Comments* (London: IISS), vol. 2, no. 1, January 1996.

19. At their bilateral summit in Freiburg, Germany, on 27 February 1996, France and Germany pledged support for 'medium-term merger' between the EU and WEU. See Peter Norman, 'France and Germany in Foreign Policy Pact', *Financial Times*, 28 February 1996.

20. See Nicole Gnesotto, 'La Défense Européenne au Carrefour de la Bosnie et de la CIG', *Politique Etrangère*, vol. 61, no. 1, Spring 1996, p. 122.

21. See the British proposals in 'Memorandum on the United Kingdom Government's Approach to the Treatment of European Defence Issues at the 1996 Inter-governmental Conference', Foreign and Commonwealth Office, 1 March 1996, paras 25–27.

22. The UK position on WEU is detailed in the 1 March 1996 Memorandum cited above and in UK Prime Minister John Major's speech to the WEU Assembly in London on 23 February 1996 (upon the new UK presidency of the WEU), text provided by FCO. Also see the article by the then Head of the Security Policy Department at the FCO, Alyson J. K. Bailes, 'European Defence and Security: The Role of NATO, WEU and EU', *Security Dialogue*, vol. 27, no. 1, March 1996, pp. 55–64.

23. The Brussels Treaty does not actually come to an end in 1998 as is often reported, but simply notes (in Article 12) that after 50 years (from March 1948) signatories can unilaterally withdraw from it, rather than having to negotiate a withdrawal with their partners. See the discussion of this point in 'L'Union de l'Europe Occidentale', *Ramsès* (Paris: Institut Français des Relations Internationales, 1995), p. 329.

Index

Contributors

Dana H. Allin is Deputy Director of the Aspen Institute Berlin.

Ronald D. Asmus is a Senior Analyst at RAND, Santa Monica, CA.

Charles Barry is a Lieutenant-Colonel in the US Army and a Senior Military Fellow at the Institute for National Strategic Studies of the National Defense University (NDU), Washington DC.

Michael E. Brown is a Senior Fellow and Co-Editor of *International Security* at the Center for Science and International Affairs, Harvard University, Cambridge, MA.

Nicole Gnesotto is a Professor at the Institute of Political Studies, Paris, and Special Adviser for European Security at the French Institute of International Relations (IFRI), Paris.

Philip H. Gordon is the Carol Deane Senior Fellow for US Strategic Studies and Editor of *Survival* at the International Institute for Strategic Studies, London.

Robert P. Grant is a Senior Research Associate at the United States–Center for Research and Education on Strategy and Technology (US–CREST), Arlington, VA.

Robert Joseph is Director of the Center for Counter-proliferation Research at NDU, and is on the faculty of the National War College, both Washington DC.

Richard L. Kugler is a Senior Analyst at RAND, Washington DC.

F. Stephen Larrabee is a Senior Analyst at RAND, Santa Monica, CA.

Robert C. Nurick is a Senior Analyst at RAND, Santa Monica, CA.

Nick Williams works in the Political Affairs Division of NATO's International Staff, Brussels.

Philip Zelikow is Associate Professor of Public Policy at Harvard University, Cambridge, MA.

Other security-related titles from the IISS:

The *Adelphi Paper* series (8–10 issues a year) analyses current and future issues of international security. It constitutes the most comprehensive series of world-wide strategic issues available in monograph form.

Strategic Comments, launched in January 1995 and published ten times annually, provides timely 1,500-word briefings on issues of international concern. Each subject is skilfully presented and accompanied by maps, graphs and diagrams.

In *Strategic Survey 1995–1996*, the major political, economic and foreign-policy developments and trends of 1995 and the first quarter of 1996 are reviewed. Articles covering regional security, proliferation and military conflict form an accessible commentary invaluable for interpreting world-wide strategic events.

Survival: The IISS Quarterly is a leading voice in the strategic-studies field. The journal provides sound analysis, authoritative information and innovative thinking on global issues with important military or security implications, and identifies emerging strategic trends.

The Military Balance 1996–1997 is an indispensable database of the military strength, organisation, equipment and defence expenditure of the world's armed forces. It contains up-to-date information on the composition, size and weapons holdings of nearly 170 countries.

For further information on the above publications, contact:
The Publications Manager, IISS, 23 Tavistock Street, London WC2E 7NQ, UK.
Tel: +44(0)171 379 7676; Fax: +44(0)171 836 3108; e-mail: iiss@iiss.org.uk